Arguments
from
Ignorance

Arguments
from
Ignorance

Douglas Walton

The Pennsylvania State University Press
University Park, Pennsylvania

Library of Congress Cataloging-in-Publication Data

Walton, Douglas N.
    Arguments from ignorance / Douglas Walton.
        p.   cm.
    Includes bibliographical references (p.   ) and index.
    ISBN 0–271–01474–1 (cloth : alk. paper)
    ISBN 0–217–01475-X (paper : alk. paper)
    1. Reasoning. 2. Ignorance (Theory of knowledge) 3. Burden of
proof. I. Title.
BC177.W3215   1996
160—dc20   94-45436
                                                                          CIP

Copyright © 1996 The Pennsylvania State University
All rights reserved
Printed in the United States of America
Published by The Pennsylvania State University Press,
University Park, PA 16802–1003

It is the policy of The Pennsylvania State University Press to use acid-free paper
for the first printing of all clothbound books. Publications on uncoated stock satisfy
the minimum requirements of American National Standard for Information Sciences—Permanence of Paper for Printed Library Materials, ANSI Z39.48–1992.

For Karen, with love

Contents

Acknowledgments

The original motivation to write this book came from twenty-five years of experience in teaching introductory courses in reasoning, argumentation, and logic, where the argument from ignorance is always introduced (as a fallacy) and where typically, it proves very hard for students to make any sense of. Trying to make sense of this kind of argument myself, in order to teach something useful about it to others, was a big help in getting started. But it would not have been possible to undertake the research in the book without the benefit of two years spent at NIAS (Netherlands Institute for Advanced Study in the Humanities and Social Sciences). During the first year at NIAS, 1987–88, Erik Krabbe and I worked together on the research project, *Commitment in Dialogue* (SUNY Press, 1995). And during this period, through many discussions, I learned much about the logic of reasoning in dialogue. During a second year at NIAS, I was a member of the research group "Fallacies as Violations of Rules of Argumentative Discourse," along with Frans van Eemeren, Rob Grootendorst, Sally Jackson, Scott Jacobs, Agnes Haft van Rees, Agnes Verbiest, Charles Willard, and John Woods. This experience was very valuable in giving me greater familiarity with the pragmatic methods currently being developed and used in the field of argumentation theory.

I also thank the Social Sciences and Humanities Research Council of Canada for a research grant in support of this work. Thanks are also owed to Dov Gabbay and Hans Jürgen Ohlbach for organizing the seminar "Reasoning and Argumentation" at the Schloss Dagstuhl International Conference and Research Center for Computer Science in August 1993. During this seminar, Erik Krabbe presented the paper, "Appeal to Ignorance"; discussion of this paper with the participants in the seminar helped to refine some of my own theories on the *argumentum ad ignorantiam*.

Many corrections and detailed comments on an earlier draft of the manuscript of this book were made by Mike Wreen and Mark Weinstein; I am grateful for their many corrections and numerous improvements.

I also thank Amy Merrett for word-processing the manuscript, including the figures and tables. Also, thanks are due Victor Wilkes, for helping to collect some of the case study materials used in Chapters 1, 2, and 3.

Finally, I thank the editors of *Argumentation,* the *American Philosophical Quarterly,* and *Pragmatics and Cognition,* respectively, for permission to reprint portions of three previously published articles, parts of which have been reprinted in various chapters: (1) "Burden of Proof," *Argumentation* 2 (1988): 233–54; (2) "Nonfallacious Arguments from Ignorance," *American Philosophical Quarterly* 29 (1992): 381–87; and (3) "The Speech Act of Presumption," *Pragmatics and Cognition* 1 (1993): 125–48.

1
Introduction

A man is sitting inside a warehouse that has a tin roof and no windows. Tin roofs are notorious for making lots of noise inside a building when it rains outside. The man in the warehouse cannot see outside, so he could not tell directly if it were raining at a given time. But he could infer indirectly, using, for example, the following argument: if it were raining now I would know it (by the noise); but I do not know it; therefore, it is not raining now. This type of argument is called an *argumentum ad ignorantiam* in the logic textbooks, usually translated as the argument from ignorance, or as the appeal to ignorance. Sometimes it is also called lack-of-knowledge inference, negative evidence, or negative proof.

The man's argument from ignorance in the warehouse case seems reasonable enough, but there are some grounds for reservation. First, it is based on ignorance, or so-called negative evidence, in the sense that the premise is he does *not* hear noise that would normally be the indication that it is raining outside. It is the absence of noise that is the basis of the argument. Second, it is an indirect argument. He does not see the rain or absence of rain outside directly. He can only infer it by presumption from what he hears, or fails to hear, inside. In drawing this conclusion he could perhaps be mistaken. For example, it could be raining softly outside, so that he does not hear any noise on the roof inside. Or for some reason that he is unaware of, it could be that the rain is not hitting the roof.

Perhaps for these reasons, arguments from negative evidence have often been mistrusted, and assigned a second-class status in logic. Indeed, in the standard treatment of the logic textbooks, the *argumentum ad ignorantiam* is classified as a fallacy. Perhaps we can appreciate why this has been so, by reflecting that you can use this same type of argument to "prove" the existence of ghosts, ESP, and all sorts of dubious entities. One standard example is: "Ghosts must exist, because nobody has ever been able to prove that they don't exist."[1] In many other standard cases like this one (studied in Chapter 2) the *argumentum ad ignorantiam* does appear to be used in a fallacious way.

Appeal to Ignorance as a Fallacy

The danger inherent in the use of arguments from ignorance is that such an argument might discourage us from going ahead to look for positive evidence to prove a hypothesis. Even worse, it might be used to deflect criticism away from one's failure to provide such positive justification for a claim one has made. The requirement of fulfilling the burden of proof for a claim one has made is a fundamental principle of argument, where two parties reason together in a sincere attempt to get at the truth of a matter.[2]

The *argumentum ad ignorantiam* is well known to anyone who has taken an introductory logic course as the fallacy of "appeal to ignorance," sometimes also called the fallacy of the "argument from ignorance." A typical textbook account of this famous fallacy that will give the basic idea of how it is generally treated in logic textbooks is that of Kelley (1994, 147–48):

Case 1.1

> Suppose I accused you of cheating on an exam. "Prove it," you say. "Can you prove that you didn't?" I ask—and thereby commit the fallacy of *appeal to ignorance*. This fallacy consists in the argument that a proposition is true because it hasn't been proven false. To put

---

1. See Chapter 2, "Ghosts, the Paranormal, and ESP."
2. See Walton (1988), and Chapter 2, "Burden of Proof."

it differently, it is the argument that a proposition is true because the *opposing* proposition hasn't been proven true.

Kelley (148) describes this type of argument as having the form below, where A is a proposition, and the symbol ⌐ stands for the negation of A.

⌐A has not been proven true.

Therefore, A is true.

This form of argument is said to be fallacious "because a lack of evidence for ⌐A does not imply that there is evidence for A" (148). Kelley gives another example to emphasize the point (148):

Case 1.2

> I cannot prove that a storm is not brewing in the atmosphere of Jupiter, but that would hardly count as evidence that a storm *is* brewing. The absence of evidence usually means that we simply don't know enough to make a judgment. Such ignorance cannot be transmuted into knowledge, any more than brass can be transmuted into gold.

Some clue to both the danger of this fallacy, and also the nature of it as a kind of failure of principles of good reasoning, is indicated by the accusation of cheating case (case 1.1). Normally, the accuser has the burden of proof—the obligation of offering evidence or justification for a claim made. The use of appeal to ignorance is an attempt to evade this obligation by shifting it onto the other party in the dialogue.

The danger of this fallacy is more graphically brought out by an example given by Kahane (1992, 64):

Case 1.3

> In 1950, Senator Joseph R. McCarthy responded to a doubting question about the fortieth name on a list of eighty-one case histories he claimed were of Communists working for the United States State Department by saying, "I do not have much information on this ex-

cept the general statement of the agency that there is nothing in the files to disprove his Communist connections."

According to Kahane this case is an example of the fallacy of appeal to ignorance: "Many of McCarthy's followers took this absence of evidence proving that the person in question was not a Communist as evidence that he was, a good example of the fallacy *appeal to ignorance*" (64). This particular example, frequently cited in the logic textbooks as a case of the fallacious appeal to ignorance (as shown in Chapter 2)[3] indicates the danger of this fallacy. Presumably, it is this very danger that justifies its treatment as such a prominent fallacy in the logic textbooks. The danger is that in a witch-hunt atmosphere, even a mere accusation, with no positive proof or evidence for it given, can be acted upon; the person accused can be prosecuted or punished, even if innocent of the wrongdoing cited by his accuser.

Certain types of allegations of wrongdoing are hard to refute, and because of a wave of popular hysteria, which may be generated politically by advocacy groups for certain interests or political views, absence of evidence comes to be taken as a kind of proof of the charge. Currently, many critics allege that charges of sexual abuse of children now function in this way. Coren (1994, A22) describes a typical type of divorce and child custody dispute case.

Case 1.4

A man was accused by his wife of sexually molesting their twelve-year-old daughter. The girl was examined at a hospital, and the man took a lie detector test, but no evidence of abuse was found. The child was questioned, and after several interviews, began to cite recalling abuse, but she also said "Mummy helps us remember." As a result of the trial, the man's name was put on a Child Abuse Register, which requires no conviction or proof.

Coren (1994, A22) describes the logic of this process where the "pointing finger," the "smoke of accusation" is sufficient, even in the absence of evidence, to conclude to an assumption of guilt.

---

3. See case 2.28 below for a slightly different presentation of this same case.

The point has been made before but it is worth reiterating: Sexual-abuse cases represent a contemporary Salem. Indeed there is now an international computer network, known as witch hunt, composed of men fraudulently accused of these crimes. The monomania of the 17th century also involved a gender-biased law, often relied on the evidence of emotionally unstable people and was built heavily upon the manipulation of children. Today accused men have to face not only the plaintiff but a wall of tendentious statistical material and an atmosphere that susurrates with rumour and innuendo.

Many feel that the conviction of some innocent persons is necessary to combat the terrible crime of child abuse, and the issue is so current that it is difficult to comment on it objectively, in historical perspective. While this type of case is comparable to other historical witch-hunt types of cases of the use of the argument from ignorance,[4] how close the parallels really are remains to be seen. Whatever the outcome, it is this type of issue that is the current focus of concern about the correctness or fallaciousness of the *argumentum ad ignorantiam* as a type of argument.

Zero Tolerance

Borrowed from the Reagan-era war on drugs, the phrase "zero tolerance" is now being applied as a judicial model by universities and government agencies in investigation and prosecution of charges of harassment and discrimination. The principle of zero tolerance is that once an accusation is made of, say, sexual abuse, violence against women, or profanity in the schools, it should be followed by immediate arrest of the alleged perpetrator, even if the accusation was made anonymously. This principle, in effect, reverses the burden of proof. The presumption of innocence is replaced by a presumption of guilt.

Examples given by Klein (1994, A7) include automatic expulsion of high school students accused of violence; automatic dismissal of a government employee by an anonymous call to the Women's Directorate, on the basis of a photograph supposedly indicating harassment, even if no corroborating evidence is available; and in the universities, zero tolerance for any action

---

4. See Chapter 4, "The Salem Witchcraft Trials."

or comment that "is known or might reasonably be known" to be "unwelcome, unwanted, offensive, intimidating, hostile, or inappropriate." Examples would include "jokes, cartoons, gestures, remarks, innuendo, exclusion, graffiti, threats, physical assault, academic penalty, hazing, stalking, and shunning" (A7).

An example given (Klein, 1994, A7) is the case of a flyer distributed at the University of Toronto that read: "Homosexuality is wrong because there are no healthy children produced from it. Abortions are wrong because children are killed." Students, invoking zero tolerance, approached university administrators, telling them to stop the flyers.

The administrators objected to having to enforce the principle of zero tolerance on the grounds that they would have to go in with a police escort, even on the basis of "a sliver of a rumor about a picture you don't like." Defenders of the policy reply that it "indicates a greater willingness to take such complaints seriously" (Klein, 1994, A7).

This type of policy of reversing the burden of proof is a species of *argumentum ad ignorantiam* of the following form: if you can't prove that you are not guilty, then it is presumed that you are guilty. Normally, the burden is on the accuser to provide evidence or corroboration of the charge. Admittedly, where an event took place privately between two people, with no physical evidence of harm, it is generally hard to prove such objective corroboration. The solution advocated by the zero tolerance principle is to shift the burden of disproof of the charge onto the side of the accused party. If he can't furnish such evidence, the conclusion we should draw by the *ad ignorantiam* argument is that he is guilty.

Is this a reasonable or fallacious use of the argument from ignorance? This is a hotly disputed question at the moment. Defenders of zero tolerance argue that the application of the argument from ignorance, as a reasonable argument in this instance, is justified by argument from consequences: namely, that women are at present suffering from abuse to such a degree that anyone who opposes zero tolerance is causing the deaths of women. Opponents of the principle also base their opposition on the argument from consequences. They argue that the policy of zero tolerance is producing many innocent victims of false charges of abuse, and having a disastrous effect on families.

Opponents of the policy also argue that the advocates of zero tolerance are focusing only on the consequences as they affect one group, and ignoring the impact on anyone who is not a member of this group. They see this as a form of self-interested bargaining or advocacy dialogue taking the place of a more rational and objective type of deliberation or critical discussion that takes all points of view into account.

At any rate, on this controversial issue, the central question directly relates to the *argumentum ad ignorantiam* as a type of argument. Is it reasonable or fallacious in this case? And what are the grounds for justifying one opinion or the other?

Recovered Memory as Evidence

Allegations of sexual abuse have recently become the subject of much litigation, and new kinds of legal arguments have come forward to support such claims based on new kinds of controversial "evidence." Although many feel now that prosecuting sexual abuse is good, the pressure to push ahead with such accusations, to which a powerful stigma is attached, has resulted in controversies that stretch the boundaries of the kinds of evidence (or lack of evidence) used to support criminal charges. The charge of sexual abuse has acquired special status at this particular time, so that questioning some of the new kinds of "evidence" on which the charge may be based has become very difficult, or perhaps even impossible, without seeming to be callous or unsympathetic.

One type of evidence currently being used to support allegations by grown children that their aging parents sexually abused them years ago is "recovered memory." According to exponents, suppressed memories that may be too painful to recall explicitly are stored deep in a person's subconscious mind, but can be recalled by a therapist's questioning. But opponents of the use of this type of evidence—who have even formed a group called the False Memory Syndrome Foundation—argue that any real memory of such a traumatic experience would be too vivid to be repressed. The question is to what extent memory lapses or lack of knowledge can be filled in by *ad ignorantiam* inferences that reconstruct what probably happened. But this question remains controversial.

Therapists argue that bringing out these repressed memories is very helpful to recovery of the patient's self-esteem. According to Makin (1993, A5), there is a growing literature that advocates the use of this evidence, and shows how to extract it.

Case 1.5

> . . . The titles include *The Courage to Heal, Allies in Healing, Victims No Longer* and *Right to Innocence*," in which author Beverley Engel advises: "If you have any suspicion at all, if you have any memory—no matter how vague—it probably happened." This is precisely the sort of statement that enrages the movement's opponents.
>
> Many authors and therapists contend that a patient's initial lack of memory is a strong sign of abuse—the kind of horror the mind would suppress. They provide a check list for indications that abuse has been forgotten, including such common feelings as low self-esteem, sexual difficulties and feelings of failure.
>
> Having read all this, the patient may begin to recall fragments of shadowy events from long ago—a hand on her shoulder, an unexplained sensation of anger toward a parent. If she should have trouble reaching back in time—or should develop second thoughts about her "memories"—the therapist need only say: "You seem to be in denial."

There are numerous problems with this kind of evidence. It has an inherent problem of verifiability, because it is repressed, and because it concerns private matters in a family that may have happened years ago. There may be no circumstantial evidence, and no testimonial evidence from anyone not directly involved in the lawsuit. These problems do not deter exponents of recovered memory evidence, however, who claim that rejecting it as legitimate evidence would provide a defense for child abusers (Makin, 1993, A5). Hence the case of recovered memory has become another fringe area of scientific evidence, comparable to the traditional cases of ESP, the paranormal, and ghosts, so often treated as examples of the *argumentum ad ignorantiam* in the past.

Early in his career, Freud elicited many childhood memory cases of women being raped by their fathers. At first, he took these memories as a veridical type of psychiatric evidence, but later in his career, he changed his mind, and became convinced that the majority were cases of fantasizing. However, in the 1980s, as more evidence of child abuse came to emerge, the view that incest is prevalent came to be accepted. Gardner (1993, 370) sketches out this development.

Then in the latter 1980s a bizarre therapeutic fad began to emerge in the United States. Hundreds of poorly trained therapists, calling themselves "traumatists," began to practice the very techniques Freud had discarded. All over the land they are putting patients under hypnosis and subtly prodding them into recalling childhood sexual traumas, memories of which presumably have been totally obliterated for decades. Decades Delayed Disclosure, or DDD, it has been called. Eighty percent of the patients who are claimed to experience DDD are women from 25 to 45 years old. Sixty percent of their parents are college graduates, 25 percent with advanced degrees. More than 80 percent of their parents are married to their first spouse.

Under drug therapy or hypnosis, the patient, typically a woman in her thirties with depression or anxiety symptoms, or inability to lose weight, begins to respond to the leading questions of her therapist. Over months or even years of treatment, shadowy figures of incest begin to appear in the woman's visions, leading to anger and a blaming of an "incest perpetrator" for causing these problems. Stunned, the parents deny everything (Gardner, 1993, 370), but against the weight of this "scientific evidence" their protestations are futile, even if no other corroborating evidence of abuse can be found. Patients are led to believe that bringing these repressed memories to light will solve their problems. But in fact, as many cases now attest, the outcome is the breaking apart of the family, which has even more negative effects in exacerbating the patient's problems.

These cases are very interesting, both for the philosophy of science and the philosophy of law, because they raise the question of whether the elicitation of recovered memory by a therapist should be counted as scientific evidence. Certainly they are based on the *argumentum ad ignorantiam.* In *Courage to Heal,* Bass and Davis (1988, xx) write that the accuser may be "grilled for details," but that "of course such demands for proof are unreasonable. You are not responsible for proving that you were abused." This is a clear waiving of the obligation to fulfill burden of proof, and a shifting of the burden to the accused party to prove his innocence. It is a classical *argumentum ad ignorantiam.*

Scientists are at present split on whether this kind of "evidence" is valid or not in scientific reasoning. A group of distinguished senior psychologists and psychiatrists have now formed the FMS (False Memory Syndrome)

Foundation to combat the growing FMS epidemic. At first, their speaking out was shouted down by enthusiasts of recovered memory, when scientific papers were blocked by catcalls and demonstrations.[5] However, now these scientists have begun writing and publishing papers on FMS.

One important factor in evaluating this type of case of the argument from ignorance is that the therapists are (supposedly) experts. Hence when they find "evidence" of abuse, the claim of discovery is taken by others, e.g. in a court of law, as expert testimony. However, according to some findings of Garry and Loftus (1994, 83), in fact there may be a shifting of burden of proof, a use of the *argumentum ad ignorantiam,* implicit in the use of such testimony as evidence:

> In-depth interviews of clinicians who had seen at least one repressed memory case revealed that the vast majority (81%) usually believe their clients' claims. "I have no reason not to believe them," one therapist said. Another maintained, "If a woman said it happened, it happened." More than two-thirds of those surveyed believed it was not the therapist's job to determine whether a memory is authentic or inauthentic. Such a position is unsurprising, because one of the long-held tenets of psychotherapy is that people construct their own reality.

The psychiatrist who is interested in finding repressed memories may in fact, after using leading questions, find them. But she may be more interested in their therapeutic value in promoting self-esteem than in the question of whether they are veridical.

However, when such a psychiatrist testifies before a court that she found such evidence as repressed memories, it has to be taken by the court that this is expert testimony, and that the evidence it represents is based on a presumption of knowledge and expertise. Thus there is a kind of *ad ignorantiam* shift here from one context of dialogue to another. The therapist may not claim to "know," but this claim of lack of knowledge will be taken as evidence of the proof of the charges anyway. Whether the therapist believes the memory is authentic or not, the court will presume that her testimony to its existence implies that it is authentic and veridical.

---

5. The case is cited by Maté (1994). Dr. Harold Lief, a Pennsylvania psychiatrist who serves as an adviser to the FMS Foundation, was prevented from speaking in 1993 by a group of angry demonstrators. Due to catcalls and interruptions, the lecture had to be cancelled.

The Problem Posed

These controversies about the use of evidence in science and law show that the underlying type of argument called the *ad ignorantiam* poses a problem. Is this type of argument reasonable or fallacious? In either case, we need to know more about the form or structure of the argument, and about the kind of evidence needed to evaluate an instance of it as correct or not, in a given case.

If this is right, a basic problem is posed. If the argument from ignorance is nonfallacious in some cases, how can we generally judge, in a particular case, whether the argument is reasonable or fallacious? And if this type of argument is sometimes reasonable or correct, what sort of structure does it have, so that we can identify it as a distinctive species of argumentation, and verify, in a given case, whether it is being used correctly or fallaciously? So far, there have only been a very small number of papers on the *argumentum ad ignorantiam,* and these questions have not been answered.

R. Robinson (1971), in a ground-breaking paper, upset the traditional wisdom that the argument from ignorance is a fallacy, by finding common examples of it in argumentation in everyday conversation that are tricky to judge, but do not appear to be (always, at any rate) so bad they should be called fallacious.

Perelman and Olbrechts-Tyteca (1969), in a section on the argument from ignorance (see Chapter 4, "Spy Cases"), portrayed it as a kind of tactic, like a dilemma, in argument, used to pare down a respondent's options for reply to two choices: that is, "You must accept my conclusion as true, unless you can prove it is false." The implication here is that there is not evidence to prove it false, therefore my claim must be accepted as true. This dialectical variant of the *argumentum ad ignorantiam* originated from the description of it as a type of argument in Locke's *Essay* (1690), where it was presented as a potentially suspicious, but not inherently fallacious argument of the form, "You must admit what I allege as a proof or assign a better [disproof] yourself" (see Chapter 2, "The Lockean Origin"). Locke is credited with introducing the *argumentum ad ignorantiam* and so naming it. At any rate, Locke claimed to have invented the term (Hamblin, 1970, 161).

In his survey of the standard treatment of fallacies, Hamblin (1970) has less than half a page on the *argumentum ad ignorantiam* (43–44). Citing the ghosts argument (above) as an instance of the fallacy, he also quotes the

qualification added by Copi (1953, 57), "this mode of argument is not fallacious in a court of law because there the guiding principle is that a person
is presumed innocent until proven guilty" (see this chapter, "Foundationalism and Scientific Reasoning"). Hamblin notes, "it must be a strange form
of argument that is now valid, now invalid, according as presumptions
change in context." This brief but pungent remark is almost eerily prescient
to indicating the solution to the puzzle of the *argumentum ad ignorantiam*
that will be proposed in this book, based as it is on a theory of the shifting
of presumptions (Chapter 7) in a context of dialogue (Chapter 6). At a
more general level, Hamblin's own theory (1970; 1971) of different structures of dialogue as normative frameworks in which to evaluate fallacious
and nonfallacious arguments, provided the basis of the new, pragmatic approach to the analysis of arguments from ignorance presented below.

Developments in the field of argumentation in more recent years have
also helped to provide a new pragmatic framework in which arguments can
be evaluated as reasonable or not in virtue of meeting implicit conversational postulates. Grice (1975) developed a theory of conversational implicature, and van Eemeren and Grootendorst (1984; 1987) developed the
critical discussion as a normative model of argumentation. These pragmatic
and dialectical approaches to argumentation created a framework in which
a new and different practical and presumptive analysis of the *argumentum
ad ignorantiam* as a distinctive species of argument in its own right became
a realistic possibility as a research project.

Schedler (1980) argued that the *argumentum ad ignorantiam* should be
seen as a fallacy of ambiguity, rather than a fallacy of relevance, as it has
traditionally been portrayed in the textbooks. But neither alternative
seemed very compelling or useful, until, as shown below in this book, dialectical relevance was defined as a pragmatic concept to be evaluated in
light of the use of a particular argument in a broader (global) context of
dialogue (Chapter 6, "Dialectical Relevance"), and ambiguity was defined
as a pragmatic concept relating to shifts in the concept of evidence in different contexts of dialogue (Chapter 7). The importance of the pragmatic aspects of argumentation in providing an adequate evaluation of common
cases of the *argumentum ad ignorantiam* was made apparent by Wreen
(1989), who argued convincingly that many examples of the argument from
ignorance are not unreasonable (and certainly not fallacious) when considered in a proper context. The problem, as Wreen rightly diagnosed, is that
too many of the textbook examples used in the past have been one-liner
(incomplete) arguments, wrenched out of any context of use that might give

enough background information to evaluate them adequately. Although in recent times, various developments are more and more indicating the importance of the argument from ignorance as a pervasive type of argumentation, the verdict on whether it is a good or bad type of argument remains mixed and uncertain. Robinson and Wreen (but see also D. Walton 1989a, chapter 7) have stood outside the logical tradition of presuming toward a general condemnation of the *argumentum ad ignorantiam*.

Generally, however, the argument from ignorance continues to be maligned; in a recent book, Gaskins (1992) portrays it as a powerful and all-pervasive but largely unnoticed strategy of modern discourse in a culture that has come to cast profound suspicion on all forms of authority. According to Gaskins, the skillful advocate reasoning, "I win my argument unless you can prove me wrong." has come to dominate not only legalistic argumentation, but also scientific inquiry, and modern moral disputes on public policy.

While it is true that arguments from ignorance are based on considerations of burden of proof, as we shall see, and true that there has been, in recent years, a weakening of respect for authority, and even for scientific reasoning as a standard of rationality, to link these things together throws suspicion on the *argumentum ad ignorantiam*. It suggests that the argument from ignorance is, if not overtly fallacious, at least a symptom of the recent preponderance of legalistic, adversarial negotiation, as a replacement for truth-seeking rational argument based on objective evidence. This makes the argument from ignorance appear very suspicious, even a kind of corruption of rationality contributing to the decline of logic.

The Value of Argument from Ignorance Defended

From ancient times, however, there have been glimmers of an opposing point of view, defending the value of arguments from ignorance. We are told by Plato (*Apology,* VI.21) that Socrates, puzzled by the pronouncement of the Oracle at Delphi that he, Socrates, was the wisest of all, investigated this claim by questioning individuals who were reputed to be wise. Socrates hoped to prove the Oracle wrong, he tells us, by finding a man wiser than himself. Socrates tells us of his experience when questioning one particular man.

> So I examined the man—I need not tell you his name, he was a politician—but this was the result, Athenians. When I conversed with him I came to see that, though a great many persons, and most of all he himself, thought that he was wise, yet he was not wise. Then I tried to prove to him that he was not wise, though he fancied that he was. By so doing I made him indignant, and many of the bystanders. So when I went away, I thought to myself, "I am wiser than this man: neither of us knows anything that is really worth knowing, but he thinks that he has knowledge when he has not, while I, having no knowledge, do not think that I have. I seem, at any rate, to be a little wiser than he is on this point: I do not think that I know what I do not know." (Plato, *Apology,* trans. F. J. Church, ed. Robert D. Cumming [Indianapolis: Bobbs-Merrill], 1956, 26)

Here Socrates exploits his own ignorance by recognizing it, and drawing appropriate conclusions concerning his own limitations in matters of politics, and other controversial areas where pretense of absolute knowledge or conclusive proof is not, for practical purposes, realistically obtainable. While we are not told here what the exact form of the argument from ignorance is, or precisely why it is valuable as a reasonable kind of argumentation, still the suggestion is that this type of argument is not worthless, and does have some sort of valuable function in dealing with important matters of controversy in everyday life. It does contribute to wisdom, or is a part of wisdom.

A historical development of some importance to the study of the argument from ignorance was the *doctrine of learned ignorance* developed by Nicholas of Cusa (1401–64), which says of the "instructed" or wise person that "the more he knows that he is unknowing, the more learned he will be" (quoted by Hopkins, 1981, 3). Nicholas is said to have formulated this doctrine on a sea journey from Constantinople to Venice in late 1437 or early 1438 (Hopkins, 1981, 1). However, he was aware of the previous use of this kind of principle by Socrates, and in fact cited Socrates as a wise man precisely because "he knows that he does not know." (Hopkins, 1981, 3). Nicholas argued that, as humans, we cannot know the infinite. But God is infinite, so he concluded that we cannot know the nature of God. Thus we can only conclude to the existence of God indirectly, by a process of learned ignorance. This philosophical view advocates and presumes the argument from ignorance as a reasonable, but presumptively valid type of indirect argument to an inferred conclusion.

Nicholas wrote insightfully (Hopkins, 1981, 4) that "learned ignorance is not altogether ignorance." It is not simply absence of knowledge or a failure to know anything. Instead he saw the argument from ignorance as a way of combining ignorance and knowledge subtly by a careful and wise reasoner: this combination functions through awareness of limitations and drawing the right conclusion from a knowledge of these limitations.

Nicholas based his doctrine on the premise that we cannot know things like God or the infinite directly, but we can conclude to their existence and nature by means of a negative, secondary type of reasoning that gives "a shadowy befiguring of some possible" but finite, superhuman being (Hopkins 1981, 4). Hence it seemed that Nicholas was portraying the argument from ignorance as a kind of presumptive or approximative, guesswork type of reasoning, that enables us to extrapolate indirectly toward conjecturing a somewhat uncertain conclusion by means of combining knowledge and ignorance.

This was a somewhat unusual doctrine in the history of ideas. Although Nicholas was aware of the doctrine previously found in such sources as Eckhart and Pseudo-Dionysius (Hopkins, 1981, 1), it was certainly not a doctrine that was in the mainstream of Western thinking. And it stands out as a somewhat unusual recognition of the argument from ignorance as a type of argument that is acknowledged to be presumptive or inconclusive in nature, but is not said to be fallacious or erroneous in all cases.

Negative Proof

In the modern treatments of the subject, as previously mentioned, it was John Locke who had the most decisive impact. Many of the subsequent textbooks quoted Locke, or followed his way of treating this type of argument. Although Locke described the argument from ignorance in a balanced way—leaving open whether it could be used fallaciously or reasonably—his treatment of it as a device for shifting the burden of proof, when two parties reason together, suggested many of the worries indicated above (for example, by the McCarthy case) that it has the potential for use as a powerful sophism. As we shall see in Chapter 2, the majority of the textbooks took up this line of its being a fallacy. Not everybody agreed, however.

Curiously, DeMorgan (1847; repr. 1926; pages from each are cited) did not treat the argument from ignorance as a fallacy. Instead, he treated this same type of argument, under the heading of *negative proof,* as a reasonable type of argument that is commonly used in everyday reasoning. DeMorgan began (262; 304) by distinguishing between proof of a negative (proposition), and negative proof. The first, DeMorgan suggested, is "easy," as easy as proving a positive proposition, but the second is difficult, and even could be said to be "hardly attainable" (262; 304). DeMorgan (262; 304) gave the following simple case to illustrate his point.

Case 1.6

> A book has been mislaid; is it in one room or the other? If found in the second room, there is proof of the negative as to the first: and almost any one who can read can be trusted to say, on his own knowledge, that in a certain room there is a certain book. But to give negative proof as to the first room, it must be made certain, first, that every book in the room has been found and examined, secondly, that it has been correctly examined. No one, in fact, can prove more than that he cannot find the book: whether the book be there or not, is another question, to be settled by our opinion of the vigilance and competency of the searcher.

According to DeMorgan then, a negative proof is harder than you might initially think. It involves a secondary, implicit assumption that may be hard to prove in some cases, and may even be unwarranted in some cases.

Consider the simple case in point cited by DeMorgan. That you didn't find the book when you looked in the room for it may be easy to prove. But suppose there were lots of books in the room. Then what can we infer from our failure to find the book? Only that you didn't, or couldn't find the book. Drawing the conclusion that the book was not there is another, and more difficult inference. To warrant this conclusion—by drawing a negative proof, as DeMorgan calls it—you have to add the additional, implicit premise that you were vigilant and competent in your search. The negative proof is only as strong as the confidence that can be placed in this additional assumption.

This analysis of negative proof is a precursor of my own analysis of this type of argument from ignorance, or failure to find something, given in Chapter 8. In my analysis, I shall postulate that this type of argument always presupposes an additional, conditional premise of the form: if the object being searched for were there (in the place where the search was conducted), it would have been found. This premise is a kind of depth-of-search assumption that needs to be satisfied for the negative proof or argument from ignorance to be reasonable as a justification for inferring the conclusion that the object was not there, in the location being searched.

Hence it is interesting to see that DeMorgan does not see the *argumentum ad ignorantiam* as a fallacy, but as a commonly used type of argument that can—under the right conditions—be quite reasonable. On the other hand, he is clearly aware that it is a harder argument to prove than is commonly assumed. And therefore it is apparent, on his analysis, that the argument could often be used in a way that would make it fallacious, or at least inadequately supported.

DeMorgan was himself a scientist of some accomplishment, and was perhaps aware of the use of negative proof in scientific reasoning. But it is interesting that he chose an everyday common example of ordinary reasoning that (like the rain on the roof example I began with) illustrates the very clear nonfallacious use of the argument from ignorance as a familiar type of reasoning.

Although the ancients seemed to have more of a recognition of the place of ignorance in the search for knowledge and wisdom, as Ravetz (1987; 1993) observed, the rise of science, and especially foundationalist and positivistic views of scientific research, seems to have swept ignorance under the rug. It is as though ignorance is no longer admissible in a view of science that sees itself as a solidly established body of verified results, a body of knowledge with all the ignorance expunged out of it.

Foundationalism and Scientific Reasoning

Negative reasoning of the *ad ignorantiam* type is, as we have seen, rarely conclusive as a type of argument. Instead, it is much better seen as a kind of plausible reasoning that is presumptive and heuristic in nature: it suggests a route of new investigation or argumentation by ruling out some of the less plausible alternatives and the less promising avenues. However, because it is fragile and defeasible in nature, this form of argument has frequently been denounced by thinkers who are inclined toward a positivistic or foundationalist view of scientific reasoning, as being inherently fallacious, in any genuine case of scientific reasoning whatsoever.

Again and again, we have seen that evaluating arguments from ignorance is highly sensitive to and dependent on the context in which the argument was used. Foundationalists, who see scientific argument as taking place within the normative framework of the model of dialogue we call the inquiry, think that all scientific arguments should be based on knowledge. Some of the more extreme foundationalists, like Descartes, thought that scientific reasoning should only be based on axiomlike bedrock first principles that can be absolutely and indubitably known to be true. The originator of this viewpoint on scientific argument was, of course, Aristotle, who defined a *demonstration* as a chain of argumentation based on premises known to be true, and proceeding by way of inference to conclusions that are less well established as true.

The basic paradigm of this model of scientific reasoning was, of course, Euclidean geometry. All the axioms are numbered, and are supposed to represent bedrock assumptions, or principles that are known to be true, beyond any reasonable doubt. Then each theorem derived from these axioms by means of logical arguments, which can be certified to be deductively valid, and hence truth-preserving, is given a lower number, corresponding to the order of derivation. The result is a well-ordered, tree-like structure that is called by Woods and Walton (1978a) a cumulative model of argumentation; it has a tree structure that outlaws any kind of circular reasoning as fallacious, and its function is to remove the need for retraction of commitments (cumulativeness). A *cumulative* model of reasoning (Woods and Walton, 1978a, 78) is one where once a proposition is verified as true at a given point in the line of reasoning, then it can be permanently accepted as true, and there will never be any need to retract it in the future. Cumulativeness characterizes the inquiry as a type of dialogue, and contrasts with the persuasion dialogue, where retraction has to be allowed in a fairly liberal way.[6]

Now from the foundationalist viewpoint, genuine scientific reasoning can always be traced back to a set of axioms or initial assumptions that are known to be true; that is, that represent positive scientific knowledge. From this viewpoint, any argument from ignorance, any argument based on a premise expressing a lack of knowledge, is simply not genuine scientific reasoning at all. By these lights, all cases of the *argumentum ad ignorantiam* can be peremptorily dismissed as fallacious.

6. These differences are more fully explained in Chapter 6.

Foundationalism is not nearly so fashionable as it once was, but its popularity for a long period in philosophy had a strong effect on how the logic textbooks and manuals on scientific method tended to regard arguments from ignorance. Foundationalism was fairly strong in the ancient world. Plato advocated that true knowledge had to be of the true and unchanging forms, and Aristotle put forward his concept of the knowledge-based demonstration as the model of good scientific reasoning.

But foundationalism really peaked with the rise of the empirical and mathematical sciences in the Renaissance period. Descartes's method of doubt is probably the apotheosis of this foundationalist point of view on scientific reasoning. But like all timely and popular philosophies, it had many influential followers. Arnauld built a very Cartesian account of scientific reasoning into the *Port Royal Logic* (1662) for example, and this had a strong influence on logic textbooks continuing right through the twentieth century. The tendency within this framework was simply to presume that all arguments from ignorance were, by their nature, inherently fallacious in any sort of reasoning that purported to represent the scientific method of verifying hypotheses based on cumulative knowledge in science.[7]

It is against this background that we can see why Gaskins (1992) is able to decry the *argumentum ad ignorantiam* as an inferior form of argument that is very suspicious, or even sophistical, on the grounds that it substitutes a method of fallible conjecture, and burden-shifting for solid scientific investigation of the "positive facts." Gaskins makes the argument from ignorance sound inherently suspicious and underhanded as a way of sophistically manipulating public opinion, because it functions as a substitute for doing a real scientific investigation of an issue, and getting down to the bedrock of positively verified knowledge.

With the rise of science being so successful, this rhetoric of "hard science" makes a popular readership rush to join in saluting the flag of positivism. From this popular point of view then, it is not hard to see why the textbooks can dismiss all arguments from ignorance as being inherently fallacious, without having to worry about too much critical questioning or serious opposition from their students.

---

7. Pascal (1941, 392) was not above using the argument from ignorance to attack casuistry, when he criticized the "grand maxim" attributed to Father Bauny, "that if an opinion has been advanced by some casuist, and has not been impugned by the Church, it is a sign that she approves of it."

Recent Recognition of Argument from Ignorance

Recently, however, the positivistic view of science has come under critical scrutiny, and it has become more widely accepted, at least in some circles, that ignorance and questioning is an essential and important aspect of how scientific reasoning works when new discoveries are made, and when scientific hypotheses are evaluated on evidence.

If some recent studies turn out to be accepted, it may even be that the argument from ignorance is characteristic of some of the most common and useful kinds of scientific reasoning. Smets (1991) has cited the necessity of arguing from ignorance in certain kinds of arguments needed to establish well-founded theories in science. Dohnal (1992) argues that arguments from ignorance and uncertainty are both common and useful in reliability reasoning in designing and testing microelectronic circuits. Ravetz (1987) and Dunn (1992) have maintained that arguing from usable ignorance has valuable and reasonable functions in knowledge transfer and utilization in policy decision-making. Recently, Witte, Kerwin, and Witte (1991) have championed the Socratic attitude of favoring skeptical questioning over a dogmatic memorizing of facts, as a better method of medical education and research. They have even set out a "Curriculum of Medical Ignorance" that systematically advocates use of the argument from ignorance as the model of medical reasoning. These proposals may appear radical and even somewhat paradoxical in light of the general condemnation of the argument from ignorance as a fallacy. But they are supported by developments in some other areas.

Another very significant factor in this equation have been the recent developments in computer science, especially in the field of artificial intelligence where knowledge-based reasoning of all kinds is beginning to be studied in considerable detail. It is a very familiar kind of reasoning in this area to search through a knowledge base, find that a particular proposition sought for is not there, and then conclude that this proposition is false. This is called *default reasoning* in computer science. A familiar example (Reiter, 1987) would be the kind of case where you look at an airport monitor listing all the stops on a flight between Vancouver and Amsterdam, and you see that Winnipeg is not listed as one of the stops (see case 3.5). When you infer that the plane does not stop at Winnipeg, you are using an *argumentum ad ignorantiam*. But this argument could be reasonable, assuming the convention that all stops are listed on this monitor (what Reiter calls the *closed world assumption*).

These developments suggest that the argument from ignorance is not the fallacy that tradition indicates, and that, in many cases, it is quite a reasonable and acceptable argument that has legitimate and common uses in scientific and medical reasoning, and in the kind of knowledge-based reasoning common in computer science.

But the tendency to dismiss the argument from ignorance as fallacious from a foundationalistic viewpoint is, arguably, based on a misconception of the argument from ignorance or negative evidence, which never was meant to be an inherently conclusive or positive knowledge-based type of argument at all. Instead, it is best seen as generally being a presumptive kind of argument that has the function of pointing the way in reasoning in certain frameworks of conversational argument, subject to retraction and correction in the future, should new information come in.

The function and value of the argument from ignorance then becomes manifest in more open-ended types of dialogue, like persuasion dialogue and deliberation, where arguments are typically based on tentative presumptions, in the absence of definitive knowledge that would resolve an issue conclusively. But it could also be perceived to be of value in scientific reasoning, if your model of that type of reasoning is something other than that of the inquiry.

Many of the textbooks (see Chapter 2, "Legal Presumption of Innocence") do, in fact, concede that the *argumentum ad ignorantiam* is not fallacious in one area in particular, and that is in legal reasoning, where, for example, it is reflected in the basic principle of criminal law (mentioned by Copi, above) that a person is presumed innocent, in the absence of proof of guilt. Just how this principle could be justified as a reasonable instance of the argument from ignorance, however, has always remained a puzzle, resulting in a bewildering and conflicting variety of views expressed in the textbooks.

Rethinking the Argument from Ignorance

All these developments taken together suggest that the *argumentum ad ignorantiam,* a basic item in the introductory logic curriculum, is at a point where it needs rethinking, reevaluating, and investigation in a broad and systematic way that covers cases of its use in many different disciplines and in everyday discourse.

The analysis given in this book will support the hypothesis that the *argumentum ad ignorantiam* is, in many instances, a reasonable kind of argument, by citing many cases of its use in everyday conversations on all kinds of practical matters, where it is used quite appropriately to infer a conclusion. Also cited are cases of the use of negative evidence in scientific research. The use of negative results in science is controversial, but it will be shown that the type of argument from ignorance used in such cases, while inherently presumptive in nature, and no substitute for positive empirical results when available, should not be condemned as inherently fallacious.

The argument from ignorance is, however, fallacious in some instances. Among the major case studies illustrating this in the book are the Salem witchcraft trials, the McCarthy hearings, the Alger Hiss case, and a criminal trial where the prosecuting attorney used the argument from ignorance very effectively to make the defendant appear to have to prove his own innocence. Another is the controversial issue of the safety of silicone breast implants, where physicians (quoted in cases in Chapter 4), used the *ad ignorantiam* argument, "There is no scientific proof that silicone breast implants are unsafe; therefore they are safe (as far as we know)."

As a result of these extensive case studies, I draw out an abstraction of the logical forms of the argument from ignorance, in Chapter 5. These forms are then used to identify various types of *ad ignorantiam* arguments commonly used in discourse. But when it comes to the job of evaluating the argument from ignorance as correct or fallacious in a given case, I shall take a pragmatic point of view, arguing that such an evaluation must be done in the context of dialogue in which the argument was used. Chapter 6 outlines several normative models of dialogue in which the logical forms of the argument from ignorance need to be placed, before they can be evaluated as fallacious or not.

Chapter 7 shows how presumptive reasoning functions in these contexts of dialogue to shift a burden of proof to the other side, when two parties are reasoning together. It is shown in the book that presumptive reasoning is a legitimate type of argumentation in its own right, alongside the more familiar, traditionally accepted types: deductive and inductive reasoning. The legitimate uses of presumptive reasoning to clarify commitment in a critical discussion are brought out, with the aim of overcoming the prejudice that traditionally attached to this type of reasoning, and also specifically, to the argument from ignorance.

Chapter 8 presents an analysis of the form, or so-called argument scheme, of the argument from ignorance. It is shown how this form of argument can be used correctly in argument provided that it is used in a way that it meets certain standards appropriate for the context of its use.

Finally, in Chapter 9, I show how the argument from ignorance is typically used as a fallacy, to try to get the best of an opponent in argument unfairly. There are various ways it is so used, and a useful classification of the most common and effective subtypes of *ad ignorantiam* fallacy is presented.

2
The Treatment in Logic

The best introduction to the argument from ignorance is through its treatment in the logic textbooks and other manuals of critical thinking meant for beginners. There have been very few scholarly articles in logic written on the *argumentum ad ignorantiam,* as it is usually called in logic,[1] but there is quite a good deal of material to be found in the textbooks (even though it is scattered, contradictory, and undeveloped).

Curiously, as Hamblin (1970) showed, the pattern of passing along the "standard treatment" of the various traditional informal fallacies through generations of textbooks, often repeating the same examples, was characteristic of the development (or lack of development) of this whole field. In general, there was little or no real scholarly work of any depth done on these fallacies as objects of research. Still, the textbooks were, and are, an excellent source of good, if briefly treated examples. The standard treat-

---

1. The Latin phrase *argumentum ad ignorantiam* is usually translated as "argument from ignorance," and these two phrases tend to be used as equivalents by the textbooks. However, *argumentum ad ignorantiam* literally means "argument to ignorance." Many textbooks also use the phrase "appeal to ignorance" to refer to what is taken to be the same fallacy, or type of argument.

ment does exhibit a distinctive point of view, and line of development of that view, on the argument from ignorance.

The Standard Treatment as a Fallacy

The modern logic textbooks and critical thinking manuals (spanning the period from the late 1920s to the present), generally take a fairly standard approach to the *argumentum ad ignorantiam,* although there are many exceptions. First, nearly all of them—more than fifty—who mention the *ad ignorantiam* deal with it in a short space, generally one page or less.[2] Second, they begin by identifying the type of argument involved, some of them even giving an explicit form or scheme (see this chapter, "Schematic Accounts of Logical Form"). Third, the examples they give are typically cases where getting evidence to prove a conclusion is problematic because of inherent difficulties of verifiability: arguments involving UFOs, ESP, paranormal phenomena, and the existence of God, are among the most common examples cited (see this chapter, "The Lockean Origin"). Fourth, although the textbooks classify the *argumentum ad ignorantiam* as a fallacy, and generally describe it as a fallacious type of argumentation, many of them hasten to add that there are special circumstances or cases in which it is nonfallacious (or at any rate, there are arguments that appear to be *ad ignorantiam* are not fallacious) (see this chapter, "Treatment in the Older Textbooks").

A survey of four widely used current textbooks—Copi (1953), Carney and Scheer (1974), Manicas and Kruger (1976), and Machina (1982)—will give the reader a very good idea of what the *ad ignorantiam* is standardly taken to be in the modern textbooks.[3] Carney and Scheer (1974, 29) outline the form of the argument as follows (using *p* to stand for any proposition, in their notation).

---

2. The search covered the 240 logic textbooks and critical thinking manuals in my personal library, and probably an equal number found in the University of Winnipeg Library. Of these, fifty-five were found to have something to say about the *ad ignorantiam*. Not all of the books surveyed had a specific section on fallacies.

3. These four were chosen because they give accounts that clearly illustrate the argument from ignorance, both as a distinctive type of argumentation, and as conceived by the logic textbooks.

1. There is no proof (or you have not proved) that p is false.
    Therefore p is true.

2. There is no proof (or you have not proved) that p is true.
    Therefore p is false.

Carney and Scheer describe this form of argumentation as a fallacy, and give the following example of it (29).

Case 2.1

> At one time there was no proof that the earth revolves around the sun. If someone had argued:
>
>> The earth does not revolve around the sun, since there is no proof that it does.
>
> this would be an instance of an *ad ignorantiam* fallacy. For, as we can see, man's ignorance of reasons for the earth revolving around the sun does not support the conclusion that the earth does not revolve around the sun.

This case does seem to be clearly a fallacious argument, but Carney and Scheer go on to cite cases of arguments about reincarnation and the existence of an immaterial soul that appear more problematic because it is unclear whether such claims could ever be proved or disproved.

The link between the *ad ignorantiam* and such cases where verifiability of a hypothesis is a problem is made right at the beginning in Copi (1953, 56).

> The fallacy of *argumentum ad ignorantiam* is illustrated by the argument that there must be ghosts because no one has ever been able to prove that there aren't any. The *argumentum ad ignorantiam* is committed whenever it is argued that a proposition is true simply on the basis that it has not been proved false, or that it is false because it has not been proved true. But our ignorance of how to prove or disprove a proposition clearly does not establish either the truth or the falsehood of that proposition. This fallacy is most often connected with such matters as psychic phenomena, telepathy, and the like, where there is no clear-cut evidence either for or against. It is curious how many of the most enlightened people are prone to this

fallacy, as witness the many students of science who affirm the falseness of spiritualist and telepathic claims simply on the grounds that their truth has not been established.

Machina (1982, 42) describes the form of the argument from ignorance in a way essentially similar to that of Carney and Scheer, as this (here, X stands for a proposition):

$$\frac{X \text{ has never been proved to be true.}}{X \text{ is false.}}$$

Or this:

$$\frac{X \text{ has never been proved to be false.}}{X \text{ is true.}}$$

Machina (42) calls either form "the fallacy of arguing from ignorance," commenting "both forms are equally fallacious."

Using another example where the problem is that "there is no clear-cut evidence either for or against," Machina (42) offers an important clue why *ad ignorantiam* arguments are fallacious in such cases. Machina (42) cites a pair of *ad ignorantiam* arguments, (A) and (B), where the conclusion of one is the opposite of the conclusion of the other.

Case 2.2

(A)   No one has ever been able to prove there is a God.
        Thus, the reasonable thing to do is to believe there is not a God.

(B)   No one has ever been able to prove atheism is correct.
        So, the best thing is to believe in God.

Both these arguments can't be right. What is suspicious then about the *argumentum ad ignorantiam* in such cases is that both sides can use it to exploit the lack of evidence. Machina (42) suggests however, that neither side is being reasonable: "Normally, when we lack adequate evidence the reasonable procedure is to draw the conclusion that at least has the best support, or else to suspend judgment and draw no conclusion at all." The fallacy violates this reasonable procedure when one side in a disputed issue tries to shift the burden of (dis)proof wholly to the other side, and thereby claim victory (too easily).

Manicas and Kruger (1976, 292) explicitly link the *ad ignorantiam* fallacy to the concept of burden of proof in the following example.

Case 2.3

> Consider this argument by Richard Nixon: ". . . Mr. Sparkman and Mr. Stevenson should come before the American people, as I have, and make a complete financial statement as to their financial history, and if they don't, it will be an admission that they have something to hide." In sum, Mr. Nixon argued that if Mr. Sparkman and Mr. Stevenson didn't prove their honesty, we would have to assume they were dishonest. Not only is this a fallacy of *argumentum ad ignorantiam* but it also violates the American legal principle that a person is presumed honest until proved dishonest. Here Mr. Nixon assumed the opposite, that a person may be presumed dishonest until proved honest.

Ostensibly, the fallacy in Nixon's argument in this case was the failure to give any positive evidence to support a charge of dishonesty. Instead, he tried to shift the burden of (dis)proof onto Sparkman and Stevenson to prove that they were not dishonest. Of course, if Sparkman and Stevenson fell into the trap of trying to give evidence of this sort, to disprove their dishonesty, it might make them look even more guilty. Their efforts might make it seem to the rest of us that they really had something to cover up.

This case convincingly shows that the *argumentum ad ignorantiam* is a serious fallacy, in the sense that it is a common type of tactic that could easily fool someone into submitting to a bad argument. But what is the basis of the fallacy? It may violate an American legal principle. But we need to dig a little deeper than this to explain why it is a fallacy in the sense of being a violation of some principle of logic.

Is It Always a Fallacy?

The logic textbooks, on the whole, operate on the presumption that the *argumentum ad ignorantiam* is generally fallacious, and treat this type of argument under the heading of "fallacies." But some of them are stronger than others in definitely describing it as a fallacy. Thomas (1977, 207), for example, defines *argumentum ad ignorantiam* as a fallacy, and makes no mention at all of the possibility that this type of argument could be used nonfallaciously in some instances.[4]

D. S. Robinson (1947, 197) describes the *ad ignorantiam* as an "attempt to prove a proposition negatively," and the word "attempt" here suggests failure. Similarly, Werkmeister (1948, 61) describes *argumentum ad ignorantiam* or "the argument based on ignorance" as an "attempt to shift the burden" or "inability to verify" that is "irrelevant to the truth or falsity" of a conclusion. This too suggests that the *argumentum ad ignorantiam* is always fallacious, and Werkmeister gives no indication of any exceptions.

Ruby (1950, 136) describes the "appeal to ignorance" or *argumentum ad ignorantiam* as an evasion, suggesting it is inherently fallacious as a type of argument. Little, Wilson, and Moore (1955, 20) categorize the *argumentum ad ignorantiam* as a fallacy because "evidence which we do not have can hardly be considered a relevant argument." They even go so far as to say that "lack of evidence . . . establishes nothing." Latta and MacBeath (1956, 780) also treat the *argumentum ad ignorantiam* as a failure of relevance that is inherently fallacious as a type of argumentation. Blumberg (1976, 47) takes the same line, but is a little more open to the possibility of qualification: "The *ad ignorantiam* fallacy is one of irrelevance because the fact that we lack premisses from which to infer a conclusion is *in general* not itself a relevant premiss with respect to that conclusion." This kind of treatment of the *argumentum ad ignorantiam* tends to be more typical of the older textbooks, or at least those of the older style.

In the more modern or "new wave" informal logic textbooks, however, more room tends to be made for the possibility that some *ad ignorantiam* arguments could be nonfallacious. For example, Richards (1977, 39) adds a warning, after describing argument from ignorance as a fallacy, using the telepathy case as an example.

> However, one needs to be careful with Arguments from Ignorance. If to the argument about telepathy we added the premiss that if telepathy occurred, then with all the effort that has gone in to looking for it we should have solid evidence by now of its existence, then the argument would no longer be fallacious. The Fallacy of ad

---

4. Admittedly, Thomas's treatment of the *ad ignorantiam* is very brief.

> Ignorantiam occurs just when a claim is denied on the sole ground
> that there is no evidence for it, not on the further ground that if it
> were true there would be evidence for it.

This warning is significant, because it suggests that even in cases we tend to
be suspicious about, like telepathy, it should not be taken for granted in
every case that the *argumentum ad ignorantiam* is fallacious. The difference
between the fallacious and the nonfallacious case seems to reside in some
element of verifiability of the hypothesis in question. Richards puts this in
the form of a counterfactual: if the hypothesis were true, there would be
evidence for it. Given this additional counterfactual premise, we do seem
to have some kind of a basis for recognizing some instances of *argumentum
ad ignorantiam* as nonfallacious (see again "Schematic Accounts of Logical Form").

It seems that this general type of argument could be fallacious in some
cases, but nonfallacious in other cases, depending on the situation. The
treatment of the fallacy of appealing to ignorance in Michalos (1970, 52)
takes this line even further, by giving an example of an ordinary type of
case where the *argumentum ad ignorantiam* would be nonfallacious.

Case 2.4

> Sometimes the failure to produce evidence *for* a claim *should* be
> counted as evidence *against* it. For example, suppose someone says
> there is an elephant in your room. If you go to your room, look all
> around, and fail to find any evidence in support of this claim, you are
> justified in treating this lack of *supporting* evidence as *disconfirming*
> evidence, i.e., the failure to find evidence for the claim may be con-
> sidered evidence for the *denial* of the claim. Such a move is justifi-
> able because a person can hardly fail to find evidence for the fact
> that an elephant is in his room *provided that* (1) he looks for it and
> (2) it is there. Hence, the failure to find evidence that an elephant is
> there must be counted as evidence that *no* elephant is there.

The difference between the fallacious and nonfallacious cases, according to
Michalos (53) has to do with the observability of the evidence: "the failure
to find evidence for a claim should be counted as evidence against it *provided that* such evidence is ordinarily observable when it exists." The growing tendency to concede nonfallacious cases of *ad ignorantiam* reasoning is

very clearly expressed in Michalos's treatment of the fallacy. Other texts in this category include Weddle (1978), Yanal (1988), Little, Groarke, and Tindale (1989), Hurley (1991), and Hughes (1992).

The case of the elephant discussed by Michalos raises a number of questions. In this case, as Michalos described it, the failure to find evidence actually counts as evidence. So we could ask, Is this really an argument from ignorance? It is in at least two respects. First, the failure to find an elephant in the room is a kind of negative evidence. And second, the evidence is for the conclusion that no elephant is there—a negative conclusion. In these respects it is an argument from ignorance in the sense of being a negative argument.

If it is an argument from ignorance, it should be counted as a nonfallacious one, it seems. But why? The answer seems tied to the observability of the evidence: the person can look around the room carefully, and then use this finding to falsify the hypothesis that there is an elephant there.

Many of the more recent textbooks, in particular, acknowledge the existence of such nonfallacious special cases of the *argumentum ad ignorantiam* as part of their treatment of the fallacy.

Nonfallacious Cases

The four textbooks here surveyed all concede that there are special circumstances in which an *ad ignorantiam* argument may not be fallacious. As Carney and Scheer (1974, 30) suggest:

> For example, in a law court if it is not proved that A is guilty, it follows that A is not guilty. Even though this argument has the form of an *ad ignorantiam,* it is not fallacious because of the wise principle employed in our law courts that a person is presumed innocent until proved guilty. In fact such an argument in a law court can be analyzed as having an additional premiss presupposed in the circumstances, so that the argument in reality is
>
> Premiss: It has not been proved that A is guilty.
> Premiss (presupposed in the circumstances): If a person is not proved guilty, then he is assumed innocent.
> Conclusion: A is innocent.

In this special set of circumstances, Carney and Scheer are suggesting, the *ad ignorantiam* is not fallacious because of the additional second premise, which is a presupposition built into the law. In criminal law, the burden of proof is on the prosecution: failure to prove guilt beyond a reasonable doubt means that the prosecution side loses the case. There is an unequal distribution of burden of proof here. The defense, to win, only needs to show that the argument of the prosecution is insufficiently strong to prove guilt.

But this is not the only set of circumstances in which an *ad ignorantiam* argument can be nonfallacious, according to Carney and Scheer (30): "Similarly, scientists sometimes conclude that a statement is false on the basis of the failure to turn up the required evidence for the statement. Such an argument is correct with this added premiss presupposed in the circumstances: The scientists are sufficiently expert in the area so that if evidence were available, they would turn it up."

Copi (1953, 56) is not this willing to admit of exceptions, conceding only the one type.

> The *argumentum ad ignorantiam* is fallacious in every context but one. The exception is a court of law, where the guiding principle is that a person is presumed innocent until proven guilty. The defense can legitimately claim that if the prosecution has not proved guilt, this warrants a verdict of *not guilty*. But since this position is based upon the special legal principle mentioned, it does not refute the claim that the *argumentum ad ignorantiam* constitutes a fallacy in every other context.

Manicas and Kruger (1976, 292) are even less generous than Copi in this respect, describing the legal presumption of innocence as a "seeming exception."

> A seeming exception to this principle is found in law, where it is held that in the absence of evidence to the contrary, every person is presumed to be innocent. But even this presumption of innocence is not without some foundation, since experience has shown that most people are innocent of any serious wrongdoing when there is no evidence to the contrary. And, of course, when there is, the presumption is rebuttable.

What they seem to be suggesting is that the argument from ignorance in the case of the legal type of presumption may not be, at least completely, a real argument based on ignorance, as opposed to knowledge, or positive evidence of some sort. This is so because the argument does have a "foundation," being supportable, at least partly, by "experience."

Machina (1982) is inclined to think the argument from ignorance even less fallacious than the other three texts, finding an important class of everyday arguments that are exceptions, outside legal cases. He gives (43) the following case.

Case 2.5

> Consider the following argument, which fits the first form [see case 2.2], but which does not seem to be fallacious:
>
> (C) I've looked all through the drawer for my pen, and I found no sign of it.
> _____
> The pen is not in the drawer.
>
> In this example, the premiss essentially says that despite my best efforts I lack evidence of the pen's presence in the drawer. The conclusion says that the pen is not in the drawer, which means that it is false to say the pen is in the drawer. Thus, argument (C) can be seen as an instance of the first form of the fallacy of arguing from ignorance. Yet argument (C) surely is not fallacious.

According to Machina (43), the argument is nonfallacious in this case because it meets the first of a pair of background conditions.

> (Background condition which, if met, prevents an argument fitting the first form from being fallacious.)
>
> X is the sort of proposition which probably would have been proved true already if it were true.
>
> (Background condition which, if met, prevents an argument fitting the second form from being fallacious.)
>
> X is the sort of proposition which probably would have been disproved already if it were false.

This analysis of what separates the fallacious from the nonfallacious cases is similar to Carney and Scheer's proposal in the legal case that there is a background conditional premise presupposed in the special circumstances of a nonfallacious argument from ignorance (see also "Schematic Accounts of Logical Form").

However, both Manicas and Kruger, and also Copi, would be less generous in conceding the extent of the nonfallacious cases of arguments from ignorance. Judging from the parallel cases they present, they would probably say that the argument concerning the missing pen is not really, at least completely an argument from ignorance. Because I looked through the drawer, I did search for the pen, and hence my conclusion that it is not there was based on observational evidence, which is a kind of knowledge (as opposed to pure ignorance).

Manicas and Kruger offer a case to illustrate this point (292).

Case 2.6

> If we get a rash and have not eaten strawberries, we may assume that the rash was not caused by eating strawberries. Here . . . however, our conclusion is based not on ignorance but on the knowledge that we have not eaten strawberries. Similarly, if we eat strawberries and do not get a rash, we may conclude that we are not allergic to strawberries. But this conclusion, too, is based not on ignorance but on the knowledge that a rash has not occurred. In the same way scientists try to find facts that will disprove their hypothesis, and only when they cannot find any do they permit themselves to have confidence in their hypothesis. But once again this confidence has been justified by a diligent search, which, though negative in its findings, still constitutes positive evidence that the conclusion may be true.

Copi too is unwilling to categorize as an argument from ignorance the kind of case where a competent search is made, and turns up an absence of proof (56):

> In some circumstances it can safely be assumed that *if* a certain event had occurred, evidence of it could be discovered by qualified investigators. In such circumstances it is perfectly reasonable to take

the absence of proof of its occurrence as positive proof of its nonoc-currence. Of course, the proof here is not based on ignorance but on our *knowledge* that if it had occurred it would be known.

The case cited by Copi (56) to prove this point is one that is fundamental to any consideration of the *ad ignorantiam.*

Case 2.7

> For example, if a serious F.B.I. investigation fails to unearth any evi-dence that Mr. X is a communist, it would be wrong to conclude that their research has left them ignorant. It has rather established that Mr. X is *not* one. Failure to draw such conclusions is the other side of the bad coin of innuendo, as when one says of a man that there is "no proof" that he is a scoundrel.

As these cases show, there is not only disagreement in the textbooks on how wide the class of nonfallacious cases of the *argumentum ad ignorantiam* is. There is also disagreement on how to define or classify what an argument from ignorance is.

Michalos, in case 2.4, described the argument about the elephant in the room as an instance of the *argumentum ad ignorantiam* (a nonfallacious one). Machina, in case 2.5, described the argument about the pen in the drawer as an instance of the *argumentum ad ignorantiam* (a nonfallacious one). But judging from Copi's account of case 2.7, he wouldn't describe either the elephant case or the pen case as *ad ignorantiam* arguments at all. His grounds would presumably be that, in these cases, "it would be wrong to conclude that their research has left them ignorant." Copi would presum-ably describe these cases by saying that the searches have established that the elephant is *not* in the room, and that the pen is *not* in the drawer.

This represents a fundamental disagreement in the textbook treatments of the *argumentum ad ignorantiam.* Michalos and Machina see it as a type of argument that can be reasonable in some cases. Hence they are faced with the problem of telling their students how to distinguish between the fallacious and the reasonable cases.

Copi manages to brush this inconvenient problem aside, however. Any case, like case 2.7 of the FBI investigation of Mr. X, where the argument does seem reasonable, can be classified as falling outside the category of *ad ignorantiam* arguments altogether. Here the argument is based not on "ignorance" but on "our *knowledge* that if" something "had occurred it would be known." Since this is knowledge, not ignorance, all three cases (the elephant case, the pen case, and the case of Mr. X) are reclassified by Copi. They are not arguments from ignorance.

The Lockean Origin

The first known occurrence of the expression *argumentum ad ignorantiam,* used in roughly the sense it is given in the modern logic textbooks, is found in a parenthetical and often omitted passage in Locke's *An Essay Concerning Human Understanding,* first published in 1690.[5] In this short passage, near the end of the chapter entitled "On Reason," Locke cites four types of arguments "that man in their reasonings with others, do ordinarily make use of to prevail on their assent, or at least so to awe them as to silence their opposition." Three of them, the *argumentum ad verecundiam,* the *argumentum ad ignorantiam,* and the *argumentum ad hominem* are nowadays generally known as fallacies. However, these types of arguments are not described as fallacies by Locke. As Hamblin (1970, 161) puts it, "Locke does not clearly condemn any of the argument-types, but stands poised between acceptance and disapproval." Locke indicates that the type of argument called *argumentum ad hominem* is already known under that name, but he indicates that he is inventing the terms for the other three.

This passage from Locke's *Essay* is now well known, and is quoted in full in Hamblin (1970, 159–160). But it is worthwhile here to quote the part where Locke introduces the *argumentum ad ignorantiam* (Hamblin, 160): "Another way that men ordinarily use to drive others and force them to submit their judgments and receive the opinion in debate is to require the adversary to admit what they allege as a proof, or to assign a better. And this I call *argumentum ad ignorantiam.*" Here it is interesting to see that Locke is using the expression in a way that has a somewhat different orien-

---

5. Aristotle frequently writes of syllogisms that are fallacious because both premises are negative in the *Prior Analytics,* and Sextus Empiricus, a skeptic, writes much on suspension of belief or acceptance where insufficient evidence is known. Curiously, however, neither of them ever appears to state explicitly the argument from ignorance as a distinctive type of error or fallacy. Note that this claim itself is an argument from ignorance. What I really mean to say is that I have not found a passage that states the idea of the argument from ignorance, after searching through the works of Aristotle and Sextus.

tation than the one it predominantly (though by no means exclusively) has in the modern textbook accounts. He is using it in a dialectical framework; that is, in a context of disagreement, or difference of opinion, where two parties are reasoning with each other. The one party is using the *argumentum ad ignorantiam* as a way of engaging in interactive argumentation with the other party. Locke even explicitly used the word "debate" as one way of describing the setup. The argument from ignorance could be described as a kind of method or tactic, used in such a dialogue framework. Hamblin (160) calls it "an assent-producing device." Clearly, "argument" is being viewed here not just as a set of premises and conclusion—as so often stressed in the modern logic textbooks—but as a contestive exchange of reasoning moves between two parties where "devices" or tactical methods can be used to support a conclusion or defend an opinion.

Another aspect of Locke's treatment of the *argumentum ad ignorantiam* (and the *ad verecundiam* and *ad hominem* as well) that is somewhat distinctive and unusual is that he sees it as a weaker or second-line type of argumentation, as compared with a stronger, or first-line type he calls *argumentum ad judicium*. Locke calls the *argumentum ad judicium* "the using of proofs drawn from any of the foundations of knowledge or probability." This type of argument has to do with knowledge, according to Locke, whereas the other three relate only to opinion. Locke writes of the *argumentum ad judicium:* "this alone of all the four brings true instruction with it and advances us in our way to knowledge." What Locke is saying here is very striking, and distinctive of his view of the *argumentum ad ignorantiam.* He is saying that it is *dialectical,* or opinion-oriented, rather than *epistemic,* in the sense of being knowledge-oriented, or of contributing to knowledge. According to Locke's account, the *argumentum ad ignorantiam* can prepare the way for knowledge or "dispose one for the reception of truth." But it does not actually contribute to, or establish knowledge directly. Locke writes: "I may be ignorant and not be able to produce a better" [argument than another man], and therefore "ought to take the same [opinion] with him," but that does not mean that the opinion is false, or that it is proved or known to be false in itself, apart from the framework of a dialectical exchange.

> [The *argumentum ad ignorantiam*] may dispose me, perhaps, for the reception of truth but helps me not to it; that must come from proofs and arguments and light arising from the nature of things themselves, and not from my shamefacedness, ignorance, or error.

Locke is here distinguishing two quite distinct senses of the term "proof." One is to prove something relative to another party in a dialogue, as an acceptable opinion or commitment in argumentation. The other meaning is to prove something in the sense of showing that it is known to be true, or that it is established by evidence drawn from "the nature of things themselves." This is a more objective sense of "proof," meaning "based on external evidence that all reasonable parties to a dispute should presumably agree to, once shown the evidence." The other is a more relative or subjective sense of "proof," meaning based on the strongest argument in a dialogue to that point.

It is evident from Locke's remarks that he is taking the point of view that the dialectical kind of proof is the weaker, or secondary, of the two types, and that it must give way to the other where the other is available and strong enough to be decisive. He is clearly ranking the two types of proof, and saying that the one is more provisional in nature, while the other is more fundamental and underlying. The one only prepares the way, or disposes a particular person for the reception of truth, while the other "helps me" directly to truth, and is drawn from "the foundations of knowledge."

Locke's point of view in drawing such a dichotomy is not original to him. In fact, as Hamblin (1970, 161) notes, his dualistic perspective here is very much reminiscent of Aristotle's distinction between dialectical (opinion-based) arguments and demonstrative (knowledge-based) arguments. Locke's point of view in this passage is also strongly Aristotelian in tone in virtue of his seeing the *argumentum ad ignorantiam* (as well as the *ad verecundiam* and *ad hominem*) as assent-producing devices in an interactive framework of two parties reasoning together, devices that have the very real potential to be used as sophistical tactics to manipulate argumentation deceptively and dishonestly.

The modern textbooks have, with a few exceptions, tended to go in a different direction from Locke's conception of the *ad ignorantiam* (with only a few exceptions). But the older textbooks can clearly be seen to have been very much influenced by Locke's account, many of them paraphrasing it, or even quoting it.

Treatment in the Older Textbooks

Richard Whately is perhaps best known as a contributor to informal logic for his theories of presumption and burden as central to argument. It is quite a surprise, therefore, to see that Whately said very little about the *argumentum ad ignorantiam,* especially in light of his more extensive treatment of many of the other fallacies. At the tail end of his comments on the various *ad* fallacies (including, prominently, three of the four Lockean ones), Whately, in his *Elements of Logic* (1859, 237), has only this to say about the *ad ignorantiam:* "Along with these is usually enumerated '*argumentum ad ignorantiam,*' which is here omitted, as being evidently nothing more than the employment of *some* kind of Fallacy, in the widest sense of that word, towards such as are likely to be deceived by it." Curiously, Whately does not seem to think that the *argumentum ad ignorantiam* is a real fallacy in its own right, and he seems reluctant to say much of anything about it.

What could explain this reluctance? A clue is in Whately's earlier remark (236–37): "There are certain kinds of argument recounted and named by Logical writers, which we should by no means universally call Fallacies; but which *when unfairly* used, and *so far as they are* fallacious, may very well be referred to the present head." Whately here refers to the Lockean tradition of including *argumentum ad ignorantiam* as a fallacy, but he is clearly disagreeing with, or indicating we ought not to follow that tradition.

Why would Whately make such a suggestion? The answer is not too hard to find, if we recall a key passage in Whately's *Elements of Rhetoric* (1846, 113–14).

Case 2.8

> A body of troops may be perfectly adequate to the defence of a fortress against any attack that may be made on it; and yet, if ignorant of the advantage they possess, they sally forth into the open field to encounter the enemy, they may suffer a repulse. At any rate, even if strong enough to act on the offensive, they ought still to keep possession of their fortress. In like manner, if you have the "Presumption" on your side, and can but *refute* all the arguments brought against you, you have, for the present at least, gained a victory: but if you abandon this position, by suffering this Presumption to be forgotten, which is in fact *leaving out one of, perhaps, your strongest arguments,* you may appear to be making a feeble attack, instead of a triumphant defense.

Whately's analysis of presumption, as expressed above, clearly presumes that at least one version of the argument from ignorance is nonfallacious.

For the advice he is giving is that if you want to defend a presumption, your best line of argument may be to refute the negative arguments brought against it, instead of marshaling positive evidence to support it. Whately is, in effect, relying on a principle of burden of proof, a somewhat similar kind of argument to the *argumentum ad ignorantiam.* This suggests Whately might recognize the *argumentum ad ignorantiam* as a reasonable, and sometimes highly appropriate type of argumentation. Small wonder then that he was diffident about categorizing it as a fallacy.

What Whately's treatment showed is that there is an important link between presumptive reasoning and the *argumentum ad ignorantiam,* a link that makes the argument from ignorance more complicated than it may appear to be. Despite this warning by Whately, the remainder of the earlier logic textbooks tended pretty much to follow the Lockean line; after a while, however, they tended to drift toward classifying *argumentum ad ignorantiam* as a fallacy, and away from Locke's more balanced point of view.

Jevons (1883, 315) describes *argumentum ad ignorantiam* as "an argument founded on the ignorance of adversaries." Veitch (1885, 547) writes of the *fallacia ad ignorantiam:*

> A man says: Here is my opinion; here are my arguments. Can you refute this opinion? Can you answer those arguments? No, I cannot; I confess I am beaten. Well, then, accept the arguments, or, at least, the conclusion. This appeal, as wholly relative to the ignorance of the hearer or reader, is entirely beside the mark. The ground of it is in no way decisive, either of the force of the arguments or of the truth of the conclusion. It amounts to this: You don't know any better, therefore accept this as true.

This is very much an account in the Lockean spirit. But it seems to make the *argumentum ad ignorantiam* come out as generally a fallacy.

Hyslop (1899, 176) is a little more balanced, although the kind of argument he cites may be different from the argument from ignorance, as we conceive it. Hyslop's version might be better called "taking advantage of someone's ignorance."

> The *argument ad ignorantiam* is an appeal to a man's ignorance in order to produce conviction upon the ground of his inability to dispute the case.
> These several forms of *argumenta* are essentially the same in their

principles and import, and though they do not accomplish real proof, and to that extent evade the issue, yet they have the legitimate use of driving a man to define his position.

But in Hibben (1906), the *argumentum ad ignorantiam* takes a sharp turn for the worse, even though here, too, what is meant by this expression may be quite a different type of argument than the *argumentum ad ignorantiam* as defined by other textbooks: "This fallacy consists in taking advantage of the ignorance of the person or persons addressed who, consequently, lack the power of discrimination between the true and the false, the relevant and the irrelevant." Here it is categorically portrayed as a fallacy, with no acknowledgment of any "legitimate use" as an argument. This fallacy here still has some Lockean flavor, but it has changed to something quite different—what Hamblin (44) derisively describes as "browbeating of ignorant people into accepting the views of the speaker." This certainly sounds fallacious, but it also sounds like a different sort of fallacy from the Lockean type of *argumentum ad ignorantiam.*

Gibson (1908, 289) quotes the key part of the Locke passage directly, but without further explanation or qualification, classifies the *argumentum ad ignorantiam* as a fallacy. Mellone (1913, 354) seems to follow Hibben's line by dismissing *argumentum ad ignorantiam* in one line as a fallacy of "trading on the ignorance of the person or persons addressed." This seems less like a specific type of fallacy than merely taking advantage of or browbeating someone who is ignorant.

In these older textbooks generally, the tendency is to treat the argument from ignorance more or less in the Lockean fashion, as a dialectical fallacy where one party in a dialogue pressures the other or exploits his ignorance in an argumentation exchange. But then there was quite a distinct shift in the modern textbooks to thinking of the *ad ignorantiam* as an epistemic failure, or failure of proof, where "proof" and "knowledge" were conceived in a more impersonal way, in abstraction from an argumentative exchange between disputants. A glimpse ahead to the modern approach is already given in the discussion of burden of proof in Sidgwick (1884, chap. 3). Sidgwick poses the following questions (157):

How far, for example, are we "bound to explain away" a so-called fact? If we already have an apparently well-established theory regarding, say, the impossibility of corpses reviving, or of "spirits" holding communication with the living, or even if our theory goes no further than to deem some given behaviour of mind or matter a physical impossibility, what is the rational attitude towards a claimed miracle, or ghost-story, or mere narration of marvellous fact for which no explanation is offered?

Although he does not mention the *argumentum ad ignorantiam* by name, he does cite what he calls a "short cut" procedure of "fair presumption" that corresponds to this type of argumentation (159):

> Where there exists a "fair presumption" in favour of a belief, or where a belief is in harmony with prevailing opinion, the assertor is not "bound" to produce evidence, but that whoever doubts the assertion is bound to show cause why it should *not* be believed.

This means that with respect to any proposition that is apparently in harmony with established scientific knowledge or prevailing opinion, if no cause is given to show why it should not be believed, then it may be accepted (without producing positive evidence to support it). Sidgwick, like Whately, was accepting the argument from ignorance as being nonfallacious, although he viewed the argument in a distinctively different context.

Ghosts, the Paranormal, and ESP

A strong and growing tendency in the modern textbooks is to use examples of arguments that are on the borders of science, that are often related to pseudoscience, or that are cases whether it is highly questionable if any clear evidence could prove or disprove the claim. This class of cases represents a very special type of problem of verifiability of the proposition in question. It is not just the argument from ignorance that is involved, but also this special aspect of nonverifiability (or questionable verifiability) that affects these cases. But it is in this problematic type of case that the *argumentum ad ignorantiam* becomes more convincing, or apparently persuasive, and also more difficult to deal with.

This class of cases is reminiscent of the kind of problem of verifiability emphasized in the discussions of the early analytical philosophers in the twentieth century. They were worried about certain speculative, sweeping claims made by idealist philosophers, about the existence of God, the nature of reality and so forth, that did not appear to be verifiable or falsifiable by any clear, specifiable, or testable evidence. It is this nonverifiability characteristic that seems to be common to this whole class of cases treated in the textbooks.

Creighton (1929, 186) used the example of spiritualistic mediums to illustrate the *argumentum ad ignorantiam*. The fallacy, as he saw it, is one of trying to prove it is possible that something is true by arguing that it is impossible to prove that it is not true (186).

Case 2.9

> Thus we cannot prove affirmatively that spirits do not revisit the earth, or send messages to former friends through "mediums."

The full argument expressed here is that spiritualistic communication must be possible, because we can't prove that it is impossible. According to Creighton (186) the fallacy in this argument is confusing what is abstractly possible with what is really possible; that is, "possible" in the sense that "we have some positive grounds for believing."

Werkmeister (1948, 61) included the similar example of "mental telepathy" in his three examples of the *ad ignorantiam* fallacy.

Case 2.10

> Belief in immortality is unwarranted, for no one can absolutely prove that the soul is immortal.

Case 2.11

> Man is predetermined in all his actions, for you can't prove that he is free.

Case 2.12

> Mental telepathy may be accepted as a fact, for nobody can prove that it is impossible.

According to Werkmeister (61), all three of these arguments are fallacious because inability to verify a proposition is not sufficient proof that the opposite proposition is true.

Ruby (1950, 136) illustrates the *argumentum ad ignorantiam* by an example of a discussion on religion.

Case 2.13

> A man may argue that the Book of Genesis gives a literal account of the creation of the world. A skeptic may state that this account appears improbable to him, though he may also admit that he cannot disprove it. The religious protagonist then asserts, "You must now admit that it is true, for you cannot disprove it." This is the appeal to ignorance or inability to disprove.

Ruby calls this an "evasion," because "ability to disprove is not equivalent to proof." To illustrate the fallacy, he provides a comparable case (136).

Case 2.14

> Only evidence gives us proof. If we accepted this evasion we should be required to believe that the Angel Gabriel visited the prophet Mohammed and informed him that God had decided that the Mohammedan religion was to supersede the Jewish and Christian religions. For how would you go about disproving this claim? We are not required to accept the improbable merely because we do not know how to disprove it. As cautious thinkers, we will withhold belief until we have positive evidence in favor of a proposition.

These two cases are not quite comparable, because the conclusion of the second case is more implausible, whereas the burden of proof/disproof in the first case is more evenly balanced. Even so, the second case does make a good point about kinds of claims that are difficult to disprove.

Purtill (1972, 61) uses the case of the Loch Ness monster.

Case 2.15

> The *Fallacy of Arguing from Ignorance* [occurs where] an argument that at best proves that a conclusion has not been disproved is used

to attempt to establish that conclusion. For example, "All efforts to show that there is no monster in Loch Ness have failed. Therefore we must conclude that there *is* a monster in Loch Ness." Even if it is true that all efforts to disprove the existence of the Loch Ness monster have been unsuccessful, our conclusion should be that the question is still open, not that the existence of the monster is thereby proved.

To illustrate the fallacy, Purtill (61) reverses the argument to get an opposite argument from ignorance (61).

Case 2.16

> Many arguments of this kind can be neatly reversed. We might just as well argue that "All efforts to prove the existence of a monster in Loch Ness have failed. Therefore, there is certainly no monster in Loch Ness." The one argument is no better than the other.

Purtill (61) sees the problem with both these cases as one of the difficulty of proving a further counterfactual premise of the form: If the monster did (did not) exist, its existence (nonexistence) would have been proved by now.

Blumberg (1976, 47) uses the examples of extrasensory perception (ESP) and extraterrestrial life.

Case 2.17

> Extrasensory perception exists because no one has been able to prove that it does not.

Case 2.18

> Extraterrestrial life does not exist because no one has been able to prove that it does.

Note that in this account of the *ad ignorantiam,* it is not the impossibility or difficulty of disproof that is cited, but the fact that no one in the past has been able to prove that something is false, or does not exist.

Richards (1977, 39) uses the examples of telepathy and astrology.

Case 2.19

> To infer that telepathy doesn't exist or that astrology has nothing in
> it *purely* on the grounds that there is no real evidence for either,
> would be an example of the fallacy [of argument from ignorance].
> All that one can infer from that lack of evidence is that neither has
> been established.

Thomas (1977, 208) mentions the existence of God, UFOs, mental telepathy, and the Loch Ness monster as examples of the fallacy of arguing from
ignorance. Weddle (1978, 28) mentions flying saucers and the Genesis account of the creation of the world. Kilgore (1979, 26) also cites the example
of flying saucers as an instance of the fallacy of appeal to ignorance.

Case 2.20

> Since you cannot disprove that there are flying saucers, you should
> accept as reliable the reports of those claiming to have seen such ob-
> jects.

Toulmin, Rieke, and Janik (1979, 174) cite the "classic illustration" of the
argument for the existence of God, and also a case concerning astrology.

Case 2.21

> The stars seem to hold the key to our destiny.
>
> No one has ever demonstrated conclusively that the stars do *not*
> hold the key to our destiny.
>
> When a hypothesis has not been conclusively disproved, that lack of
> proof by itself can be taken *as evidence for* the hypothesis.

This argument from ignorance is fallacious, they say (174), because citing
lack of proof as "itself a kind of evidence" would "trivialize" the concept
of evidence "beyond recognition."
    Fearnside (1980, 22) cites belief in the existence of God, based on inabil-
ity to disprove, as an example of the argument from ignorance. Engel (1982)
cites the following pair of cases.

Case 2.22

> There is intelligent life in outer space, for no one has been able to
> prove that there isn't (188).

Case 2.23

> The chiropractors have failed entirely in their attempts to establish
> a scientific basis for their concepts. This question can therefore be
> settled once and for all. Chiropractic has no basis in science (189).

Halverson (1984, 63) uses the example of UFOs "being piloted by beings
from other planets," and Moore, McCann, and McCann cite cases of flying
saucers and ghosts. Pirie (1985, 96–97) cites examples of ghosts, extraterrestrial life, Bigfoot, the Yeti, and the Loch Ness monster. Davis (1986, 59)
cites an example concerning life on Mars. And Seech (1987, 96) takes up
the case of psychic phenomena, as well as mentioning (97) the existence of
spirits, life on other planets, the existence of God, and astrology. Govier
(1992, 168) mentions ghosts, life on other planets, UFOs, telepathic communication, and the following example of fallacious appeal to ignorance.

Case 2.24

> In some New Age religions, it is fashionable to believe in reincarna-
> tion. People practice something they call "channeling," and think
> that they are connected with spirits informing them of lives of past
> selves. To critics they may reply "you can't prove I'm wrong; prove
> that I didn't have past lives as a Mongol warrior and a Greek slave
> maiden." But the fact—if it is a fact—that a conclusive disproof is
> unavailable is no reason to believe the claim true. Ignorance as to
> disproof is not proof; it is just lack of knowledge.

This sort of case does represent a real fallacy, in the sense of a deceptive
tactic of argumentation used in everyday reasoning. It is often used by
cranks and defenders of crackpot theories to defend their speculative theories on the grounds that evidence is not available to disprove them. But the
problem in these cases of pseudoscientific claims seems to be one of scientific verifiability (or falsifiability) of a hypothesis. What led the textbooks
away from the Lockean conception of the *argumentum ad ignorantiam* as

a shift in the burden of proof, and toward these scientific preoccupations about verifiability?

Two explanations are likely. One is that this preoccupation just reflected the overriding concern with empirical science and with scientific method during the first half of the twentieth century. The other is that this concern very much affected philosophy as a discipline. Much of the literature in analytical philosophy during this period was centrally concerned with questions of verifiability.

In another respect, however, the modern textbooks have continued, at least implicitly, to reflect a particular aspect of the argument from ignorance that seems to be related to the Lockean conception: the legal presumption of innocence.

Legal Presumption of Innocence

Many of the textbooks mention the legal presumption of innocence in their discussions of the *argumentum ad ignorantiam.* However, there seem to be differences of opinion on how this should be dealt with. As mentioned above, Copi (1953, 56) held that the argument from ignorance is fallacious in every context but this one (see "Nonfallacious Cases" above).

Little, Wilson, and Moore (1955, 20) draw a distinction between "legal" and "actual" ignorance, presumably to discount the presumption of innocence as an exception to the rule that all arguments from ignorance are fallacious: "In order to give protection to the innocent, we assume that everyone is innocent until he is proved guilty. This assumption does not mean that a person is *actually* innocent in the absence of convincing evidence of guilt, but that he is *legally* innocent. We are certain that many guilty men have been declared innocent as far as the law is concerned simply because there was not enough evidence to establish guilt." Chase (1956, 166) not only thinks the legal context is compatible with the fallaciousness of the *ad ignorantiam,* but actually supports it: "[the argument from ignorance is] strictly forbidden in court. It amounts to forcing the accused to prove his innocence."

Runkle (1978, 291–92) seems to agree with Little, Wilson, and Moore that the word "innocent" is ambiguous in a way that makes the legal presumption of innocence no real exception to the fallaciousness of the *argumentum ad ignorantiam*.

> It is presumptuous to say that a claim is false because unproved or that a claim is true because not disproved. Is this presumption ever justified? It is sometimes said that such presumption is properly made in courts of law: if a person's guilt cannot be proved, he is presumed innocent. This presumption, however, is made possible by a special legal principle and establishes the fiction that the defendant is innocent. Failure to prove guilt does *not* mean that the person is innocent; it only means that society is directed by law to treat him *as if* he were innocent.

No doubt it is true that the expression "presumption of innocence" is somewhat misleading to describe the general rule of burden of proof in the criminal trial. Even so, however, it is less than clear why the rule of burden of proof in a criminal trial is not a species of argument from ignorance.

Fearnside (1980, 22) helps clarify the matter a bit.

> Under our law a person charged with crime must be proved guilty before he may be punished, and if guilt is not proved to the satisfaction of the jury it will bring in a finding of "not guilty." Such a finding does not mean that the accused has been shown *not* to have committed the offense; it signifies merely that his guilt was not proved. He may be guilty in fact or he may be innocent, but whichever he is, the evidence to show guilt is inadequate. Since we punish only those proved guilty of wrongdoing, where proof fails, a defendant is not guilty in a legal sense and we misleadingly announce "not guilty" where we may mean "not proved."

But what conclusion should we draw? Does the legal rule really come out to be an instance of arguing from ignorance, or not? And if so, how can it be shown to be an exception to the general rule that such arguments are fallacious? These questions remain puzzling, and do not appear to have been answered.

Engel (1982, 189) further clarifies the matter by bringing in the concept of presumption. In a fallacious appeal to ignorance (188), inability to disprove a conclusion is used as "proof that the conclusion is true." However, in a criminal case, the defendant is only *presumed* innocent. The failure to prove guilt is not taken as *proof* of innocence (189).

> It should be noted, however, that this mode of argument is not fallacious in a court of law, where, if the defense can legitimately claim that the prosecutor has not established guilt, then a verdict of not guilty is warranted. Although this claim may seem to commit the fallacy of appeal to ignorance, it does not really do so. The relevant legal principle in this case is that a person is presumed innocent until proven guilty. We do not say that defendants *are* innocent until proven guilty, but only that they are presumed to be so. Clearly, not every person whose guilt has not been proven is innocent; some are later proved, in fact, to be guilty. But until this is done, they are regarded as legally innocent, whether they are actually innocent or not. Practice in court is therefore not really an exception to our rule.

Here again the ambiguity of the term "proof" seems to be a problem. In one sense, a defendant who has won her case has not *proved* that she is innocent, or not guilty, in some broad sense of this word. This is just a presumption that has been successfully defended against the prosecution's attack. But isn't that a kind of "proof" as far as the law is concerned? Perhaps the key is that the legal notions of proof and disproof do not "prove a conclusion true," so much as to hold up or overturn a presumption.

But can't we still have fallacious *ad ignorantiam* arguments that conclude in presumptions? If I argue that we should presume that ghosts exist, because nobody has proved that they don't exist, couldn't this still be a fallacious *ad ignorantiam* argument, even though I never claimed that it "proved the conclusion true?" There still seems to be some uncertainty about whether or why the legal rule setting burden of proof cannot fall under the heading of the generally fallacious *argumentum ad ignorantiam.*

Halverson (1984, 63) thinks that the presumption of innocence principle does not lead to a conclusion that something is *proved* at all: "these principles do not make the absurd claim that in the absence of evidence the falsity of the statement of alleged fact or the innocence of the accused are *proved.* They merely establish the convention that under these circumstances proof will not be required." The suggestion here appears to be that the term "proved" is entirely inappropriate, in case of this legal principle.

Moore, McCann, and McCann (1985, 294) take the approach not of claiming that the principle is a nonfallacious argument from ignorance, but of claiming it is not an argument from ignorance at all.

> The principle that in American courts those accused are to be presumed innocent until proven guilty may seem to be an argument from ignorance, but in fact it is not. There is a difference between legal innocence and actual innocence. Legal innocence means that not enough evidence has been found to convince a jury "beyond the shadow of a doubt" that the accused has committed the crime. Many guilty persons have been declared innocent by law simply because there was not enough evidence to establish guilt.

This argument, like some of the others above, does not seem too convincing. Even after we disambiguate between "legal innocence" and "actual innocence," it still seems that inside the legal system, failure to prove (legal) guilt, leads to the conclusion "not guilty" (meaning no legal guilt was established). This still seems to fit the general form of the argument from ignorance.

Another argument that this legal principle is not really an argument from ignorance is to be found in Davis (1986, 59–60). The argument here seems to be that failure to find guilt in a proper legal trial is actually a sufficient form of proof, and not merely an ignorance, or lack of proof.

> Failure to find something after a thorough search constitutes proof that it is not there. One of the cornerstones of American law also appears to be an argument from ignorance—namely, the principle that a person is innocent until proven guilty. Taken at face value, such a statement would represent an argument from ignorance. But in the context of the law, this statement means that conviction requires proof of guilt, whereas failure to prove guilt suffices for acquittal. In opposing legal systems ("guilty until proven innocent"), acquittal must be based on proof of innocence, while failure to prove innocence is sufficient for conviction. Neither system sanctions the argument from ignorance.

This argument seems to be based on a good premise, because a failure to find evidence can, in the right circumstances, be described as itself a kind of evidence (or even proof). Nevertheless the argument seems to muddy the waters even further, because the jumping back and forth between positive descriptions of the same action or process seems arbitrary. "Failure to prove guilt" can, it is true, be described as a positive finding or type of evidence. But it can also be described in negative terms. And since the negative description is perfectly accurate, and indeed revealing and informative, it still seems quite appropriate to describe this process of legal reasoning as an instance of the *argumentum ad ignorantiam.*

The long and the short of this is that these varying treatments of the subject of presumption of innocence in law are very confusing. The problem is that most of the textbooks feel compelled to say something about it, presumably in order to head off the criticism that the *argumentum ad ignorantiam* is not a fallacy in this context. But dealing with the somewhat technical legal question posed by the issue seems to defeat the textbooks: they can't seem to decide whether this really is an instance of the argument from ignorance; or, if it is, whether it is fallacious or not, and in general how to describe it as a species of argument.

Whately (1846, 112–13) clarified this problem very well, and should have the last word, for the moment.

> It is a well-known principle of the Law, that every man (including a prisoner brought up for trial) is to be *presumed* innocent till his guilt is established. This does not, of course, mean that we are to *take for granted* he is innocent; for if that were the case, he would be entitled to immediate liberation: nor does it mean that it is antecedently *more likely than not* that he is innocent; or, that the majority of these brought to trial are so. It evidently means only that the "burden of proof" lies with the accusers; —that he is not to be called on to prove his innocence, or to be dealt with as a criminal till he has done so; but that they are to bring their charges against him, which if he can repel, he stands acquitted.

This dispels some of the confusion, and rightly points out that the root notion is that of burden of proof.

Burden of Proof

The argument from ignorance is clearly connected in some kind of important and revealing way to the underlying concept of burden of proof.

Many of the textbooks in fact indicate that the *argumentum ad ignorantiam* is a fallacy when the burden of proof has been reversed, or unfairly shifted to the other party, in a dialogue exchange of arguments. Among the modern textbooks stressing burden of proof as central to the *argumentum ad ignorantiam* are Werkmeister (1948), Michalos (1969), Munson (1976), Wright and Tohinaka (1984), Makau (1990), and Govier (1992). Waller (1988) provides a much fuller treatment of how burden of proof is central to the *argumentum ad ignorantiam*.

Werkmeister (1948, 61) sees the fallacy of *argumentum ad ignorantiam* as an attempt to shift the burden of proof to the other side in an argument. Michalos (1969, 370) sees burden of proof as a kind of responsibility for defending an assertion one has made: "Now, usually one who makes an assertion must assume the responsibility of defending it. If this responsibility or *burden of proof* is shifted to a critic, the fallacy of appealing to ignorance is committed." Such a shift occurs, according to Michalos (370) when one party in a dialogue asks another for a reason to prove his view, and he replies "Prove I'm wrong."

Munson (1976, 299) also explains burden of proof as a kind of responsibility or "job" an arguer incurs when she "puts forward an assertion, announces a position, or takes a stand." However, this responsibility to support a claim with evidence is abandoned when the arguer tries to shift it to the other side. In a case of this type, the "sophistic defender" of a claim "shirks" her responsibility, as shown in the following case (Munson, 1976, 300).

Case 2.25

CHALLENGER: One of the premises of your argument was that college students don't have the kind of perspective necessary to participate in determining university policy. Why do you believe this is true? It's certainly not obviously true.

ARGUER: Well, I should have thought it was obvious. Will you please tell me what reasons you could possibly have for believing that college students *do* have the necessary perspective?

One can certainly see how this type of case illustrates the *ad ignorantiam* fallacy. But what is burden of proof, and how exactly does it arise in an argument? The idea certainly seems to be dialectical in nature. That is, it presupposes a context of dialogue in which two parties are arguing with each other, and each of them has certain obligations or jobs assigned.

This idea is brought out a little further by Wright and Tohinaka (1984, 223) who write that it is part of the nature of an argument that it contains a conclusion which "must be appropriately connected to a set of sentences that support that claim." Thus the arguer who makes the claim has a responsibility "to support it with reasons." On the other hand, the party who questions the claim or doubts the argument does not have a positive burden of proving it wrong.

A problem, however, is that the burden of proof analysis of the *ad ignorantiam* does not seem to apply equally well to all cases. Consider the following case from Little, Groarke, and Tindale (1989, 274).

Case 2.26

> Commonplace examples of arguments from ignorance are found in everyday reasoning. "I've looked everywhere for Lulu, my pet chicken, and can't find her, so she must have left the yard." Here the failure to show that Lulu is in the yard prompts the conclusion that she is no longer there.

The first problem here is that there appears to be only one party involved in the reasoning; it is not explicitly a dialogue or dispute between two speakers, one of whom has the burden of proof. But perhaps, even so, we could say that a conflict of opinions is implicitly involved, because the question at issue is whether Lulu has left the yard or not. The speaker does not know the answer, so she could take turns considering the evidence on either side. So perhaps there is an implicit context of dialogue involved, and thus it can be said that there is an implicit shift in the burden of proof so that the person has wound up disproving that Lulu is in the yard.

But the second problem with this case is that it appears to be a nonfallacious argument from ignorance. Little, Groarke, and Tindale call it a good argument from ignorance (274).

> The criteria for good arguments from ignorance are implicit in these examples. The key to a good argument from ignorance is a responsible attempt to garner evidence that confirms or disconfirms the claim in question. Accordingly we define a good argument from ignorance as:

An argument that, after the failure of a responsible attempt to find evidence that some claim, x, is true (or false), concludes that x is false (or true).

It is only after such an investigation is completed that we can legitimately conclude that the claim in question is mistaken. It would not be convincing to argue that Lulu is not in the yard on the basis of our not seeing her unless we have made some effort to locate her—by looking behind the mulberry bush that blocks our view, and elsewhere.

Is the case of Lulu (2.26) really an argument from ignorance? It seems partly an argument from ignorance, and partly a case of positive evidence collected by an investigation. But if it is an argument from ignorance, how does the burden of proof concept apply to it?

The concept of burden of proof is recognized in law, so it may seem that it is a clearly defined concept that can be firmly set down or determined. Ilbert (1960, 15) defines burden of proof in law as follows:

In modern law the phrase "burden of proof" may mean one of two things, which are often confused—the burden of establishing the proposition or issue on which the case depends, and the burden of producing evidence on any particular point either at the beginning or at a later stage of the case. The burden in the former sense ordinarily rests on the plaintiff or prosecutor. The burden in the latter sense, that of going forward with evidence on a particular point, may shift from side to side as the case proceeds. The general rule is that he who alleges a fact must prove it, whether the allegation is couched in affirmative or negative terms.

This seems like a clear enough idea, in principle, but as Govier (1992, 169) has shown, in fact, in many common cases of controversy, it can be open to question on which side the burden of proof should lie. There are many open questions of burden of proof that have arisen in connection with new products, particularly drugs and medical treatments, that may possibly have harmful side effects. On the assumption of a free market economy and an individual's personal freedom to do what she likes with her body, it has often been argued that the burden of proof should be on those who would restrict or ban a new product. But as Govier (169) notes, this issue is complicated.

> In the past few years, public thinking on this matter has changed, partly due, no doubt, to well-publicized cases of drugs and other products with unforeseen harmful effects. We may see a shift to the idea that those who wish to market new products should first prove, to a rigorous degree, that these products are safe. The burden of proof, with a stringent standard of proof, would shift to those who would introduce a new product rather than to those who would restrict it.

Which side has the burden of proof in this kind of case can be controversial and complex. Both sides may share something of the burden, and government rulings may shift the burden at different times and in different circumstances.

Although legal rules of evidence may define where burden of proof lies in legal arguments, outside the law it may be more difficult to determine burden of proof in a given case. This is a fundamental problem for analysis of the *argumentum ad ignorantiam*. For surely, in a given case, whether the argument from ignorance is fallacious or not depends on the determination of burden of proof in that case.

The McCarthy Hearings

In the early 1950s Joseph R. McCarthy, a senator from Wisconsin, slanderously accused many innocent people of being Communists, subversives, or Communist sympathizers, making the subject of security risks a national obsession in the United States. According to an executive order of 1947, an employee could be removed as a "loyalty risk" on grounds of "espionage, advocacy of revolution, and membership in, or association with organizations deemed subversive by the Attorney General" (Matusow, 1970, 4). This led to a number of hearings and tribunals in which McCarthy, in a witch-hunt atmosphere, reversed the burden of proof, forcing many accused persons to prove that they were loyal Americans.

It is not hard to see how the *argumentum ad ignorantiam* flourished as a fallacy in this atmosphere. McCarthy would typically show up for one of these hearings with an impressive-looking bulging briefcase full of files on accused individuals. But in fact, the files often contained nothing more than slanders and innuendoes, based on little or no real evidence (Rovere, 1959, 130–33).

Several of the textbooks cite examples of the *argumentum ad ignorantiam* fallacy characteristic of the type of argumentation that took place in the interrogations of the McCarthy era when accused individuals were found guilty of being Communists. The first example of this type—other than that of Kahane, cited as case 1.3—is found in Chase (1956, 166).[6]

Case 2.27

"The State Department is full of Reds!"
"Prove it."
"I don't have to, let's see you disprove it."

Chase (164) describes the context in which this argument was used with such powerful force.

> "McCarthyism" . . . attempted to set up a different kind of law in a different kind of court, to replace, if not reverse, the principles of Anglo-Saxon justice. Cases which would not be admitted in the regular courts have been brought under administrative jurisdiction, i.e., loyalty boards, or before investigating committees of Congress and State legislatures. Many an accused person has been declared guilty with no proof beyond the charge, and then tried for his associations, ideas, suspected intentions, family connections, rather than for his specific acts.

As Chase notes (164) these tribunals "looked like a Hollywood version trial" when viewed on television. But in reality, accusations were made on

6. Copi (1953), in case 2.7 above, did use the example of an FBI investigation failing to unearth evidence that Mr. X is a Communist in his discussion of the *argumentum ad ignorantiam*. But Copi was making the point that if such a search were thorough enough, it would be based not on ignorance but on knowledge, and would not, therefore, be a genuine case of argument from ignorance. This case is presented and discussed in detail in Chapter 4. In the fourth edition (1972), Mr. X was still a communist, but in the sixth edition (1982), he had become a "foreign agent." In the seventh edition, he was still a foreign agent, but he disappeared in the eighth edition (Copi and Cohen, 1990).

the basis of little or no real evidence, so that the proceedings were really a kind of "inquisition" or "kangaroo court."

This type of case is quite an effective illustration of the *argumentum ad ignorantiam* as a fallacy. For one thing, the argument was used here with great force, and the consequences of its use were enormous. For another thing, it is clear that something is badly wrong with this type of tribunal, and therefore very easy to convince students (readers of the textbook) that the *argumentum ad ignorantiam* is fallacious here, without having to raise further questions or make qualifications.

Copi (1982, 112) used this example as an exercise, and continued to use it in subsequent editions up to and including Copi and Cohen (1990, 107–8. The case is from Rovere (1959, 132).

Case 2.28

> On the Senate floor in 1950, Joe McCarthy announced that he had penetrated "Truman's iron curtain of secrecy." He had 81 case histories of persons whom he considered to be Communists in the State Department. Of Case 40, he said, "I do not have much information on this except the general statement of the agency that there is nothing in the files to disprove his Communist connections."

This very interesting case of the *argumentum ad ignorantiam* was subsequently taken up by other textbooks. The same example (case 2.28) was used in Carter (1977, 144), and used as a leading example by Davis (1986, 59):

> This fallacy [the argument from ignorance] is committed whenever the conclusion that something is false is drawn from the premise that it has not been shown to be true, or whenever the conclusion that something is true is drawn from the premise that it has not been shown to be false. Such arguments were very common during the McCarthy era, when people were accused of being communists merely because they could not prove they weren't.

It is evident from this example that the fallaciousness of the argument from ignorance is linked to burden of proof somehow, and to the presumption of innocence in the law. The procedures used in the McCarthy tribunals appear to have reversed burden of proof so that the exact opposite applied:

you were presumed guilty, once accused, and the burden then lay on the accused party to provide evidence of being innocent. However, given the difficulty of rebutting the vague charge of being a "Communist sympathizer," this burden would be heavy indeed.

The notion that the fallaciousness of the argument from ignorance is tied to an inappropriate attempt to shift the burden of proof is brought out in the use of this example by Bonevac (1990, 79).

Case 2.29

> A lack of knowledge shows something only if there has been a competent, thorough, unfrustrated attempt to secure that knowledge. Otherwise, pointing toward a lack of knowledge is an unfair attempt to shift the burden of proof onto one's opponents.
>
> Some dramatic examples of this kind of fallacy arose in the context of Senator Joseph McCarthy's crusade against Communists in government. Presenting a list of alleged Communists in the State Department, he said about one official, "I do not have much information on this except the general statement of the agency that there is nothing in the files to disprove his Communist connections." Lack of disproof, clearly, is not tantamount to proof.

But since the McCarthy hearings were not legal proceedings, or court cases bound by legal rules of evidence, what in fact was fallacious or unfair in his use of innuendo to make accusations on the basis of little or no real evidence? What burden of proof should have been required here, and why was it a requirement that should have been adhered to? These are not easy questions to answer. But these are the questions that need to be investigated if we are to have any sound basis for determining in a given case whether an argument from ignorance is fallacious or not.

In hindsight, it is easy to dismiss the argument from ignorance as used by McCarthy as a dubious tactic or tool, used in a witch-hunt interrogation. But at the time, the argument was amazingly effective and convincing to many people. It seems that in an atmosphere of popular emotional hysteria for a "cause," aided by a widespread fear or threat to security of some sort, this type of argument from ignorance is swept forward, and can be very convincing for a time, with devastating effects on affected individuals.

The fundamental problem for us, however, is not the crowd psychology of the *ad ignorantiam,* but the question of finding some sort of normative basis or structure of argumentation that would enable us to decide, on good evidence, in a particular case, whether the argument from ignorance is fallacious or not. The first step in this process is to identify some characteristic logical form of the argument from ignorance exhibiting its general structure as a type of argument.

Schematic Accounts of Logical Form

Several of the textbooks give a schematic account of the logical form of the *argumentum ad ignorantiam.* Carney and Scheer (1974, 29), as already outlined above, express their scheme in the form: there is no proof (or you have not proved) that *A* is false (true); therefore *A* is true (false). Here we adopt the standard of using capital letters, *A, B, C, . . . ,* to stand for propositions.

The scheme given by Machina (1982, 42), as we saw already, is slightly different, taking the form, "*A* has never been proved to be true (false); therefore *A* is false (true)." This scheme refers to proofs given in the past, whereas the Carney and Scheer scheme refers alternately to the existence of a proof, or to the person to whom the argument was addressed (presumably this is the "you" of their scheme) not having proved the proposition.

Similarly, the scheme presented by Kilgore (1979, 26) contains a "you," perhaps suggesting a dialectical or burden of proof framework where two parties are engaged in argumentation together: "*A* is true because you are unable to show convincingly that *A* is false." This scheme is quite different from the previous two, because it is based on the inability to prove, rather than just on the failure to prove, something in the past.

According to the account given in Nolt (1984, 256), the argument from ignorance has two forms.

There is no proof that *A*.
Therefore not-*A*.

There is no proof that not-*A*.
Therefore *A*.

In this scheme, the negation particle (not) is used instead of the terms "true" and "false." However, in other respects, the scheme is similar to the one of Carney and Scheer.

Similarly, the account of Kelley (1994, 128) uses a negation prefix for the denial, negation or opposite of a proposition.

Not-A has not been proven true.
Therefore A is true.

Kelley's version uses the term "true" as well as the negation particle.

Govier's scheme (1992, 167) is quite different from any of the above, because it phrases everything in terms of knowledge, as opposed to proof or proving. She gives the following pair of forms (167), which she sees as representing a fallacious type of argument.

We do not know that A is true.
Therefore, A is false.

We do not know that A is false.
Therefore, A is true.

Johnson (1992, 242) gives two forms of argument he calls the fallacy of appeal to ignorance that are essentially identical to those of Govier above.

Many other textbooks, that do not give so explicit accounts of the form of the argument from ignorance as those above, explain ignorance as meaning lack of knowledge. But there are others that rely more on the concept of proof than knowledge.

Some textbooks define the *argumentum ad ignorantiam* without even referring to knowledge or lack of knowledge. According to Creighton (1929, 186), "The *argumentum ad ignorantiam* is an attempt to gain support for some position by dwelling upon the impossibility of proving the opposite."

Castell (1935, 372) defines the *argumentum ad ignorantiam* as "the fallacy of arguing that [a proposition] p must be admitted because its disproof is difficult or impossible." Robinson (1947, 197) defines the *argumentum ad ignorantiam* as "an attempt to prove a proposition negatively by showing that its opposite is an absurdity or an impossibility or very undesirable." This definition is questionable on the grounds that it makes *argumentum ad ignorantiam* indistinguishable from *reductio ad absurdum* (as pointed out by Mike Wreen). But it does suggest (favorably, in my view, as indicated in Chapter 8, below) that *argumentum ad ignorantiam* does have a *modus tollens* structure in outline. Werkmeister (1948, 61) characterizes the *argumentum ad ignorantiam* by the statement, "The fact that a certain proposition or theory cannot be demonstrated to be true is not in itself sufficient proof that an opposite proposition or theory is true." Blumberg (1976, 47) writes that to commit the *ad ignorantiam* fallacy is "to argue that a conclusion should be accepted because it has not been disproved or that it should be rejected because it has not been proved."

None of the forms proposed above are explicitly dialectical. Generally they presume a framework in which knowledge or proof can be described in impersonal terms, as a cumulative buildup of evidence perhaps. However, as noted, the use of "you" in two of the accounts at least implicitly suggests a dialectical framework of two parties.

Some other accounts have been more explicitly dialectical in giving account of the form of the *argumentum ad ignorantiam*. Ruby (1950, 136) offers the following sequence, or as I shall call it, "profile" of dialogue (in Chapter 4, "Stonewalling").

Profile 2.1

A is true.

Why?

Because you can't disprove it.

Here, it is the inability to disprove that is cited as the basis of the *argumentum ad ignorantiam*. But another feature is the explicitly dialectical format of the question-reply sequence of a dialogue between two parties engaged in arguing interactively.

Other textbooks have suggested an additional dimension of the structure of the *ad ignorantiam* argument in the form of another consideration. W. E. Moore (1967, 304) suggests a counterfactual proposition that is implicit.

Case 2.30

> The lack of knowledge or evidence is significant only in proportion to the probability that the evidence would have been found if it existed. Suppose you argue that Joe Smythe was not in the library last week on the ground that you did not see him there. The fact that you did not see him there is significant only in proportion to the probability that you would have seen him had he been there.

Copi (1953, 57) also recognized this additional counterfactual premise when he wrote, "In some circumstances it can be safely assumed that *if* a certain event had occurred, evidence of it could be discovered by qualified investigators." Purtill (1972, 61) also mentions additional premises of this sort. In discussing the Loch Ness monster case, he writes that "we unconsciously add some further premise": for example, "If the monster did exist, its existence would have been proved by now." These considerations suggest that, in addition to the explicit forms of argument expressed by the various schemes above, there may be a nonexplicit type of premise as well, presumed by the context of an *ad ignorantiam* argument in a given case.

What is key in the textbook accounts is that they presume that the *argumentum ad ignorantiam* is generally fallacious, or at least is a fallacy in many cases: they also admit, nonetheless, that it is nonfallacious in some cases. The basic problem then is to prove some sort of basis for distinguishing between the fallacious cases and the others. Clearly the accounts of the logical form of the *argumentum ad ignorantiam* are not sufficient in this regard, and some sort of additional premises or structures are needed to get anything like an adequate analysis of this type of argument.

Before we go on to that project, however, it will be useful to survey the traditions on the argument from ignorance in disciplines other than logic. In these disciplines, the perspective is quite different, and provides quite a contrast with the view of philosophy expressed in the logic textbooks.

3

—————————————————Uses
Outside Logic

For those familiar with the standard treatment in logic, as outlined in Chapter 1, it may come as quite a surprise that the argument from ignorance is widely used, and presumed to be nonfallacious, in scientific and medical reasoning, in other academic disciplines like history, and in practical reasoning in everyday, common argumentation and deliberation. At first it may be difficult to believe this, but part of the reason it is not evident is terminological. In these uses outside logic as a discipline, the *argumentum ad ignorantiam* is known by a variety of other names.

In the natural sciences and medicine, experimental studies often report "negative evidence" or "negative results." In psychology and the social sciences, "lack-of-knowledge inferences" have been recognized as reasonable kinds of inferences that experimental subjects often make. In history, *ex silentio* reasoning is common, where there is absence of positive empirical evidence, but where the failure of something to happen, or to be recorded, can be a basis for drawing a conclusion about the past. In computer science, the subject of negative reasoning by default from what is *not* in a knowledge base, has been the subject of recent research. The study of so-called nonmonotonic and autoepistemic reasoning in artificial intelligence is centered exactly on the kind of reasoning a computer uses when it searches through a knowledge base and, not finding a specific item of knowledge there, draws some sort of conclusion from this absence of knowledge.

As will be shown in this chapter, all these cases do fall under the category of argument broadly sketched out in Chapter 1 as the *argumentum ad ignorantiam* of traditional logic. This traditional treatment of the *ad ignorantiam* poses a big puzzle, because all of these arguments outlined in the cases in this chapter are generally presumed to be reasonable and appropriate, in the disciplines and contexts in which they are used. They certainly don't seem to be fallacies. How then, can we reconcile this apparent disparity? How can we judge when an argument from ignorance is reasonable or fallacious? This is the ultimate question, but for the present, let us try to get some grasp of these nonfallacious uses of the *argumentum ad ignorantiam* outside logic.

Negative Arguments *Ex Silentio*

Fischer (1970) does not list the *argumentum ad ignorantiam* in *Historians' Fallacies* among the many fallacies listed. Nevertheless, he does cover this area by splitting what amounts to the *ad ignorantiam* into two separate fallacies: the fallacy of the negative proof (47) and the fallacy of the presumptive proof (48).

The fallacy of the negative proof seems to correspond to what historians usually call the *ex silentio* argument, except that Fischer is highly negative about this type of argumentation, classifying it as not "correct" as an empirical procedure suitable for use in collecting historical evidence (47).

> The *fallacy of the negative proof* is an attempt to sustain a factual proposition merely by negative evidence. It occurs whenever a historian declares that "there is no evidence that X is the case," and then proceeds to affirm or assume that not-X is the case. He may have spent all the years of his youth in the Antiquarian Society, feverishly seeking the holy X and never finding it. He may have examined every relevant scrap of evidence in every remote repository, without reward. He and every other reasoning being on this planet may know in their bones that not-X is the case. But a simple statement that "there is no evidence of X" means precisely what it says—no evidence. The only correct empirical procedure is to find affirmative

evidence of not-X—which is often difficult, but never in my experience impossible.

This is a fairly strong stand on the *ex silentio* or "negative proof" type of argument, which is more often taken by historians to be a weaker type of argumentation, and only appropriate where stronger, positive evidence is not available, but is not taken to be so wholly defective that it can be generally categorized as fallacious (see case 3.1).

The fallacy of the presumptive proof, according to Fischer (48) "consists in advancing a proposition and shifting the burden of proof or disproof to others." This fallacy is much closer to the traditional conception of the *argumentum ad ignorantiam* as a fallacy found in the logic textbooks, and is especially reminiscent of the Lockean *ad ignorantiam* type of argument.

It is interesting then that Fischer, writing from a viewpoint of the discipline of history, does not use the expression "argument from ignorance" at all. It is also interesting to see how he splits this type of argumentation in two separate species of arguments, one emphasizing the negative aspect, and the other centering on shifts in the burden of proof.

The following case (Maxfield, 1981, 138) is a particularly good example of a reasonable use of the *ex silentio* type of argument from ignorance. This case concerns the giving of military medals or awards for courage (*dona militaria*) by the ancient Romans.

Case 3.1

> The Romans do not appear to have awarded medals posthumously. The evidence regarding posthumous awards is entirely negative; there is no positive statement to the effect that the Romans honoured only their live and not their dead heroes, but neither is there any statement to the contrary nor any single case of a soldier who must have been decorated after death. There is no reason to believe that the fine decorations illustrated on the cenotaph of Marcus Caelius who died in the Varus disaster of AD 9 were awarded to him posthumously. On the contrary, the circumstances of his death in one of the most ignominious defeats ever suffered by the Roman army preclude the award of decorations. The *dona* must belong to an earlier stage in his career. It is notable that, of the two Canuleius brothers who fought for Caesar in Gaul, both serving in legion VII, only Caius who survived received military decorations. Quintus who

was killed did not. To deny the possibility of posthumous awards is to accept an argument *ex silentio* with all its inherent weaknesses, but the total quantity of evidence on the whole question of *dona militaria* is such as to justify the belief that had such a practice existed it would have been reflected in some way in the available evidence.

The argument in this case is an *ad ignorantiam,* because the conclusion that the Romans did not award medals posthumously, is based on a negative finding: there has never been a single known case of a soldier decorated after death, nor is there any statement of the existence of such a case. The premise of the argument is based on absence of knowledge of any instance of such an award.

Maxfield's use of the *argumentum ad ignorantiam* in this case is very judicious, in several respects. She cautiously expresses the conclusion by claiming only that the Romans did not *appear* to have awarded medals posthumously. She recognizes that she is using a negative argument *ex silentio,* "with all its inherent weaknesses." And she cites three more positive supporting arguments to back up the argument from ignorance: (1) she rebuts the apparent conclusion that the decorations on the cenotaph of Marcus Caelius represented posthumous awards; (2) she cites the positive evidence of the case of the two brothers, where the one who died did not receive an award; and (3) she cites the "total quantity of evidence" as supporting the counterfactual—if the practice of giving posthumous awards existed, we would know about it. These three supporting arguments back up the central *ad ignorantiam* argument very convincingly, by taking the larger picture of known, relevant evidence into account.

This case suggests that the *ex silentio* argument is a species of *ad ignorantiam* argument that can be used reasonably in the discipline of history, and probably is a very common kind of argument that historians often have to use. It would be an exaggeration, then, to say that this type of argument is inherently fallacious.

What is also indicated by this case, however, is that the argument from negative evidence tends to be an inherently weak argument, used where there is absence of positive evidence. It tends to be weaker, all else being equal, than an argument from positive evidence. It tends to be a presumptive type of argument, meaning that it is provisional on the given evidence, and subject to default or correction should new evidence that is stronger (or more positive) come to be known.

Fischer, then, is not wrong in emphasizing this presumptive nature of *ex silentio* arguments by having a separate fallacy of presumptive proof. But are presumptive arguments inherently fallacious in nature? It depends on what Fischer means by "advanced." If you put in "asserted" for "advanced," what is described is a fallacious argument. But not if you put in "presumed" instead of "asserted." The second half of this chapter is devoted to showing how and why presumptive arguments (from ignorance) can be reasonable in many instances.

Negative Evidence in Science and Medicine

What is called negative evidence in scientific research arises where an outcome that may be expected is tested for, but does *not* occur. Until recently scientific articles reporting negative results were not generally regarded as publishable, but now such articles are on the increase. On June 24, 1993, in a search in the UNCOVER data base, then including more than four million titles (and in some cases, abstracts) of articles, thirty-two articles were found that reported conclusions based on negative evidence in scientific or medical research.[1]

Some feel that more publishing of negative results is a good thing. David Pullinger, electronic product manager at Institute of Physics Publishing, is quoted by Holderness (1993, 23) as saying, "Greater publishing of negative results will be very helpful—they don't receive so many citations, but are essential to stop others wasting time and money." Others disagree. Lynne Brindley, librarian at the British Library of Political and Economic Science, is skeptical (Holderness, 1993, 26): "I suppose they're useful—but I think personal pride will inhibit progress in that area." This remark suggests that the publishing of negative evidence may not be altogether a good thing. Another assumption is that negative evidence is not so good as positive evidence.

On the other hand, surely it would be too strong to say that negative evidence is so bad that it is worthless or fallacious. In medical research, for

1. Under the joint word search "negative" and "evidence," 112 titles were listed. Of these, thirty-two were definitely found to give or discuss negative evidence in scientific or medical research. However, not all abstracts of these articles were available in UNCOVER, and it was not always possible to determine whether an article was about negative evidence by the title alone. So the real number is likely larger than thirty-two.

example, in the testing of new drugs or treatments, negative results can be quite important. This has already been noted by Copi and Cohen (1990).

Case 3.2

> In some circumstances, of course, the fact that certain evidence or results have not been got, after they have been actively sought in ways calculated to reveal them, may have substantial argumentative force. New drugs being tested for safety, for example, are commonly given to mice or other rodents for prolonged periods; the absence of any toxic effect upon the rodents is taken to be evidence (although not conclusive evidence) that the drug is probably not toxic to humans. Consumer protection often relies upon evidence of this kind (94).

In this type of case, assuming the investigation was a thorough one which met scientific standards of correctness, the negative conclusion that the drug is, as far as is known, not toxic to humans could be justified. Here the failure to prove does provide a nonfallacious kind of argument for arriving at a conclusion, at least on the basis of the known scientific evidence. It is not conclusive proof that the drug is safe. But it is scientific evidence that could provide a basis for further testing on human subjects, as part of a continuing inquiry.

If negative evidence is not conclusive, what is the "substantial argumentative force" it provides? How is it different from positive evidence? It seems to function indirectly by excluding or denying some outcomes that we are concerned about, or have some reason to expect. For example, Zweig, Singh, Cardillo, and Langston's (1992) study arose from recent interest that had focused on the possibility that Parkinson's disease is transmitted by a gene that is inherited exclusively through the maternal line. But this study, as indicated in the abstract quoted in case 3.3 below, found results that did not support the hypothesis of maternal inheritance.

Case 3.3

> A questionnaire concerning the occurrence of Parkinson's disease in parents was administered for 252 patients with Parkinson's disease. Eleven fathers and five mothers of patients were reported to also have had this disease. These data fail to provide support for the hy-

pothesis that Parkinson's disease is the result of maternal inheritance of an abnormal mitochondrial gene. This conclusion is further supported by a review of similar studies in the literature and an additional unpublished study, which revealed that of 922 patients with this disease, 37 fathers and 19 mothers were reportedly affected.

These findings do not refute the maternal transmission of Parkinson's disease (at least conclusively). But by failing to provide evidence for this hypothesis, after screening a large population, the study provides a substantial argument against it. This is evidence of a sort.[2]

One can see the element of the argument from ignorance here. Not enough is known at present either to definitively support or refute the hypothesis that it is the result of maternal inheritance of the mitochondrial gene. But since there has been support for the hypothesis in the past, and nothing so far rules it out, the negative finding of the study outlined in case 3.3 can perform a function of guiding researchers in future work on searching for the cause of this disease. The function here is one of guiding a search which is still open at this initial stage because of absence of knowledge established so far.

In the kind of searching process characteristic of a scientific inquiry, ignorance is relative. Certain facts are known, and ultimately the inquiry will only be successful when the target proposition is proved or disproved, based on these known facts. But at the earlier stages of the inquiry, there may be much that is unknown; that is, the conjectures may be based on little evidence, one way or the other. At these stages, it may be very useful in guiding the search, in directing the efforts to make empirical studies, to know what is not known. Here, negative results have a function in guiding the search.

In some cases, however, the *argumentum ad ignorantiam* can be very weak and tentative, because data is very hard to come by. John Anderson, a NASA research scientist, at a press conference at the Ames Research Center in California in July 1988, advanced a conjecture that a Planet X, five times as heavy as earth, could be traveling in a very elongated elliptical orbit perpendicular to the orbits of the other planets in our solar system. The orbit of Planet X could explain mysterious irregularities in the orbits

2. Another typical title from the UNCOVER search is J. Hey (1989), Speciation via hybrid dysgenesis: Negative evidence from the *Drosophila Affinis* subgroup, *Genetica* 78:97–104.

of Neptune and Uranus in the nineteenth century. But what evidence did Anderson base his hypothesis on?

Case 3.4

> Anderson bases his belief in Planet X on a *lack* of evidence gleaned from the flights of the two Pioneer spacecraft, now heading into the farthest reaches of the solar system. Back in the last century astronomers noticed that something was causing odd changes in the orbits of Uranus and Neptune. One possible explanation was the tug of gravity from an undetected planet. But if Planet X cruised in a typical orbit, it should have exerted its gravitational tug on the tiny, free-floating Pioneers. That didn't happen.[3]

It is true that Anderson's argument here was based on a lack of evidence. But it was also based on the observations of the movements of the two Pioneer spacecraft, which could be described as (positive) observational data of a sort. Moreover, a fuller description of the nature of the argumentation involved reveals a *modus tollens* structure. If Planet X were cruising in a typical orbit, the free-floating Pioneer spacecraft would have shown perturbations. But they did not. It may be concluded that if Planet X exists, it is not in a typical orbit, similar to the other planets. A possible explanation is that Planet X is too far away to affect the spacecraft, and this leads to the hypothesis that Planet X is in a very big orbit that may take a thousand years to circle the sun. If that hypothesis is right, then future perturbations in the orbits of Neptune and Uranus may be observed in the next century.

Case 3.4 is interesting as an instance of the *argumentum ad ignorantiam* because it is a case of scientific investigation, yet at the same time it verges on speculation precisely because of the lack of evidence. Does Planet X exist? We don't know, but the presumption of the scientific community is not to include Planet X in the scientific accounts of our solar system. This presumption has to do with standards of burden of proof for scientific inquiry. There is some positive evidence for the existence of Planet X—the reported perturbations of Uranus and Neptune in the nineteenth century.

3. William D. Marbach and Michael D. Cantor (July 13, 1987), The search for Planet X, *Newsweek*, 55.

And there is some negative evidence—the lack of perturbations in the Pioneer spacecraft trajectories. But this evidence appears to be minimal, in the sense that both observations could just as easily be accounted for by all kinds of other factors, without postulating the existence of Planet X. Therefore, the hypothesis that Planet X exists is only a plausible speculation, not an established scientific hypothesis. It is not pure speculation, however. It is a falsifiable hypothesis. There is observational evidence relevant to the hypothesis, which would confirm or disconfirm it. The problem is that the evidence is hard to come by at the present time, and what evidence is available can only be regarded as supporting the hypothesis of the existence of Planet X to a very small degree. Thus this case is different from the fallacious cases of pseudoscientific reasoning concerning UFOs and so forth.

We have seen then that the argument from negative results (negative evidence) can range from cases where it has substantial (but not conclusive) argumentative force, to cases where it has only a very small or slender argumentative force. Yet within this range, it can be a reasonable kind of argument that has a useful function in a scientific inquiry. On the other hand, it seems that positive evidence—evidence that either supports a hypothesis by positive findings, or refutes it—is preferable to negative evidence (when positive evidence is available). This type of argument is an argument from ignorance then, in two senses. It is a negative argument, based on something you didn't find, and it is a type of argument appropriate at the earlier stages of an inquiry, where conclusive knowledge, or hard evidence, tends to be lacking.

Negative Reasoning from a Knowledge Base

There is one form of the *argumentum ad ignorantiam* that has been recognized as a legitimate, reasonable, and very common way of drawing conclusions from a knowledge base in computer science. A *knowledge base* is any collection of propositions taken to be true in a given domain of knowledge at a given time, containing various facts and/or rules in that domain. Negative reasoning from a knowledge base can take place where it is inferred that a particular proposition is false because it is not in the knowledge base.

Presenting an interesting example, Reiter (1987) linked negative reasoning to what is called the *closed world assumption* in computer science, the assumption stating that all relevant, positive information has been presented in a knowledge base. This assumption licenses any respondent to infer that if a proposition is not explicitly stated, its negative may be assumed to hold (Reiter, 1981, 119).

Case 3.5

> Consider the simple example of a database for an airline flight schedule representing flight numbers and the city pairs they connect. We certainly would not want to include in this database all flights and the city pairs they do *not* connect, which clearly would be an overwhelming amount of information. For example, Air Canada flight 103 does not connect London with Paris, or Toronto with Montreal, or Moose Jaw with Athens, or . . . (Reiter, 1987, 150).

Hence if we look at the flight schedule for flight 103 and see that it does not contain a proposition saying this flight connects Moose Jaw with Athens, we can conclude that flight 103 has no such connection. The basic principle behind this way of presenting the information, according to Reiter (150) is that there is far too much negative information to present explicitly. So this negative information is presented indirectly by licensing the respondent to draw conclusions by negative reasoning.

It is very interesting to note that Reiter's presentation of the problem of negative reasoning in computer science reveals an important link with the literature on informal fallacies. For it is clear that case 3.5 is an excellent example of the use of the *argumentum ad ignorantiam* as a type of inference. Although this type of argument has traditionally been treated in logic textbooks as a fallacy, the kind of case cited by Reiter suggests that it also has correct uses as a reasonable type of knowledge-based argumentation.

In cases where the closed world assumption is in place, the inference drawn by *ad ignorantiam* may be regarded as conclusive. For example, if we know the airline schedule lists *all* the stops for flight 103, then it is possible to conclusively infer that any stop not listed is not connected to other stops on the flight. But even where the knowledge base is assumed to be incomplete (i.e., the closed world assumption does not hold), a reasonable but nonconclusive inference can be drawn by *argumentum ad ignorantiam*. Such a species of inference has been recognized in the social sciences as a common type of argumentation.

Researchers in cognitive science have studied *ad ignorantiam* argumentation by constructing computer programs that are designed to model certain kinds of inferences structured like human memory. A *lack-of-knowledge inference* (Collins, Warnock, Aiello, and Miller, 1975, 398) occurs where a respondent fails to find a queried item of information that a certain proposition is true, stored as knowledge in his memory, and concludes that, as far as he knows (the conclusion is "hedged" and "uncertain"), this proposition is false. In other words, in some cases, respondents will say "no" rather than "don't know" to a question, even though they lack enough knowledge to be certain about their answer.

What factors are important in leading a respondent to give a negative answer, rather than a "don't know" reply, even if he is reasoning from an incomplete knowledge base? One factor is the respondent's depth of knowledge of the subject.

An example from Collins, Warnock, Aiello, and Miller (1975, 398) shows how the AI program, called SCHOLAR (which has a geology knowledge base) answers the question, "Does Guyana produce rubber?" SCHOLAR does not know whether Guyana produces rubber (neither this particular proposition nor its negation are in SCHOLAR's knowledge base). SCHOLAR does know, however, that Peru and Colombia produce rubber. But how much does SCHOLAR know about Guyana? The important thing is that the more SCHOLAR knows about Guyana, the more confident it can be that if Guyana produced rubber, SCHOLAR would know it. In this case, SCHOLAR knew enough about Guyana to conclude, with a moderate degree of confidence, that Guyana does not produce rubber.

Case 3.6

> Is rubber an agricultural product of Guyana?
> RUBBER IS AN AGRICULTURAL PRODUCT OF PERU AND COLOMBIA. I
> KNOW ENOUGH THAT I AM INCLINED TO BELIEVE THAT RUBBER IS
> NOT AN AGRICULTURAL PRODUCT OF GUYANA. THE AGRICULTURAL
> PRODUCTS OF GUYANA ARE SUGAR AND LUMBER.

Yet in other cases, SCHOLAR will reply that it doesn't know whether a queried proposition is true or not. What is the key difference between these two kinds of responses?

The difference seems to relate to SCHOLAR's depth of knowledge of the subject matter. Where SCHOLAR replies "I don't know," it is because it doesn't know enough about the subject of the query to say, one way or the other. But where SCHOLAR replies "This is not the case," even though it does not know for sure, one way or the other, it has enough depth of knowledge that it has an inclination to draw a conclusion, one way or the other.

When one takes into account the knowledge-based character of the reasoning in advice-giving contexts of dialogue where a user is consulting a computer program that is an expert system, the *argumentum ad ignorantiam* begins to make a good deal of sense as a legitimate, correct, and important kind of argumentation. If the computer program has a certain proposition A contained in its knowledge base, then in reply to the question "Is A true?" the computer can say yes. But suppose A is not contained explicitly in the computer's knowledge base. Should it always reply "I don't know whether A is true or false" in such a case? Presumably not. In some cases, the expert system can draw an inference on whether A is presumably true or not, based on what it does know about related propositions in its domain of knowledge. The greater our confidence is that the expert knows all there is to know about the subject of our query, the greater our confidence is that the closed world assumption applies to our reasoning.

Thus here we have two species of *ad ignorantiam* argumentation, both of which are inherently reasonable, at least under the right conditions. When the closed world assumption holds in a knowledge base, the argument from ignorance is a conclusive type of argumentation, relative to that assumption. In cases where the closed world assumption does not hold, the *argumentum ad ignorantiam* takes the form of a lack-of-knowledge inference, based on a weaker assumption that there is enough knowledge to say that a particular proposition would be in the knowledge base, if it were true. In these cases, the *argumentum ad ignorantiam* is not a conclusive type of argumentation. Instead it is a kind of presumptive reasoning based on how confident we are that if something were true, it would be known to be true.

In knowledge-based AI systems like PROLOG, an assumption of complete knowledge is embodied in the negation rule, which states that a proposition may be said to be "false" if it cannot be proved true by the system (Aida, Tanaka, and Moto-Oka, 1983). The assumption is that the system is a closed world; that is, that its knowledge is to be regarded as complete in the given domain of inquiry. In this framework, the argument from ignorance is generally a conclusive type of argumentation.

Nonmonotonic Reasoning

Classical deductive logic has the property of *monotonicity,* meaning that if you have a valid argument, no matter how many new premises you add (even to the point where they form an inconsistent set), the argument still remains valid. However, practical reasoning tends to be nonmonotonic, because if new information comes in which changes the circumstances of a given situation, the rational conclusion may be to opt for a different course of action which takes this updating of information into account. Practical reasoning is dynamic or variable in a sense in which the reasoning modeled by classical deductive logic is static or "fixed."

Nonmonotonic reasoning is currently an intense topic of interest in artificial intelligence, where the following example of an argument is so often cited as the illustrative case.

Case 3.7

> Birds fly.
> Tweety is a bird.
> Therefore, Tweety flies.

This argument, as we would normally interpret it in everyday conversation, is nonmonotonic in just the following way. If the premises are true in a given instance, then one would be entitled to presume that the conclusion is true, provided the case is a normal one, in the sense that there is no knowledge that certain special circumstances are present that would invalidate the inference. For example, suppose we know that, in this particular case, Tweety is a bird that has an injured wing in a sling. Then, of course, in these special circumstances, we know that although Tweety is a bird, at least for the present he does not fly.

Case 3.7 is a typical example of nonmonotonic reasoning because it is not a deductively valid argument, but nonetheless it does seem to be a reasonable or correct argument in some sense. It is reasonable in the sense that the conclusion is true, given that the premises are true, and that there is an absence of knowledge that the conclusion is false. But what kind of argument is this? What does "reasonable" mean here, if it does not refer to deductive validity?

The problem concerns the interpretation of the first (major) premise. To make the argument deductively valid, you need to construe this premise as a universal (strict) conditional of the form, 'For all x, if x is a bird then x flies.' But what if Tweety has an injured wing? Or what if Tweety is a penguin, a type of bird that does not fly? The conclusion "Tweety flies" is false, but the second premise is true, therefore the major premise must be false, assuming the argument is deductively valid.

But this interpretation is problematic, because the major premise, in reality, still seems to be true, if interpreted in a less strict way. The major premise does not seem plausibly interpreted in this case as a universal conditional that asserts that all birds (without exception) fly. As Reiter (1987, 149) puts it, a more natural reading of this premise is one that allows for possible exceptions, and allows for the possibility that Tweety could be an exceptional type of bird with respect to the property of flying; that is, "Normally, birds fly," or "If x is a typical bird, then we can assume by default that x flies." What is meant here by *default* is that in the absence of evidence that Tweety is atypical, we can provisionally (subject to correction) assume that he flies. Thus the inference is *defeasible*, or subject to default, in the sense that it only goes forward provisionally, subject to defeat or rebuttal, should information come in showing that Tweety is not typical.

What is revealed here is that there are, broadly speaking, two types of reasoning, conclusive and nonconclusive. The conclusive type of reasoning, characterized by the closed world assumption, is monotonic; no matter how much new knowledge comes in, the inference in question must always hold. It is never overturned or invalidated. The nonconclusive type of reasoning, however, has the property that it only holds in relation to the given state of knowledge at a particular time, or stage of development of the argument. It is always subject to revision or correction, should new knowledge come in that might be contrary to what is already given.

The *ad ignorantiam* argument, therefore has revealed three key characteristics. First, it is a kind of knowledge-based reasoning. Second, it is a negative kind of knowledge-based reasoning that is based on negative evidence, on a given proposition's *not* being included in a knowledge base. Third, it divides into two subtypes: the conclusive type, characterized by monotonicity and the closed world assumption, and the nonconclusive type, characterized by nonmonotonicity and the open world assumption.

The nonconclusive type of *ad ignorantiam* often tends to be presumptive in nature, and this aspect of it needs to be studied further. But before going on to this examination, let us look at another kind of reasoning currently the subject of much attention in computer science.

Autoepistemic Reasoning

Nonmonotonic reasoning seems a possible species of *argumentum ad ignorantiam*, at least initially. Given the premise that Tweety is a bird, the conclusion "Tweety flies" follows only if we do not know that Tweety is some sort of special bird, like a penguin or an ostrich that does not fly. Only in the absence of this knowledge does the inference go through. Thus the reasoning here does have to do with the absence of a certain kind of knowledge in a given case, and therefore it does seem to be partly a kind of *ad ignorantiam* reasoning.

Konolige (1988, 344) gives the following example of nonmonotonic reasoning, which illustrates this point very well. To analyze this type of reasoning with reference to the expression "Power corrupts," Konolige presents the following default structure.

Case 3.8

It is provable from a knowledge base that x (some individual thing) is powerful.

It is consistent with this knowledge base that x is corrupt.

Therefore, x is corrupt.

The way Konolige (344–45) sees this inference is one that requires not only essential reference to a knowledge base (KB) of an agent, but also a negative kind of reference that is clearly of the *ad ignorantiam* type.

If we take the sentences of a KB to be the knowledge or beliefs of an agent, then defaults can be expressed by referring to what an agent *doesn't know.* The default that "power corrupts" could be stated informally as:

> If x is powerful, then assume x is corrupt, *if nothing known contradicts it.*

It is easy to see that such reasoning is defeasible in the presence of additional information about the integrity of x.

This kind of reasoning is clearly of a kind that requires reference to what is not present in a knowledge base.

But what is even more characteristic of nonmonotonic reasoning is the default aspect itself. Nonmonotonic reasoning is always based on a premise of the form "Generally if x is a bird (subject to exceptions), x flies." It is the nature of this special type of generalization, one that holds only subject to certain exceptions, that is characteristic of nonmonotonic reasoning.

However, because nonmonotonic reasoning does have a significant *ad ignorantiam* aspect to it, an aspect that is important to understanding how it functions as argumentation in everyday reasoning, researchers in artificial intelligence have been led to consider another type of reasoning that is equivalent to the *argumentum ad ignorantiam*. Robert C. Moore (1985, 78–79) defines this type of reasoning, called *autoepistemic reasoning*, using the following example.

Case 3.9

> Autoepistemic reasoning, while different from default reasoning, is an important form of commonsense reasoning in its own right. Consider my reason for believing that I do not have an older brother. It is surely not that one of my parents once casually remarked, "You know, you don't have any older brothers," nor have I pieced it together by carefully sifting other evidence. I simply believe that if I did have an older brother I would know about it; therefore, since I don't know of any older brothers, I must not have any. This is quite different from a default inference based on the belief, say, that most MIT graduates are eldest sons, and that, since I am an MIT graduate, I am probably an eldest son.

So defined, autoepistemic reasoning comes very close to meaning the same thing as the *argumentum ad ignorantiam,* or being essentially the same type of reasoning. It has the same characteristic form as the argument from ignorance, according to Moore's description of the case he uses to illustrate it. This inference takes the following form.

I do not know that I have an older brother.

If I did have an older brother, then I would know about it.

Therefore, I do not have an older brother.

Here we have the characteristic form of argument typical of the *argumentum ad ignorantiam*. The first premise is an absence of knowledge claim. The second premise is a counterfactual that links the first premise to some relevant knowledge that is available. The conclusion is a simple assertion that something is true (or false), not modified by any knowledge or lack of knowledge condition.

Another characteristic of autoepistemic reasoning is its reflexive nature: it is a kind of reasoning where an individual is reflecting on her own knowledge base. As Moore (1985, 80) puts it, "Autoepistemic logic is intended to model the beliefs of an agent reflecting upon his own beliefs." There have been many different ways of formalizing autoepistemic reasoning now in the artificial intelligence literature, but the way advocated by Konolige brings out this reflexive aspect very clearly. This formalization uses an operator M on propositions α, β, . . . where $M\alpha$ reads, "α is consistent with a knowledge base" (344). The L-operator is the dual of the M-operator, i.e. $L\alpha$ is defined as $\neg M \neg \alpha$.

The following example from Konolige (1988, 346) gives an idea of how the formalization works.

Case 3.10

Autoepistemic (AE) logic was defined by Moore (1985) as a formal account of an agent reasoning about her own beliefs. The agent's beliefs are assumed to be a set of sentences in some logical language augmented by a modal operator L. The intended meaning of $L\phi$ is that ϕ is one of the agent's beliefs; thus the agent could have beliefs about her own beliefs. For example, consider a space shuttle flight director who believes that it is safe to launch not because of any positive information, but by reasoning that if something were wrong, she would know about it from her engineers. This belief can be expressed using sentences of the augmented language. If P stands for "It is safe to launch the shuttle," then

$$\neg L \neg P \supset P \qquad (5)$$

expresses the flight director's self-knowledge. Equation (5) is a logical constraint between a belief state ($L \neg P$) and a condition on the world (P).

The details of the formalization are not important here, but what is important is to see how autoepistemic reasoning is generally understood in artificial intelligence research, and how it represents a distinctive kind of reasoning that is essentially the same as the underlying pattern of the reasoning characteristic of the *argumentum ad ignorantiam* of the tradition of the logic textbooks.

In case 3.10 above, one can clearly see this pattern of the *argumentum ad ignorantiam*. The shuttle director reasons on the basis not of "positive information," but on the lack-of-knowledge premise that she has received no information that the shuttle is unsafe. Then too there is the typical *ad ignorantiam* counterfactual premise that if something were wrong, she would know it. In the formalization (5), the use of the negation sign ($\neg$) in front of the L-operator clearly indicates the negative knowledge aspect.

Another interesting aspect of this case that foreshadows a very common characteristic of *ad ignorantiam* arguments featured in Chapter 3 is the basing of the reasoning on an appeal to expert opinion. In this case, the shuttle director bases her inference on what she would know from her engineers; that is, expert consultants who are the sources of the knowledge base used to support the reasoning.

Balance of Consideration Arguments

The *ad ignorantiam* argument often comes into play where there is a conflict of opinions on some controversial issue, and there is very little strong evidence to resolve the issue, one way or the other. Frequently, in such a case, a number of very weak arguments are combined together to build up a case for the one side or the other. Although each individual argument may be weak and inconclusive by itself, still it may have a part to play, as part of the larger case being made. Where an *ad ignorantiam* argument is used in a case like this, it may be quite correct to say it is a weak or inconclusive argument, taken by itself. Yet it could be incorrect to leap to describing it as a fallacy, or as a fallacious argument.

A case in point concerned the controversy that arose about the World War I fighter pilot, Billy Bishop, a Canadian hero who was credited with seventy-five aerial victories. Bishop won the Victoria Cross for a lone attack on a heavily fortified German airfield well beyond the enemy lines. The stories of his exploits in aerial combat are legendary, and he is probably the most celebrated war hero that Canada has ever produced. However, there had been some rumors about Bishop's victory claims, some of which, especially during a certain period, were not very well supported by witnesses or by other available evidence. In 1982, these doubts were openly expressed in the National Film Board of Canada movie *The Kid Who Couldn't Miss,* where it openly suggested that Bishop was a fraud, and even that he had made up the story of his lone attack on the German aerodrome. The film was attacked by critics, but the controversy was intensified by the problem that "no one seemed able to prove that Bishop really had done the things for which he had been credited for so long" (McCaffery, 1988, vi). The lack of evidence seemed to fuel the controversy.

Even among the surviving pilots who had flown with Bishop, opinions were divided. One of these veterans said that "everybody in the corps" knew that Bishop was lying about victories, while another claimed, "I never heard a whisper of criticism against him, and it is nonsense to suggest that it was common knowledge he exaggerated" (McCaffery, 1988, 208). Many of the pilots praised Bishop's character highly, while others indicated reservations. One incident concerned a commemorative cover that some of the pilots refused to sign.

Case 3.11

> While it is true that three former 60 Squadron pilots refused to sign a British RAF Museum "flown cover" commemorating Bishop's raid when asked to do so in 1977, it is also a fact that another squadron member, Edgar Percival, did put his signature to the cover. And squadron member Tim Hervey has indicated that he, too, would have signed, had he been asked.
>
> Percival died just before the author could contact him, but his brother, Robert, did respond to a letter. He wrote: "I feel Edgar must have respected Bishop for I have never heard Edgar criticize

him. Edgar was one who always expected the highest standards to be kept and I feel sure that if Bishop had fallen short in this respect one would have heard it from Edgar."

It would appear that the main reason why only one of four pilots would sign the cover was that Bishop's critics simply outlived his supporters (McCaffery, 1988, 208–9).

The problem here was the absence of any really solid evidence after such a long time, especially when there had been little evidence in the first place. The situation at this point was a balance of considerations that turned on not very decisive factors, like the opinions of Bishop's character according to the testimony of the surviving pilots who had flown with him.

In this kind of situation, the *ad ignorantiam* argument is one that, despite its slender nature as a type of proof, is useful and appropriate. Robert Percival replied that if Bishop had fallen short, one would have heard it from his brother Edgar. The inference can be completed by adding the negative evidence premise, "There was no report of this kind from Edgar." Therefore, the conclusion implied is "Bishop did not fall short."

We can no longer get direct testimony from Edgar, so the best that can be done here is to draw an *ad ignorantiam* argument based on what he did not say, according to the knowledge of his brother. This is an inherently weak and fragile type of argument. But it would be inappropriate to dismiss it as fallacious. It plays a legitimate part in building up a larger body of evidence on one side of the issue presented in McCaffery's account. Then the reader can decide for herself.

Ultimately, McCaffery, in the book, does find some stronger evidence, especially some eyewitness testimony of French civilians living near the German aerodrome Bishop attacked, that supports his account of the action (196–210). But at the point in the book where case 3.11 fits into the larger picture of the evidence marshaled throughout McCaffery's book, the *ad ignorantiam* argument used in case 3.11 does have a legitimate function as supporting the one side. In such a balance of considerations argument, where hard evidence is inconclusive on both sides, even a slim and subjective *ad ignorantiam* argument can have a legitimate place in the larger picture of weighing the many considerations on both sides.

Negative Reasoning from Normal Expectations

The following type of dialogue will be familiar to viewers of vintage western movies. Two cowboys, Clint and Luke, are sitting beside a campfire.

Case 3.12

> Clint: It's quiet out there tonight, Luke.
> Luke: Yeah! Too quiet—I don't like it.
> Clint: I don't hear the crickets, or anything.
> *(They look at each other significantly, and both reach for their rifles.)*[4]

This familiar type of conversational exchange contains an *argumentum ad ignorantiam*. The negative premise that is the basis of the argument is that Clint and Luke don't hear anything. You could say that all they hear is silence—absence of any sound. This is the basis for their practical inference to the conclusion that something is wrong, that danger lurks in the darkness—as a result, they take the prudent, precautionary action of reaching for their rifles.

The key to understanding the logic of Clint and Luke's reasoning is that normally, there is the familiar nighttime background noise in the wilderness: the chirping of the crickets, or perhaps the noises of birds or other creatures. It is the absence of this noise that is their explicit premise. But their nonexplicit premise is a conditional: if things were normal (i.e., indicating safety) there would be background noise. But by *modus tollens,* one can reason that since this background noise is not present, things are not normal. This means that conditions may be unsafe, and Clint and Luke act accordingly.

Clint and Luke's reasoning is not an argument from ignorance in the sense that they are uncertain or do not know anything. In one sense, at any rate, they know something very definitely. They know that the crickets are not chirping. But that is a negative finding. So we could say their conclusion is based on negative reasoning of the following sort: they looked for something positive (crickets chirping and other noises of the woods) and found they were not present. Therefore they draw the conclusion that something was wrong. This could be called an argument from negative evidence. And

---

4. This dialogue is my own invention.

in this case, it seems to be a reasonable kind of argumentation. It is a practical kind of reasoning that could be fallible—Clint and Luke could be wrong—but it would seem to be inappropriate to describe it as fallacious.

Another example of this same kind of reasoning is the following case (transcribed by memory from a televised news program).

Case 3.13

A: Is Leona Helmsley still in jail? She's probably out by now.
B: Maybe she's still in there, because we'd probably hear about it if she got out.[5]

Leona Helmsley, the widow of deceased New York hotel magnate Harry Helmsley, was convicted of income tax evasion, and the story was widely reported by the news media. Leona Helmsley was portrayed as a rich person who abused her power as a wealthy hotel owner, and there was intense national interest in her "fall." Any new development in the story would be widely reported by the news media.

Hence you can see the logic of the *ad ignorantiam* argument in this case. *A* ventures the opinion that Helmsley is "probably out by now." But *B* counters by the argument that we would normally be expected to hear about it if she did get out, because there would be wide media coverage of such an "interesting" event. This argument rebuts the conclusion that Helmsley is out of jail by now. The argument from ignorance is based on normal expectations of media coverage of this type of event, if it were to occur. Once again it is an argument from negative evidence, based on something that did not occur, or was not perceived to occur, and drawing the appropriate conclusion from this negative finding.

This nonconclusive and nonmonotonic type of *ad ignorantiam,* based on normal expectations in a particular situation, would be too subject to error to meet standards of acceptable proof in a scientific inquiry. But it does have a legitimate place as a common and useful type of argument in practical reasoning (D. Walton, 1990b), where decisions for prudent action typically have to be taken in the absence of hard evidence or conclusive knowledge. Here, presumptive *ad ignorantiam* arguments are both useful and

---

5. This wording probably corresponds roughly to that of the original broadcast, but the source was not recorded.

reasonable in tilting a burden of proof to one side or the other in a balance of considerations situation.

Practical Reasoning and Presumption

One type of context where the nonconclusive *argumentum ad ignorantiam* often appears to have reasonable instances is the kind of case where a conclusion must be drawn as a reasoned presumption concerning how to act in a situation characterized by lack of conclusive knowledge. In this type of case, the decision to draw a conclusion on one side of an issue may be influenced by considerations of safety or prudent judgment (practical reasoning).

Case 3.14

> It is a rule of safety in the handling of firearms that if you do not know for sure that a weapon is unloaded to act in accord with the presumption that the weapon is (or may be) loaded.

Let's say that John is a member of a shooting club, and he is approaching a firing point where several pistols are laid out. When John picks up one of the pistols, he refrains from pointing it anywhere except down the range toward the targets, and he carefully opens the chamber to see whether the weapon is loaded or empty.

Presuming that John's actions are guided by the principle stated in case 3.14 above, we can say that his conclusion to act in the way he did flows from a set of premises that include the presumption stated in this important principle of gun safety. The principle of safe handling of weapons in this context sets a weight or burden of proof. You must be absolutely sure that a gun is empty before you can handle it in any way that might be potentially dangerous. And if you are not sure, then you must presume that the gun is not empty.

The reason for distributing the burden of proof in this one-sided way in relation to case 3.14 is one of safety. Since the possible consequences of mistakenly presuming that a gun is unloaded are highly significant—loss of life or limb—where you don't know whether the gun is loaded or unloaded, the requirement for proving that it is unloaded is set high. But this burden of proof is asymmetrical, for you automatically presume that the gun is loaded, and no proof to draw this conclusion is required at all.

This case is typical of presumptive reasoning where you do not know whether a particular proposition is true or false on the basis of the objective evidence, supplied by observation, experiment, or other direct sources of knowledge. But where you may have to act on the presumption that it is true, or not true, despite your lack of knowledge, your conclusion to opt for one side or the other may be determined by requirements of practicality, prudence, or safety, which set a burden of proof on one side or the other.

Actually, this type of case is not dissimilar to the kind of *argumentum ad ignorantiam* implicit in the legal requirement of burden of proof in the criminal trial rules of evidence. Ultimately, the justification of this type of rule is that it is more important to minimize the number of innocent persons who are wrongly convicted than it is to minimize the number of guilty parties who escape conviction because the case against them is not strong enough. Both types of possible outcomes are dangerous and threatening to us, but the possibility of imprisoning or executing an innocent person is particularly odious. Therefore the burden of proof is set higher on the one side by requiring proof of guilt "beyond reasonable doubt." The burden of proof in this case too is influenced by matters of safety, because of the possibility of error in a legal trial. The danger of convicting an innocent person can never be completely eliminated, but the asymmetrical burden of proof in the criminal trial is set in order to minimize the danger, or to narrow it to a range of tolerable proportions. Remedies of appeal are built in, further along the process, to reverse errors that are found through the introduction of new evidence. But the system is designed to be as safe as practically possible through the device of the asymmetrical burden of proof.

So the *argumentum ad ignorantiam* is, in many instances, both in law and also in other nonlegal contexts of practical reasoning where knowledge is fallible, incomplete, or unavailable, a nonfallacious argument. In these types of cases of plausible presumption, the expression *argumentum ad ignorantiam* is particularly apt because considerations of prudence direct the line of inference to one course of action, or to one conclusion rather than to the other, precisely because ignorance of the "real" underlying facts leaves open the very real possibility of significant error.

It is important to recognize, however, that the correctness or incorrectness of *argumentum ad ignorantiam* in practical reasoning is highly dependent on the context of the dialogue and situation. What might be a reasonable kind of *argumentum ad ignorantiam* in one situation may turn out to be a fallacious *argumentum ad ignorantiam* in another context.

Consider the case where George is a soldier in wartime. He is in an infantry support unit that has just been engaged in a successful battle to take over a building.

Case 3.15

> George finishes eating a can of rations when his sergeant tells him to get ready to move out. They are moving to advance against another enemy strongpoint. George looks at his rifle. Is it loaded or not? He can't remember.

In this case, it is George's duty to see to it that his rifle is loaded, preparatory to the attack his sergeant has notified him about. Therefore, George should presume that his rifle is (or may be) unloaded, and see to it that it is loaded, before moving out.

Both this case and the previous one were based on a premise of lack of knowledge about whether the weapon in question was loaded or not. In case 3.14, the conclusion drawn was the presumption that the gun is loaded. But in case 3.15, the correct presumption is that the gun is unloaded. Both inferences are drawn on a basis of burden of proof as requirements of safety. However, in the first case, the important danger was the possibility of accidentally discharging a loaded firearm and hurting or wounding oneself or another person. In the second case, the danger was the possibility of confronting hostile enemy forces with an empty rifle. This too, could be dangerous or fatal to self or companions, in the situation. In one case the danger is posed by the possibility that the weapon is loaded. In the other, the danger is posed by the opposite possibility.

Consider then the following pair of arguments.

(P1) I don't know that this weapon is not loaded.
Therefore, I presume that it is loaded.

(P2) I don't know that this weapon is loaded.
Therefore, I presume that it is not loaded.

Both (P1) and (P2) are instances of the *argumentum ad ignorantiam*.[6] In the case of John, in the first of the two cases above, (P1) is a reasonable and appropriate argument, whereas (P2) is unreasonable and fallacious (or would at least be an error or blunder in John's reasoning). But for the case of George, in the second of the pair of cases above, the opposite is true. For George, (P1) is incorrect and (P2) is correct.

In short, here we have two cases that appear to be legitimate instances of some form(s) of *argumentum ad ignorantiam*. But the *argumentum ad ignorantiam* that is a reasonable or correct sequence of argument in the one instance is fallacious in the other (or at least not correct). The difference lies in the allocation of the burden of proof appropriate for the context of dialogue.

It is also interesting to see that precisely this kind of *ad ignorantiam* reasoning is used in real cases of military deliberations in war where lives are at stake, but there is absence of knowledge. In the following case, related in the autobiography of General Chris Vokes, the Canadian advance against the Germans in the Italian campaign was checked by the strategic location called "Grizzly." Were the Germans still holding "Grizzly" or not? The brigade was under orders to move ahead, but if "Grizzly" was held by the Germans, and the Canadians moved in on it, they could be shelled, and there would be considerable loss of life. General Vokes records the following deliberations at this point (Vokes, 1985, 116).

Case 3.16

> The "Grizzly" objective seemed now too wide for an assault by only one battalion if, as was probable, it was held in strength by the enemy. There was no real indication it was indeed so held, but I could not prove the Germans would *not* be holding it. I thought they

---

6. Not everyone agrees with this analysis. Mike Wreen thinks that these arguments are better seen as arguments from negative consequences that do not have a distinctively *ad ignorantiam* element. He would reconstrue (P1) as follows:

I'm not certain that the gun is not loaded.
Loaded guns can pose great harm to myself or others.
Therefore, I ought to act as if the gun is loaded (and thus check it to make sure it's unloaded if I can).

Thus as Wreen renders the argument, he sees it as not being so much an argument from ignorance as a prudent argument from negative consequences. (Personal communication.)

would be, because there was excellent defensive ground to delay us on the way to Agira just beyond.

Here the *argumentum ad ignorantiam* is the form of reasoning used in these deliberations. There was no empirical evidence that the Germans were holding "Grizzly," but in the absence of evidence that they were *not* holding it, General Vokes concluded that he should act on the presumption that they were holding it. This *argumentum ad ignorantiam* was backed up by the premise that since the Germans were very capable defenders, and "Grizzly" provided excellent defensive grounds for delaying the Canadian advance, it was a good presumption that the Germans would hold it. On the basis of this reasoning, General Vokes pulled back temporarily, delaying the attack until the next morning. Just after the Canadians pulled back, the hill they had vacated came under shellfire. The next morning "Grizzly" was cleared, and occupied by the Canadians.

In a case like this, the balance of considerations must be acted upon, one way or the other. For even doing nothing (staying on the hill) is a significant action, with consequences for life or death. Here you have no choice but to act on the basis of an argument from ignorance, and hope your conclusion is justified by the way things work out, as it was in this case.

Explicit and Nonexplicit Presumptions

In some cases, an *argumentum ad ignorantiam* takes the form of an explicitly formulated presumption, used to set the parameters for conducting a conversational exchange. In these cases, presumption is used to expedite a discussion, so that it can go ahead in a more practical way. In this kind of case, the presumption is explicitly set out, the assumption being that, now pronounced, it is set in place, in the absence of any strong or concerted challenge to it by those affected. An example is the following memo circulated to all department heads at the University of Winnipeg from the office of the Supervisor of the Library Circulation Department on August 12, 1986.

Case 3.17

The Library Staff are reviewing the policy of keeping old university exams on file for student use. It has been found that the majority of exams are more than 10 years old. For some departments, we have only 2–3 exams. Please discuss this with other members of your department. Please report back to me by September 22, 1986. *If no response has been received by this date, it will be assumed that you are in favor of disposing of the practice of keeping university exams.*

The librarian who circulated this memo was making a stipulation that might or might not have been reasonable, depending on how faculty felt about the question of student exam files, and how adequate an opportunity for their responses was being given. But the sender of the memo is stipulating the rule in italics as a general requirement. It follows that any nonresponse by the given date *must* therefore be taken as agreement (exceptional circumstances aside). So the rule purports to define a required presumption on responses to the memo. The sender of the memo has stipulated, in effect, that the closed world assumption will fall into place on September 22. Such a presumption could be reasonable if enough room is left open by that ruling for contrary arguments that might arise.

Reasonable presumptions used in other cases of *ad ignorantiam* arguments are often based on standard or routine ways of doing things that are familiar, shared practices. They are based on normal expectations and plausibility, because their inference is not required. In many such cases, the presumption is not explicit, as it was in case 3.17, but is tacitly understood as part of the context of the conversation.

Reiter (1987) presented a survey of the range of different formal (deductive and inductive) systems that have been advanced in artificial intelligence studies to solve the problem posed by nonmonotonic reasoning. However, he concluded that the solution would not appear to be found in any single deductive or inductive system of logic, but rather in implicit conventions "of cooperative communication of information where it is understood by all participants that the informant is conveying all of the relevant information" (180). In such an interactive framework of communication, any relevant proposition not conveyed is, by default, assumed to be false.

An example Reiter gave (180), interestingly, links it with yet a further traditional informal fallacy, the fallacy of many questions (complex question).

Case 3.18

For example, if someone were to tell you that John has not stopped beating the rug, you would justifiably infer that John was beating the rug despite the fact that the original statement might be true precisely because John never was beating the rug to begin with. The point is that if this were the case, your informant should have told you. Since she didn't, convention dictates the appropriateness of your conclusion, despite its defeasibility.

Another type of case of nonexplicit default reasoning cited by Reiter is the use of pictures and diagrams where the contention is that an entity is not present if it is not depicted in the diagram or picture. Reiter (180) comments that statistical reasoning does not seem to account for this kind of inference, because it is difficult to imagine "what it could mean to assign a probability to the failure of a circuit diagram to depict a device's power supply, or what advantages there could possibly be in doing so." The conclusion to be drawn from these cases then is that the understanding of nonmonotonic reasoning is not to be sought in deductive or inductive formal systems of inference but in a more broadly pragmatic account of how conventions function in licensing one participant to draw legitimate inferences in cooperative communication with another participant who conveys information, both directly and indirectly, through a dialogue.

Case 3.18 links several factors together in a way that reveals the fundamental importance of presumptive reasoning in argumentation. It shows that the fallacy of many questions is linked to the argument from ignorance and that the latter underlies the former. To understand how the rug-beating question functions as a fallacy you have to see the underlying inference as the drawing of a conclusion *ad ignorantiam* from something unsaid. If something is not specifically stated as an item in a knowledge base as true (false), then we can go ahead and presume it must be false (true), given the right conventions of conversation.

Hence case 3.18 shows how such presumptive arguments from ignorance are involved in argumentation at the metalogical level of conventions of successful communication between two or more participants in argumentation. At this level Gricean maxims of communication (Grice, 1975) both govern presumptions and are, at the same time, themselves kinds of presumptions that typically license inferences on a basis of what is left unsaid in a discussion. To understand how presumptive reasoning works, we need to ascend to a higher level of seeing how it is used in dialogue, to indicate to a responding participant the right sequence of moves to make in answering a question or request. In such a case, no response at all (a null move) can count as a significant contribution to the dialogue. See case 9.1 below as an illustration of how a null move in a dialogue can function as a warrant to draw a conclusion attributed to the other party.

This matter of implicature shows how fundamental the *argumentum ad ignorantiam* is to the study of fallacies, and to the whole area of the normative evaluation of arguments in pragmatic contexts of use generally. The *ad ignorantiam* not only underlies the kinds of arguments associated with other traditional fallacies although it may not be explicitly expressed as such; it is also the key to understanding how the Gricean maxims function in conversational implicature.

Knowledge, Ignorance, and Reasoning

The cases studied in this chapter have thrown serious doubt on the hypothesis that the *argumentum ad ignorantiam* is a fallacy. Not only is this type of argumentation accepted as having argumentative force in historical, medical, and scientific research: it has come to be recognized even more explicitly in computer science, as researchers in artificial intelligence have begun to explore the kind of reasoning used in searching through a knowledge base.

Also, apart from reasoning used in scientific research and academic disciplines, there is another important kind of evidence that the argument from ignorance is a commonly accepted, useful, and reasonable type of argumentation. This evidence is from cases of practical reasoning in everyday life, where conclusions often have to be drawn on the basis of absence of knowledge. The cases studied in the second half of this chapter show that this type of *ad ignorantiam* reasoning is a type of argumentation we often have to rely on, and use intelligently. It is not, at any rate, always fallacious. Indeed, we could not get by without it, in the ordinary, practical affairs of daily life.

Fischer, as already seen, is highly negative about negative evidence, writing that the "only correct empirical procedure" is to find affirmative evidence that the event in question did not happen (positive evidence of nonexistence). He is right here, to some extent, in the sense that positive knowledge of a negative proposition is logically stronger than negative knowledge of the same positive proposition. That is, "It is known that not-A" implies, but is not implied by "It is not known that A." If it is known that not-A is true (i.e., that A is false), then it is not known that A is true.

So there is a sense in which Fischer is right to say that positive evidence is preferable to, or at least stronger than negative evidence.

But the problem is that, for many reasons, positive evidence is not always available. We may be at the early stages of an inquiry, for example, where negative evidence can function as a way of ruling out unpromising avenues, in order to guide us toward eventually finding positive evidence at the end of the inquiry. Or in the history, for example, of ancient civilizations (case 3.1), positive evidence may simply no longer exist, or for some reason be unavailable. And in practical affairs, we may have to make a prudent decision to take some action, even though positive evidence is not yet available.

Perhaps the basis of the skepticism or rejection of negative evidence here is the feeling that only knowledge is worth having, in any academic pursuit, scientific research, or as a basis for informed action. But the *ad ignorantiam* is only ignorance, or lack of knowledge. Hence arguing from ignorance yields only absence of knowledge, and is therefore worthless as a type of argumentation.

The rebuttal to this argument is that we can have knowledge of our lack of knowledge, and this itself can be at least a provisional but intelligent basis for action, or for continuing the process of questioning in a research inquiry. This rebuttal is the basis of the Socratic definition of wisdom as a kind of knowledge of one's lack of knowledge. Knowledge of one's lack of knowledge is a sophisticated, somewhat subtle concept, and perhaps therefore easy to overlook or denigrate. But the cases in this chapter have shown how often this knowledge of lack of evidence of something is vital to so much intelligent reasoning in scientific research and to practical deliberations in everyday life.

Smets (1991) distinguishes three categories of ignorance: incompleteness, imprecision, and uncertainty (138), and argues that each of these three has correct models of reasoning. This suggests that arguing from ignorance is very often correct as a type of reasoning in science, provided there is an understanding of the forms of ignorance, and the nature of how they work in scientific reasoning.

An interdisciplinary group in the departments of surgery and humanities at the University of Arizona is even more enthusiastic about the argument from ignorance in medicine. As an alternative to the traditional approach to teaching medicine where students are "taught" and "knowledge" and "answers" predominate, C. L. Witte, A. Kerwin, and M. H. Witte (1991, 296) propose a new Curriculum on Medical Ignorance that fosters open-mindedness, constructive skepticism, humility, and the ability to deal with uncertainty and explore ignorance. As their model, they cite Socrates, a philosopher who "railed against presuming to know, lest complacency preclude questioning, inquiry and learning" (296). They advocate an infusion of the recognition of ignorance in the core curriculum of medicine as a way of creating a more receptive climate for breakthroughs in medical research (298).

Witte, Kerwin, Witte, and Scadron (1989, 25) have summarized the goals of the Curriculum on Medical Ignorance as follows.

> Our goals were (1) to facilitate and enlarge understanding of the shifting domains of knowledge, ignorance, uncertainty, and the unknown through the examination of philosophical and psychological foundations and approaches, the study of the history of the evolution of selected ideas and practices, and mastery by in-depth multidimensional exploration of a timely medical topic; (2) to aid in the recognition of, and to deal productively with, ignorance, uncertainty, and the unknown, including the ability to question critically and creatively from different points of view, communicate clearly in different media, and collaborate effectively to tap and mobilize relevant resources; (3) to reinforce Socratic attitudes and values of curiosity, optimism, humility, self-confidence, and constructive scepticism.

The philosophy behind this approach is very interesting because it advocates the point of view that the *argumentum ad ignorantiam* is a pervasive and constructive (nonfallacious) type of reasoning in medical research and treatment. Far from being a fallacy, as it has so often been treated traditionally, the argument from ignorance is a reasonable and very useful type of reasoning that ought to be made explicit in medical education, according to this approach.

What is highly characteristic of the *argumentum ad ignorantiam* as a distinctive species of reasoning is its autoepistemic nature. In the simplest kind of case, a reasoner using the *argumentum ad ignorantiam* is looking into her own knowledge base, and then using negative reasoning to draw a conclusion on the basis that some particular proposition is *not* in that knowledge base. However, there is also a secondary type of case where the type of reasoning used in the *argumentum ad ignorantiam* is not *autoepistemic,* but *extraepistemic,* meaning that the reasoner bases the conclusion drawn not on looking into her own knowledge base, but by making a judgment on what is in the knowledge base of another party. This kind of extraepistemic reasoning is used where one person's argument is supported by appeal to the expert opinion of a second party. As we saw in case 3.6, the *ad ignorantiam* is an underlying part of the argumentation structure of the *argumentum ad verecundiam*. The use of appeal to expert opinion in argument, like the argument from ignorance, is a type of argumentation that is very common and useful in everyday reasoning. Neither of these types of argument should be classified (categorically) as fallacious.

However, there is some truth in the traditional wisdom that the *argumentum ad ignorantiam* is a fallacy, as we shall see in Chapter 4. Now that we have at least some idea of how the argument from ignorance functions as a reasonable type of argumentation in some cases, we can use this as a basis for studying what goes wrong when it is misdeployed, and should be subject to negative evaluation.

4

Case Studies

In this chapter, a number of important cases are examined where the *ad ignorantiam* argument has gone wrong, is a fallacy, or at any rate is shown to be a very dangerous kind of argument that can go badly wrong. These new case studies will supplement the traditional cases already covered, go beyond the standard treatment of the textbooks by indicating new areas of concern, and go into some longer cases in more depth. In analyzing these case studies, we shall diagnose the general problem associated with the fallacious use of the *ad ignorantiam* in that case, get a general idea of where and how the argument from ignorance can go wrong, and see where the dangers of its misuse lie.

Closure of the Knowledge Base

In many of the cases of argument from ignorance in Chapter 2, the argument was reasonable because a given knowledge base could be said to be closed or complete. Then we could reason that since a particular proposition was not to be found in that knowledge base, we could infer that it is not true. The correctness of the inference depended on the closed world assumption.

Indeed, in cases where the closed world assumption is merited, the *argumentum ad ignorantiam* can be not only correct, but a highly conclusive type of argumentation. By contrast, the erroneous or fallacious type of *argumentum ad ignorantiam* occurs where the knowledge base is not complete (closed), but the argument ignores or overlooks this lack of knowledge, pressing ahead more confidently than the inquiry merits. In the following case, for example, the danger of a fallacious *argumentum ad ignorantiam* exists precisely because the knowledge base is incomplete in one important respect.

Case 4.1

> According to Benoit (1990, 25), some of Aristotle's works on rhetoric—e.g., the *Synagoge Technon,* the *Gryllus,* and the *Theodecta*—are not extant: "Hence, the absence of a topic from the surviving corpus . . . is insufficient evidence that [Aristotle] failed to discuss it."

In this case, our list of topics written on by Aristotle is incomplete, due to the failure of some works to have survived. Hence Benoit warns of the danger of succumbing to the erroneous *ad ignorantiam* argument of concluding that Aristotle failed to discuss a topic simply because it is not discussed in his extant works.

This seems to be the most basic and straightforward type of *ad ignorantiam* fallacy. If, in fact, a knowledge base is incomplete, or a thorough investigation has not been carried out, then it may simply not be warranted to infer that if a proposition is not known to be true (false), it must be false (true).

Often such dubious instances of the *ad ignorantiam* argument occur in conjunction with the so-called *argumentum ad verecundiam,* or fallacious appeal to expert opinion in argumentation.

The problem is that the nature of the appeal to expert opinion tends to make it, in most cases a weak kind of argument, subject to exceptions and reservations. Most often, the knowledge base is incomplete, and does not by any means justify a conclusion "beyond reasonable doubt." This incompleteness is often revealed when the nature of the evidence used to back up the expert opinion is critically examined by subsequent questioning.

The subject of the following case concerned the trial of John Demjanjuk, the retired Ohio autoworker who was accused of being Ivan the Terrible, a guard at the Treblinka death camp in Poland.

Case 4.2

> An Associated Press article that had the headline, "Expert on prison camp unable to find record of Demjanjuk," cited the statement of a lawyer whose files (she claimed) are the only source of any historical material on the training camp where the guards for Treblinka were trained. According to Helge Grabitz, the lawyer, who is said to have spent twenty-one years prosecuting war criminals from this particular camp, she never came across the name Demjanjuk.[1]

One might be tempted to conclude from this expert opinion that it represents strong evidence for Mr. Demjanjuk's contention that he was never at the Treblinka camp. If Ms. Grabitz was unable to find evidence linking him to the training camp for Treblinka guards, and if she is an expert on the subject, then by an *ad ignorantiam* argument from this lack of evidence, backed up by her knowledge of the subject as an expert, should we not conclude that weight should be given to the doubts about the accusations against Mr. Demjanjuk? The *ad ignorantiam* and the appeal to expert opinion dovetail very nicely here as a combined argumentation technique to shift a burden of proof.

Once the evidential basis of Ms. Grabitz's knowledge in this case is revealed, however, the argument is shown to carry less weight. According to the article, "Grabitz told the court she reviewed 161 files of documents and interviewed 110 witnesses about Trawniki. She said the names of only about ten per cent of the estimated 4,000 guards trained there are known, and Demjanjuk's is not among them."[2] It seems then that Ms. Grabitz's negative finding has at least a ninety per cent chance of turning out to be unfounded as an indication of the truth of Mr. Demjanjuk's contention. While it still carries some weight, by itself it is hardly a powerful argument.

This case shows that an *ad ignorantiam* argument backed up by an appeal to expert opinion can often look very powerful initially, but crumble under

---

1. Associated Press Report (April 1, 1987), Expert on prison camp unable to find record of Demjanjuk, *Winnipeg Free Press,* 56.
   2. Ibid., 56.

critical questioning once the basis of the expert judgment is revealed. In such a case the *argumentum ad ignorantiam* is shown for what it usually is, at bottom: a plausible but weak species of argument that can serve to shift a burden of proof slightly where reliable knowledge is hard to come by. It is some evidence, but not conclusive evidence.

In this type of case, where the *argumentum ad ignorantiam* is used, there is always a premise that there is some knowledge that has been collected, and there is always (or should be) some estimate of how complete that knowledge is, with respect to some proposition at issue that supposedly comes within the domain of that knowledge. In both cases 4.1 and 4.2, the *ad ignorantiam* can be judged fallacious on the grounds that the knowledge base was less complete than it initially appeared to be.

In case 4.1, Benoit is warning us that if someone were to argue, "Aristotle did not discuss topic T in his surviving corpus, therefore Aristotle did not discuss topic T," she would be committing an *ad ignorantiam* fallacy. The reason is that the knowledge base, the Aristotelian corpus, is not complete. Hence the counterfactual premise, "If proposition A is not in the knowledge base, then A is not true" is not true, in this case. Hence the argument from ignorance is not strong, or not strong enough to meet the standard of proof required. It is properly said to be fallacious to the extent that there is an initial or surface appearance that it is a strong argument, but the actual argument given does not live up to this appearance. In this case, the fallacy Benoit warns us about is clear because (1) we have a definite knowledge base (the Aristotelian corpus of writings) and can see whether a topic is in there or not; and (2) it is known that this knowledge base is incomplete. Hence what constitutes the *ad ignorantiam* fallacy is also quite clear.

Another lesson brought out by these two cases is the importance of the context of dialogue. In scientific or scholarly reasoning, *argumentum ad ignorantiam* tends to be viewed with suspicion, because scientific method requires that a hypothesis should be based on empirical data, and tends to discourage "speculation," based on lack of knowledge. When the *argumentum ad ignorantiam* is allowed as an acceptable kind of reasoning in science, it is because it is really a mixed inference, based partially on ignorance, but partially also on some known propositions. Often these known propositions are related by *modus tollens* transformations to other propositions about things not known to be true or false. There is a positive premise that certain things are known. And also a counterfactual or completeness premise to the effect that if such-and-such a proposition were true, it would be known. If this counterfactual premise is firm, then so is the argument from ignorance.

By contrast, in cases of critical discussions on subjects of controversy where established knowledge is hard to come by, and not decisive in ruling on the issue, the *argumentum ad ignorantiam* can be perfectly appropriate and acceptable as a kind of plausible reasoning, but is less conclusive. Indeed, it reflects the principle of burden of proof that is the central mechanism making persuasion dialogue a useful and reasonable kind of argumentation in settling an issue. The lesson ultimately to be drawn from these observations is that while the *argumentum ad ignorantiam* can be a reasonable and effective argument in one context of dialogue, the same kind of argument can be ineffective and fallacious in a different context, where the goals and appropriate methods of argumentation are quite different. Much may depend on the standard of evidence required in order to meet a burden of proof.

A Legal Case

As we saw in Chapter 1 ("Foundationalism and Scientific Reasoning") the status of the *argumentum ad ignorantiam* in law is somewhat unclear. It does seem that this type of argument is involved in the legal presumption of innocence, and that the argument from ignorance, as expressed in the legal principle of setting burden of proof, can be a reasonable (nonfallacious) type of argumentation. It says in a criminal trial, for example, that if the prosecution fails to prove guilt, then the outcome of the trial is that the defendant is concluded to be "not guilty." In this framework, the argument from ignorance seems to be quite legitimate, and simply reflects or embodies a certain principle or weighting of burden of proof (Chapter 1, "Recent Recognition of Argument from Ignorance").

On the other hand, it is possible to show that in some cases in legal argumentation, the argument from ignorance can quite definitely be used in an improper way that would merit its being called a fallacy. The following case (Clinton, 1897, 135–36), used as a textbook exercise in Waller (1988, 44–45) is from a famous nineteenth-century New York criminal trial. The basic facts of the case are the following. Mrs. Emma Cunningham, charged with the murder of Dr. Harvey Burdell, claimed to have married Dr. Burdell in a secret ceremony. Dr. Burdell had been found murdered in his office, adjoining his house. He had been stabbed fifteen times. Mrs. Cunningham, a widow, was known to have been Dr. Burdell's lover. Her two daughters and two sons, as well as some other people, all lived in the house. It was known that Dr. Burdell and Mrs. Cunningham had quarreled shortly before the murder.

The discourse quoted in case 4.3 below is the closing passage of the opening speech to the jury given by the district attorney (Clinton, 1897, 135–136).

Case 4.3

> The prosecution will bring before you such circumstances [that will prove that the murder] was done by somebody in that house. Away with justice forever, if circumstances like these do not call, trumpet-tongued, upon the defence to reverse the rule of law; let the innocent prove that he is not guilty if he can. . . .
>
> And then, if it come to appear, as I think it must, that that deed was done by someone in that house, we ask who did it, who had the motive? Was it she who hated him, who scorned him? And he had scorned her, and had cast her off, and was about to cast her homeless into the world. Was it she who had threatened him . . . ? Was it she who went into mock-heroics over his body? I shall greatly mistake your comprehension if you do not arrive at the conclusion that it was done by some person in the house, and by her who had a motive, who expressed a motive by threats, upon the very eve of its consummation, who had the ability to do it and to conceal it; and having spread these facts before you, we shall call upon our learned friends upon the other side to say what of this motive? Who has a greater? What of this hatred and revenge and malice? Where is there another who had greater ability to do and to conceal? How could entrance have been obtained to that house? And if they shall fail in that, we shall claim hereafter, when the evidence which I have outlined shall be fitted together, to say that woman, whether she be called Emma Augusta Cunningham or Emma Augusta Burdell, whether she be the mistress or the wife, whether she had the simulated or the real marriage, that she—woman though she is—was guilty of the crime.

In this case, the prosecutor actually gives away his strategy by explicitly telling the jury to reverse the burden of proof, and "let the innocent prove that he is not guilty if he can." This, of course, is directly contrary to the principle, in my criminal trial, that the burden of proof is on the prosecution, not the defense.

The prosecutor then proceeds in his speech to go forward with the *argumentum ad ignorantiam* he has announced. First he gives some not very convincing evidence of the guilt of the defendant. She went into "mock-heroics" over his body, she had threatened him, and so forth. Then he calls on the defense to prove that someone else had a "greater" motive to kill Dr. Burdell then the defendant did. The implication here is that if they fail to come up with such a proof, it follows that Mrs. Cunningham must be the guilty party. He goes on to charge the defense with proving that somebody else had a greater ability to carry out and conceal the act, once again suggesting that if they don't prove this, it is evidence of Mrs. Cunningham's guilt. Finally, he even explicitly claims that if the defense doesn't prove all these things, then it follows that Mrs. Cunningham was guilty of the crime, once the evidence is "fitted together." Here then, not only has the prosecutor outlined his intention to use the argument from ignorance as a burden-reversing strategy, he has explicitly carried out the announced strategy in his actual sequence of argumentation.

In this case then, we seem to have quite good grounds for calling the *argumentum ad ignorantiam* a fallacy. The argument took place within the framework of a legal proceeding, a criminal trial, where the burden of proof for both opposing sides was fixed in advance by the rules of evidence for this type of trial. Presumably the judge would be obliged to make the burden of proof clear to the jury, as the basis for their arriving at a conclusion. However, the prosecutor deliberately tried in his argumentation to twist this around, so that it would appear to the jury that the burden of proof was on the other side. Here we have a deliberate tactic of argumentation used in an attempt to violate one of the rules governing what constitutes successful proof or evidence, set down at the beginning of the proceeding, and to which all parties to it are bound.

In other cases, like the McCarthy tribunals cited in Chapter 1, the *ad ignorantiam* is not just one localized argument that inappropriately shifts the burden of proof. It seems instead that the whole proceedings itself is systematically based on a reversal of the proper burden of proof.

The Salem Witchcraft Trials

The expression "witch hunt" commonly refers to a particular type of proceedings where charges are made, and in a wave of public hysteria and fear
relating to this type of charge at a particular time, the accused party or
parties are convicted on the basis of little or no real evidence. The McCarthy tribunals, often cited as one famous instance of the witch hunt, were
not court cases. But the Salem witchcraft trials of 1692 were actually legal
proceedings. During the height of these proceedings between June and September of 1692, fourteen women and five men were hanged in Salem as
witches, and one man was tortured to death (Shapiro, 1992, 64). The main
evidence on which these convictions were based was the testimony of young
girls who were seized with fits identified as satanic possession, and who
named the accused parties as witches, blaming them as the cause of their
torments.

   An outline of how the most famous of these trials originated in the house
of the Reverend Samuel Parris, the minister of Salem Village, is given in
Shapiro (1992, 65).

Case 4.4

   During the winter of 1691–92, a few girls, mostly teenagers, started
gathering in Parris's kitchen. There they listened to stories, perhaps
voodoo tales, told by his West Indian slave Tituba; they also tried to
discern their future husbands by fortune telling—dropping an egg
white into a glass and seeing what shape it took. For girls raised
in Puritanism, which demanded lifelong discipline and self-control,
these sessions with Tituba represented a rare and risky bit of indul-
gence in pure fancy. Too risky, perhaps. Suddenly one after another
of the girls was seized with fits. Their families were bewildered: the
girls raved and fell into convulsions; one of them ran around on all
fours and barked. Dr. William Griggs was called in and made his
diagnosis: the "evil hand" was upon them.

   Fits identified as satanic possession had broken out among adoles-
cent girls at earlier times in New England. Often their distress was
traced to local women who, it was said, had entered into a compact
with the Devil and were now recruiting new witches by tormenting
the innocent until they succumbed. So the adults in Salem Village

began pressing the girls with questions: "Who torments you? Who torments you?" Finally they named three women—Tituba, Sarah Good and Sarah Osborne—all of them easily recognizable as Satan's handmaidens. Tituba was seen as a shameless pagan, Good was a poor beggar given to muttering angrily as she went from house to house and Osborne was known to have lived with her second husband before they were married. The three were arrested and jailed, but the girls' torments did not cease. On the contrary, fits were spreading like smallpox; dozens more girls and young women went into violent contortions, flailing, kicking and uttering names.

What was most interesting about the trials in which these accused persons were convicted is the nature of the "evidence" brought against them. Much of this was "spectral evidence," based on visions or otherworldly experience not visible to anyone except the person testifying. While testifying, the girls went into shrieking torments, and their distress seemed to increase if there appeared to be any sign that the jury might be ready to acquit someone. In the preliminary investigation interrogation of Sarah Good, for example (Boyer and Nissenbaum, 1977, 8), the girls testifying against her were described as "all dreadfully tortured and tormented" when she was brought in. This kind of performance put psychological pressure on the proceedings.

The problem of evidence posed in the Salem witchcraft trials is described by Boyer and Nissenbaum (19) as "ticklish": "although witchcraft was one of the most heinous of all crimes, it was also one of the most difficult to prove, since so much of it took place in the mind of the witch." Witchcraft was defined as a contract made between the witch and the devil, and the so-called spectral evidence used to identify it referred to the shape or specter of the devil, as he took the witch's bodily shape. Thus the witness would report some vision of the accused, who allegedly caused some mischief and appeared devilish. The peculiar problem of verifiability of this type of testimonial evidence is well documented by Boyer and Nissenbaum (19–20).

Such testimony possessed a superficial resemblance to firm empirical evidence. But, as people came increasingly to recognize in 1692, spectral evidence was seriously flawed in at least two ways. The first problem was a practical one: spectral testimony remained almost impossible to verify, since often only the person experiencing the

vision could see it—others in the same room might look and discern nothing. . . .

But spectral evidence posed a still more fundamental problem—
a theological one, really: how could one be certain that Satan, in his
vast and malevolent power, was not able to assume the shape of an
innocent or even a godly person? Had not the Biblical witch of En-
dor, after all (as accused witch Susannah Martin shrewdly pointed
out during her examination in 1692), called up the devil in the shape
of the sainted prophet Samuel?

Interestingly, this kind of evidence seemed to *be* empirical evidence, because the witness appeared to be reporting facts that could be verified. One
thing the judges looked for was some sort of unexpected misfortune, like
the death of a cow, which could be cited as evidence (Boyer and Nissenbaum, 21). Another physical sign of guilt was the "witch's tit," an "unnatural
body excrescence" through which the witch suckled a demon (22). These
things could presumably be verified by observation, and so they seemed
during the trial to be forms of empirical evidence.

Another aspect of these trials was the intense psychological pressure produced by the agonies of the afflicted witnesses. However, once the suspect
confessed, the afflicted girls were relieved of their torments (Boyer and
Nissenbaum, 23). Moreover, in 1692, those who insisted on their innocence
were hanged, and only those who "confessed" were spared (Shapiro, 1992,
64). Thus while confession could be, in principle, a legitimate type of evidence of having committed a crime, in this type of proceeding it is questionable what kind of evidentiary value should be given to it. It could be better
compared to prisoners of war, who are forced to "confess" crimes against
humanity before a camera, for propaganda purposes.

Such witch-hunt cases are commonly cited as the very paradigm where
accused parties are convicted unfairly once they have been "fingered." A
pressure to convict on little or no real evidence has become part of the very
framework of the proceedings, in such a case. Typically because of some
public fear or hysteria, suspicion alone becomes enough of a basis to point
the finger of guilt, and the burden of proof somehow becomes shifted onto
the accused party to prove she is innocent. The problem is that it may be
extremely difficult, or even impossible to do this, for various reasons. The
inherent problems of arguing from ignorance in such cases are greatly exac-
erbated where, because of the vague nature of the charge, or the lack of

accessibility to evidence, the accused party cannot (in reality) defend herself successfully against the charge.

Spy Cases

In his treatment of the *ad ignorantiam,* Copi (1982, 102) cites an interesting type of exception to the rule that this type of argument is fallacious: in a case where a search has been made by qualified investigators "it is perfectly reasonable to take the absence of proof of [the] occurrence [of an event] as positive proof of its nonoccurrence." To illustrate such a reasonable use of the argument from ignorance, Copi (102) offers the following case, a variant of Case 2.7, cited above from an earlier edition (1953) of Copi's textbook.

Case 4.5

> For example, if a serious security investigation fails to unearth any evidence that Mr. X is a foreign agent, it would be wrong to conclude that their research has left us ignorant. It has rather established that Mr. X is not one. Failure to draw such conclusions is the other side of the bad coin of innuendo, as when one says of a man that there is "no proof" that he is a scoundrel. In some cases not to draw a conclusion is as much a breach of correct reasoning as it would be to draw a mistaken conclusion.

Failure to draw the conclusion that Mr. X is innocent, in such a case could itself be a kind of bad reasoning, or form of innuendo. This type of case is interesting for many reasons. Certainly it shows that negative evidence (failure to unearth any evidence) can be a reasonable (i.e., nonfallacious) type of argumentation that can strongly oblige a reasonable person to draw a particular conclusion.

But one significant problem in such a case is that it may not be so easy or straightforward to draw such a conclusion as Copi suggests. The Alger Hiss case is a famous example of exactly this sort of problem. A serious investigation failed to unearth any evidence that Hiss was a foreign agent. Yet that was still not enough to establish that he was not one. This famous case continues to be the subject of controversies.

The early years of Alger Hiss showed every indication of an illustrious career of distinguished achievement. After prep school and receiving his bachelor's degree from Johns Hopkins University, he had graduated with honors from Harvard Law School (1929). After being secretary to Justice Oliver Wendell Holmes, he practiced with prominent Boston and New York law firms, and then went on to hold important government positions during World War II, culminating in the post of president of the Carnegie Endowment for International Peace (Zeligs, 1967, 3). But his career in government was stopped short when he was accused by Whittaker Chambers— testifying before the House Committee on Un-American Activities in 1948—of having been a Communist spy. A confessed Communist agent, Chambers charged that Hiss had passed along classified State Department documents, copied on a typewriter that could be allegedly identified as belonging to Hiss. Hiss voluntarily appeared before the Committee, and under questioning by a young lawyer named Richard Nixon, steadfastly denied all the accusations. Nixon was appointed head of a subcommittee to investigate further.

During a subsequent investigation, Chambers produced five rolls of microfilm of State Department documents from a hollowed-out pumpkin in the garden of his farm. Nixon alleged that this was proof that Hiss had been a Communist espionage agent (Cook, 1958, 18). The case then went to trial, and the jury was shown that the documents produced by Chambers showed a type similar to that in letters written on an old typewriter once owned by Hiss. Two more trials followed. The jury was divided in the first one. In the second one (1949–50), the jury (eight to four), returned a verdict of guilty (of perjury) and Hiss was sentenced to five years in prison.

Over the years since the trial, there has been a flood of literature on the subject, including books by both Hiss and Chambers. But Hiss has always maintained his innocence, and there have been many doubts expressed on whether he really was a Communist spy, or whether he was simply a victim of political persecution. Many have suspected that he was framed or falsely accused, during the heyday of this sort of accusation in the McCarthy era. At age eighty-eight, Hiss has spent a lifetime protesting his innocence, but his quest has turned out to be practically impossible, despite the gathering of much evidence.

In November 1992, General Dmitri Volkogonov, adviser to Russian President Boris Yeltsin and chairman of the Supreme Council Commission on KGB and military intelligence archives, agreed to search for any relevant files on the Hiss case and to inspect them personally. After weeks of searching through the archives, Volkogonov concluded, "We have analyzed a huge amount of documents and determined as a result that Alger Hiss . . . was never a spy for the Soviet Union" (Post, Rogers, and Lin, 1992, 31). Since, presumably, the Soviet sources would be the ones to definitively know about this issue, one might think that this *ad ignorantiam* argument would be sufficient to prove that Hiss was innocent. But curiously enough, doubts remain (Post, Rogers, and Lin, 1992, 31).

Case 4.6

> Last week's revelations failed to convince everyone of Hiss's innocence. Some longtime Moscow watchers found it hard to believe that Volkogonov, who also co-chairs the U.S.-Russian joint commission on POWs, had seen all relevant documents. "There's at least a strong suspicion that some intelligence files were burned or destroyed" during the first few days after the failed coup last year, says Prof. Alexander Dallin, a Russian specialist at Stanford University. Allen Weinstein, author of the 1978 "Perjury: The Hiss-Chambers Case," argues that little pertinent evidence exists in the KGB files scoured by Volkogonov. Of the Russian agents and defectors Weinstein has interviewed, "all said Chambers was with the GRU," or military intelligence. But the GRU might not be so forthcoming if it has records on Hiss. Weinstein says he was told by Yevgeny Primakov, director of Russia's foreign intelligence service, that Moscow "will never release files on foreign agents from the 1930s and 1940s because they might still be alive."
>
> Will the world ever know the truth about Alger Hiss? Probably not. Volkogonov—a highly respected general, historian and politician—has no reason to lie. He has recently released damning information about Soviet cover-ups in the Katyn massacre and the downing of KAL Flight 007. But, as Marshall Goldman, a Russia expert at Wellesley College, points out, searching the archives to establish innocence "is like trying to prove there's no God."

The curious thing here is that although Volkogonov is certainly expert on this question, and has access to a lot of data, his conclusion seems to be open to questioning by other experts. No matter how strong his argument could be, there would always seem to remain some room for grounds for doubting it. It seems that to prove innocence the *ad ignorantiam* argument can never really be conclusive. Even after a serious security investigation doubts remained, in this case, and could not seem to be put to rest, despite the failure to unearth any evidence that Hiss was a Soviet spy.

Stonewalling

In the Hiss case, the prosecutors had the wave of Red hysteria on their side, and an impossibly heavy burden of disproof pressed down on the side of the accused. In other cases, the *argumentum ad ignorantiam* gets turned the other way around. It seems that the accusers can make no headway even where they have some very convincing evidence. In these cases, somehow the defenders are able to set a burden of proof in a way that the attackers have no real chance of fulfilling it.

The following case is a good illustration.

Case 4.7

> A particular model of car was accidentally slipping into gear while the car was parked, and many accidents were occurring, causing damage and even allegedly injuring people in some cases. Owners of the car wanted an investigation, and demanded a recall of all models of this car. The manufacturers argued that it was not established that these accidents were the fault of the design or manufacture of the transmission, and that they could be due to driver error. They claimed their engineers could find no fault in the transmission, and that further investigation or recall of these vehicles were not necessary. Eventually, as the reported number of accidents of this sort began to mount, the issue became an intense subject of public controversy. In the end, the car had to be modified so that it could not be put into gear without pressing the brake pedal first.[3]

During the public controversy part of this debate, the argument took the form of a dispute between the owners and consumer advocates on the at-

---

3. This description of the case is an outline from memory of a televised report viewed by the author sometime around 1990. However, this case has been extensively documented and analyzed in Huber (1991, chap. 4).

tacking side, and the manufacturers and their representatives on the defensive side. The arguments on both sides took *argumentum ad ignorantiam* forms. The defense argued that the attacking side could not prove that the accidents were caused by a fault in the transmission, and that, from their (the defenders) point of view, the problem was not a mechanical fault of the transmission. The attackers argued that the other side had not proved this adequately, given the danger and frequency of the accidents, all of which left no other conclusion than that of a faulty and dangerous vehicle.

As the evidence mounted that the problem was very serious, the manufacturers came under more and more pressure. Yet they continued to argue, on the basis of the expert testimony of their engineers, that no mechanical fault could be found. The owners and consumers brought in opposing experts who concluded that there had to be some sort of mechanical defect. The opposed use of *ad ignorantiam* tactics was a tug-of-war. Each side tried to put the burden on the other side, by claiming that the other side should dig up the information required to solve the problem, and was at fault for its failure to do so. But unlike the case of a legal trial, it was somewhat unclear exactly what kind of evidence was needed to meet the burden of proof, and who should have the burden.

However, eventually such evidence was brought in by independent agencies. According to Huber (1991, 62), there was a sort of vicious circularity driving the allegations forward in this case: "The publicity attracted suits, the suits generated publicity, and the more people heard about sudden acceleration, the more they came to believe in it." This led to a rolling wave of lawsuits that peaked after each television program on the subject. In the end however, scientific investigations by the National Highway Traffic Safety Association, the Center for Auto Safety, Transport Canada, the Japanese Ministry of Transport, and other agencies, concluded that there was nothing wrong with the car, and that the cause of the accidents was drivers putting their foot on the wrong pedal.

In Hamblin games of dialogue, the question 'Why A?' is a request for the hearer to give some evidence or proof to justify A; that is, to fulfill a burden of proof. But the problem, in a hotly disputed type of case, is that the other party turns this request for proof on its head, replying, "You prove that *not-A*." The sequence could be repeated indefinitely where a questioner in dialogue asks a respondent 'Why A?' and the respondent replies 'Why *not-A*?' In this type of case, the questioner asks the respondent to back up his contention that A is true, but the respondent shifts the burden of proof back onto the questioner by demanding that he prove that

A is not true. The resulting stalemate could be a very real obstacle to making progress in dialogue on an issue.

In such a case, the one party may even explicitly admit that he can't prove *A*, but instead of backing down, may insist that *A* should be accepted anyway, because the other party cannot disprove *A*. The *ad ignorantiam* argument is used: "You can't disprove *A*, therefore I am justified in accepting *A* as true." The tactic used in such a case is the attempt to shift the burden of (dis)proof to the other side in a dialogue.

It is precisely this dialectical form of the *argumentum ad ignorantiam* that was identified by Locke before 1690 and given the name *argumentum ad ignorantiam* by him. In the passage quoted by Hamblin (1970, 160; see Chapter 1), Locke gives this name to one of the kinds of arguments that, he says, men use "in their reasonings with others" in order to prevail on assent. Locke describes it as a "way that men ordinarily use to drive others and force them to submit their judgments and receive the opinion in debate." The tactic, according to Locke's description, is to "require the adversary to admit what [one alleges] as a proof, or to assign a better." Notice, however, that the kind of argument Locke describes here is not necessarily fallacious, although he does seem to suggest that it could be abused. Certainly Locke is suggesting or indicating how such a powerful tactic of persuasion could be misused in a dialogue, or deployed in a manner that might not contribute to the aims of the dialogue.

Judging from the last two cases, serious problems with the *ad ignorantiam* arise when one side or the other somehow gets the upper hand, so that the other side cannot make headway in discharging the burden of proof. In case 4.7, the car company is successfully stonewalling, by insisting that there is no proof that their cars are unsafe. Another recent case of this kind is studied next.

Safety of Silicone Breast Implants

Over the past thirty years, more than two million women have had silicone breast implants, either for cosmetic reasons or as part of reconstructive surgery. These women have reported many cases of the implant's rupturing, allowing the silicone to leak and disperse throughout the body, followed by severe illnesses such as cancer and autoimmune diseases. This led to controversy over whether the implants should be regulated, or even taken off the market. Through the controversy, the companies who made the implants and the physicians who inserted them consistently argued that there was no hard scientific evidence proving the allegedly harmful effects of these devices.

In 1982, the U.S. Food and Drug Administration (FDA) reclassified implants as "potentially risky," but not risky enough to warrant removing them. Their argument, along with a supporting argument from one of the manufacturers, was reported in *Newsweek* (Seligman, Yoffe, and Hager, 1991, 56).

Case 4.8

> The FDA has known for months about the research questioning the safety of the foam implants, but the agency didn't acknowledge the troubling findings until last week. Although still exploring what level of cancer risk the implants might pose, the agency said: "It is clear that the cancer risk is very small—certainly too small to warrant removing the implants." In fact, the FDA contended, removal might be more hazardous than retention, since it can involve delicate excision of breast tissue to which the disintegrated foam has adhered.
>
> Bristol-Myers Squibb also tried to allay the fears of women who have the implants. "Medical literature contains no reported cases of human cancer associated with polyurethane foam," said a company statement. But many women are worried. Sybil Goldrich and Kathleen Anneken, founders of Command Trust Network, a national information and support group for women with implants, report that their 24-hour hot line has been flooded with hundreds of calls since last week.

Here the statement of Bristol-Myers Squibb that the "medical literature contains no reported cases of human cancer associated with polyurethane foam" is the premise of an argument from ignorance. The implied argument is that since no cases of implants causing cancer have been proved in the medical literature, we can conclude that the implants do not cause cancer. At least, that conclusion is being put forward as the working presumption that the company finds it reasonable to act on.

However, this *ad ignorantiam* argument seems a little peculiar. Although it may be true that there is no scientific proof or hard evidence of the harmfulness of the implants, there were plenty of cases of women complaining that the silicone leaking from their implants was responsible for their severe health problems. And critics of the implants had showed how the silicone had leaked through the container in many of the cases when the implants were later removed. This seemed to be "evidence" of a sort. But physicians or manufacturers of medical products would call it "anecdotal" as opposed to "scientific" evidence. Their argument was that as long as there was no scientific evidence proving the harmful effects of the implants, they could not declare them unsafe.

During an ABC News *Nightline* program, "Are Silicone Breast Implants Safe?" several physicians were interviewed by Judy Muller and Chris Wallace. Some excerpts from these interviews are quoted below (ABC News, January 3, 1992, 1–3).

Case 4.9

> Muller began by stating to Dr. Garry Brody that the FDA is investigating complaints, including reports of ruptures, painful lumps and leakage, believed to be related to cancer. Dr. Brody replied:

> Dr. GARRY BRODY, Plastic Surgeon: Breast implants are one of the safest devices we know. Certainly nothing is 100 percent safe, but in the scheme of all the available devices and medications, it certainly ranks among the safest.

> Wallace then asked Dr. Norman Anderson, an internist who has been advising the FDA on breast implants what he would tell a patient who asked about them.

> Dr. NORMAN ANDERSON, Johns Hopkins Hospital: Chris, I would have to start out saying that 30 years experience, we still don't know the long-term effects of the silicone in the body. We have not established the safety long-term. Any decision about moving ahead with breast implants is lacking that knowledge.

> Wallace then asked Dr. Anderson whether he would recommend against using the implants.

Dr. ANDERSON: At this time, I would not recommend augmentation. I think there might be a rare situation where one would do that. Reconstruction, the women are largely answering that question by themselves. Nine out of 10 women today say no after they've had a mastectomy. The other 10 percent, it may well be a question of education.

Wallace then asked Dr. Harry Glassman, a plastic surgeon who had done many breast implantations over a period of seventeen years, whether there is "hard scientific evidence linking these implants to these serious diseases?"

Dr. HARRY GLASSMAN: Dr. Anderson, I would agree with you that, in fact, it's a very sad state of affairs that we don't have the answers to this. However, I don't necessarily believe that that lack of information should at this particular point lead to the removal of the implants from the market. Your advisory panel found that the implant manufacturers failed to prove that these implants are safe. That's quite a different matter than the implants having been proved unsafe. Thus far—

At this point, Dr. Anderson interjected, "there is no convincing proof" of the worry that these implants are unsafe. Wallace then went on to ask whether this operation "shouldn't be banned until proven safe, rather than allowed to stay on the market until proven unsafe?" In answer to this question about the burden of proof, Dr. Glassman replied as follows.

Dr. GLASSMAN: Well, if it's banned, if in fact the implant is not made available to patients and to surgeons, my concern about this, really, Chris, is that the manufacturers will obviously drop out of the marketplace, the research funds for this will dry up, and two million women who are now calling and asking very valid questions will not find out the answer. We will have nothing to say to them concretely over the ensuing years. We won't have anything to hang our hats on. And so I want to see that the implants continue, only because I want further research

> to be done, so that I can turn to my patients and say, "This is definitely what I suggest you do."

What comes out very clearly in Dr. Glassman's point of view in this case is the use of the argument from ignorance, on the basis of lack of "hard scientific evidence linking these implants to these serious diseases." This failure "to prove that these implants are safe" is used as his premise to argue for the conclusion that their use should not be regulated on the grounds that they are unsafe.

We can see that the issue here is one of burden of proof. The defenders of the implants argue that it is necessary to prove that they are unsafe, before they should be taken off the market, or their use restricted. Some time later, the U.S. government issued warnings about silicone breast implants, and restricted their use, even though they still had not been proved unsafe by hard scientific evidence. We can see in a subsequent interview with Dr. David Kessler, head of the FDA (ABC News, *Primetime Live,* June 3, 1993) that the burden of proof can be placed the opposite way. Renee Poussaint interviews Dr. Kessler and another physician.

Case 4.10

POUSSAINT:	Are breast implants safe?
Dr. COLE:	Yes.
POUSSAINT:	You can say that without qualification?
Dr. COLE:	Breast implants are safe, in as much as we count any sort of medical device as safe.
POUSSAINT:	[*voice-over*] Dr. Cole was president of the American Society of Plastic and Reconstructive Surgeons a year and a half ago when the FDA held hearings about the safety of silicone breast implants. Under his leadership, the society spent close to $4 million for a high-powered lobbying campaign to keep silicone breast implants on the market. [*interviewing*] I'm still not understanding why it is that you feel that these implants should continue to be placed in women if there is no scientific proof that they are safe.

Dr. COLE:	There is no scientific proof that they're unsafe.
Dr. DAVID KESSLER:	What the plastic surgeons wanted to convince people of was there is not evidence 100 percent conclusive to show that these are harmful. That's not the standard. If that's the standard, then you're going to wait till there are bodies out there.
POUSSAINT:	[*voice-over*] Dr. David Kessler, head of the Food and Drug Administration, says the standard for the implants has to be proven safety and the implant manufacturers, he says, are responsible for the testing to get that proof. The restrictions he placed on the use of silicone breast implants last year will stay in force, he says, until all of the testing is done, a process that could take another two to five years.
	[*interviewing*] Why does it have to take that long?
Dr. KESSLER:	I can't allow these devices to be marketed until the time when we have the answers. Can we speed up getting the answers? We're working as hard as possible. (ABC News, June 3, 1993, 6)

Here Dr. Cole takes the same point of view as that of Dr. Glassman in the previous case, using the *argumentum ad ignorantiam* to the effect that the breast implants have not been proven unsafe; therefore they are safe. Poussaint turns this argument on its head, asking why they should continue to be used "if there is no scientific proof that they are safe." This puts the burden of proof on the other side.

Kessler agrees with this using an *argumentum ad ignorantiam* in direct opposition to the type of argument from ignorance used by Cole. He argues that we do not need "evidence 100 percent conclusive" to show that the implants are harmful. His counterargument is that since we don't have the answers, we should not allow the devices to be marketed. In effect he is arguing that since they haven't been proved safe, until the testing is done, we should operate on the presumption that they may be unsafe, and should not be marketed.

This controversy is interesting because the physicians defending the continued use of silicone breast implants persistently used the *ad ignorantiam* stonewalling argument, dismissing the abundant evidence as "anecdotal" and not "scientific." But, at the same time, they were not providing the required scientific evidence by testing the implants.

In September 1993, studies confirmed that "breast implants with polyure-thane plastic coatings break down and send potentially cancer-causing chemicals into women's bodies in small amounts" (Implant danger confirmed, 1993, A5). The research, conducted by Bristol-Myers Squibb, showed that women who have the implants exhibit a substance in their blood or urine that is known to cause cancer in rats (A5).

The *Ad Ignorantiam* Tug-of-War

Investigation of cases of *argumentum ad ignorantiam* in serious debates that involve controversies about public safety and scientific evidence will show that reasonable distribution of burden can be a subtle and tricky matter requiring careful analysis of the context of dialogue. It can turn out, in some cases, that a burden of providing information could be applied to both sides. Here the *argumentum ad ignorantiam* is used as a tactic to try to press a weight of presumption against an opponent to gain the upper hand in argumentation. It functions as a kind of pressure tactic.

The following debate arose in the Question Period of *Hansard* (*Canada: House of Commons Debates,* September 30, 1985, 127:7149), through opposition concern that the embargo on the export of Canadian uranium for "non-peaceful purposes" was not being respected. A recent television report had quoted American energy officials as conceding that Canadian uranium was being used in U.S. nuclear weapons.

Case 4.11

NUCLEAR ARMAMENTS
Canadian Exports of Depleted Uranium

Ms. Pauline Jewett (New Westminster-Coquitlam): Mr. Speaker, my question is directed to the Secretary of State for External Affairs and is with regard to this very troublesome matter of Canadian depleted uranium being used in the United States for both nuclear and conventional military purposes. Can the Minister now give us the reasons why he is absolutely certain that depleted uranium is not being used for those purposes?

Right Hon. Joe Clark (Secretary of State for External Affairs):   Yes, Mr. Speaker, I can. The matter was raised both by television reporters and the other day in the House of Commons in a very general way by the Leader of the New Democratic Party. I consequently looked into it. I have informed myself on the principle of fungibility and other arcane matters that are involved in this question. I have learned that there is, in the treaty, a requirement for administrative arrangements to be put into place that deal with the residue as well as with the original uranium. I have learned that those administrative arrangements are in fact in place. I am satisfied, on the basis of the information I now have available, that the treaty is being respected.

Mr. Blackburn (Brant):   What is your proof?

Mr. Clark (Yellowhead):   I am asked for proof. The proof is that I have looked for any weakness in the treaty and I have found none. If Hon. Members have any information that that treaty is not being respected, I ask them for the fourth time not to be so secretive. Come forward with your allegations so that we can find out whether they are true or false.

Mr. Axworthy: Do a proper investigation.

This case exhibits the structure of an *argumentum ad ignorantiam* of the dialectical type. When asked for proof that Canadian uranium is not being used for military purposes, Mr. Clark replies that he has found no violations of the treaty barring such uses of Canadian uranium. Mr. Clark is arguing that since he has found no violations of the treaty, we may conclude that the treaty is being respected. But is this *argumentum ad ignorantiam* fallacious?

Globally, the requirement of burden of proof is set by the rules for Question Period set in *Beauchesne,* the manual of rules for parliamentary debate. These rules define the Question Period as a speech event. The purpose of Question Period is to allow the opposition to pose short questions that ask for information from the government, or that press for action by the government, on the issues of the day. This means that the opposition spokesperson, Ms. Jewett, has the right to ask this question about uses of exported uranium in possible violation of the treaty.

Mr. Clark replied that he had looked into the matter, and that he is satisfied, on the basis of his investigation, that the treaty is being respected. However, the opposition demands a high standard of proof. Ms. Jewett, in her question, asked whether Mr. Clark can "give us the reasons why he is absolutely certain" that uranium is not being used for military purposes. And Mr. Blackburn follows up Mr. Clark's reply by insisting "What's your proof?" We might raise the question here of how high reasonable standards of proof should be in this case. Ms. Jewett has asked for "absolute certainty," but it seems dubious that Mr. Clark (or anyone in Canada) is in a position to prove "absolutely" the universal negative proposition that Canadian uranium is not being used by anyone in foreign countries for "non-peaceful" purposes. Absolute certainty—whatever that might mean in this context— does not seem to be a realistic standard of burden of disproof to impose on Mr. Clark in this case. Realistically, all Mr. Clark could be expected to do is to monitor any indications of specific violations that are drawn to his attention, or that he can find with the resources at his disposal. How many resources of this sort should be proper for government expenditure depends on the seriousness of the problem posed by possible violations of this treaty.

Following up Mr. Blackburn's repeated request for proof, Mr. Clark follows up his *ad ignorantiam* response that he has found no violations by asking the opposition to come forward with any specific information that they might have on violations of the treaty. This seems like a reasonable request, in the circumstances, but instead of responding to it, another opposition critic simply reiterates the demand for a more rigorous government search for possible violations by saying, "Do a proper investigation." However, here the real issue is not so much the standard of the government investigation, as the failure of the critics to cite any specific violation that would justify a government investigation, and more likely to be productive. If the critics do not supply proper evidence of violations suspected, the best Mr. Clark can say is that, as far as he knows, the treaty is being respected, on the basis of the information that is available at present.

What case 4.11 suggests is that even if a respondent has a global burden of proof to prove some proposition that is legitimately queried by a questioner, at the local level, the questioner may also have a burden to be as informative as is useful or helpful to the respondent in guiding his investigation into providing an answer. Such a burden on the questioner is particularly appropriate in an information-seeking dialogue where the questioner needs to guide the answerer by asking helpful questions to support the inquiry.

This raises the general question of what type of dialogue the Question Period of the House of Commons Debates should be taken to be. Basically, the Question Period is an information-seeking and action-seeking type of dialogue, but the Speaker of the House will allow argumentative questions (to some extent) that turn the question-reply sequence into a kind of persuasion dialogue. Indeed, something like this dialectical shift is apparent in this case. Mr. Clark and his critics keep trying to shift the burden of proof back and forth, and the result is a kind of argumentation ping-pong, where each side is merely sniping at the other instead of investigating the issue of treaty violations. We can detect a strong element of eristic dialogue here. The information-seeking goal of the dialogue is thwarted by turning it into a contestive series of attempts to shift the burden of proof to the other side. It is a collaborative failure of interactive reasoning, but a good deal of the fault, in this instance, must be placed on the questioner's failure to ask more specific and helpful questions.

The dialectical form of the *argumentum ad ignorantiam* is interesting because it shows how a dialogue could go on and on in an endless cycle of questions and replies without ever resolving an issue. When White asks the question "Why *A*?" Black could reply, "Why not-*A*?" bouncing the ball back to White's court. But then White could come back with the same form of reply "Why not not-*A*?" and then Black could repeat the process, and in theory, the sequence could cycle on endlessly without ever resolving the issue of the dialogue. This procedure would not advance the argument in any way. It is a kind of futile attack and counterattack that resolves nothing.

Essentially the same kind of problem underlies the dialogue of case 4.11 above. The critics demand that Mr. Clark give reasons why he is "absolutely certain" that Canadian uranium is not being used for military purposes. Mr. Clark then asks the critics to come forward and give the basis of information for their allegation that Canadian uranium is being used for military purposes. The discussion is going nowhere. They are merely shifting the burden back and forth.

What is lacking here is some clear indication of where the burden of proof should lie. Once that is known, the stalemate of the dialectical *argumentum ad ignorantiam* could be resolved. Here then is a very real danger in debate. If the burden of proof is not clearly established and known, the debate can cycle on endlessly in an unproductive manner. And from a point of view of a critic or evaluator of a text of argument discourse of this type, it cannot be determined whether the *argumentum ad ignorantiam* is fallacious or not.

Case 4.11 is a good illustration of a familiar and characteristic kind of *ad ignorantiam* argumentation which could be called the *ad ignorantiam tug-of-war:* in this kind of situation, each side of the argument uses the tactic of pushing the burden of proof or further inquiry onto the other side. Generally, in the tug-of-war, one side is pushing to have some matter investigated, claiming that there is a serious problem, and that the other side is at fault for not investigating it; this first group or individual could be called the attacking side. The other participant, which could be called the defensive side, tries to stave off the attack of the first side, claiming that further investigation is not necessary, by using the argument that there is insufficient evidence that the problem exists, or is serious enough to warrant action or inquiry.

So far, we have seen that there are always two sides to an *ad ignorantiam* argument, and there is nothing wrong with this type of argumentation, in principle, when it is used by one side against the other. But the danger of a fallacy comes in when the one side tries to get the upper hand by pressing ahead too aggressively. In public controversies, scientific evidence of some sort is often cited (also in legal cases), with the result that the *ad ignorantiam* often overlaps with another of the traditional fallacies, the *ad verecundiam*.

Combining *Ad Ignorantiam* and *Ad Verecundiam* Arguments

Several of the cases of *ad ignorantiam* arguments studied in this chapter are cases where expert testimony is being used to back up an argument. In case 4.2, Grabitz's statement about absence of evidence on Demjanjuk was based on her knowledge of prosecuting war criminals from a particular camp over a period of twenty-one years. In case 4.7, the engineers were testifying that they could find no evidence of a fault in the car, based on their expertise. In the breast implant cases 4.8–4.10, the physicians reported, as medical experts, that there was no scientific evidence of cancer caused by polyurethane foam. In all these cases, the evidential basis for the alleged lack of knowledge is the expertise of some person or group. We saw too in Chapter 3, that the knowledge base cited in arguments from ignorance is often that of an expert. The traditional name for the type of argument where an argument is supported by appeal to an expert opinion is the *argumentum ad verecundiam.* However, the use of the Latin name for this type of argumentation suggests or implies that it is fallacious.

Things get tricky when *ad ignorantiam* and *ad verecundiam* intersect with each other in argumentation. *Ad ignorantiam* arguments are strongest, from a logical point of view, when a knowledge base for an argument is closed. If the relevant information in a knowledge base is complete, then from our failure to find a given proposition as an item of information there, after an exhaustive search, we can reasonably conclude that this proposition can be rejected as not known to be true. We could even conclude, in some cases, that, relative to a background context of inquiry, this proposition may be taken as false. But this inference is considerably strengthened to the extent that the knowledge base utilized was reliable and complete.

Characteristically, a knowledge base is reliable and complete if the source cited is known to be a highly reliable expert in that domain of knowledge. Thus an *ad ignorantiam* can be supported very effectively by an appeal to expert opinion in argumentation. If a real expert says that it is definitely and conclusively true that there is no known evidence that a particular proposition in her field is true, it creates a strong presumption that this proposition is in fact not true. Given the right context of dialogue and allocation of burden of proof, it may be very reasonable to draw the conclusion that this proposition can be presumed, for the purpose of an argument, to be false. In this sort of *ad ignorantiam* argumentation, the completeness of the knowledge base, backed up by the appeal to expertise, supports the argument from ignorance strongly.

On the other hand, appeals to expert opinion are rarely closed, deductively valid arguments. Typically they are presumptive arguments that are inherently weak, open to critical questions, and subject to errors. That does not mean that they are fallacious. But the attempt to back up an *ad ignorantiam* argument by using an appeal to expert opinion to support it is often a suspicious move that should be subject to all kinds of reservations. Bringing expert opinion into a persuasion dialogue on a controversial topic of discussion is often a sophistical tactic for trying to bring inappropriate pressures to bear on an audience or respondent.

The following case occurred in a political discussion on *Frontline,* called "The Politics of Prosperity" (Network of Public Television Stations, October 1988); the topic was the American economy prior to the 1988 federal election. The speaker was Jeff Faux of the Economic Policy Institute.

Case 4.12

> Well, bankers, of course, are always worried about inflation. They're worried about supporting the incomes of the bond holders. And what you have is a classic point of view. What we have here is, I think, the worry over inflation as a cover for a decision to slow down the economy and impose austerity on the American people. It is beyond, I think, any reasonable doubt that we have no evidence that we're going into an inflation the way we had in the late 1970's. It's just not there. Real wages are declining. So we've got a situation where people are already tightening their belts.

This is an *argumentum ad ignorantiam,* because Mr. Faux states that, in his opinion, it is beyond reasonable doubt that we have no evidence that we are going into an inflation like that of the 1970s. The claim is that *we have no evidence* that we are going into this kind of inflation. The implied conclusion is that *we are not* going into this kind of inflation.

But prefacing the no-evidence claim is a rider that this absence of evidence is *beyond reasonable doubt.* Although this seems a little odd, the argument from ignorance is in fact prefaced by a statement of certainty, of absence of reasonable doubt or ignorance. Now such a claim can be made relative to a closed knowledge base. But does it make sense here, where the issue concerns predictions of the financial market and inflation, topics that are always inherently open to uncertainty and doubt?

The argument seems on the surface implausible, and perhaps even inconsistent. But what may help to make sense of it as an effective argument is the implicit support Mr. Faux is claiming for his premise as beyond reasonable doubt through his own expertise as a spokesman for the Economic Policy Institute. Possibly he is making such a strong claim in virtue of his own expertise as a financial analyst, and on the basis of his interpretation of what the financial experts are now saying about the state of the U.S.

economy. If so, the claim that his assertion is beyond reasonable doubt begins to make more sense as a coherent type of argument that could be supported strongly, even though it is an argument from ignorance.

If this is the basis of the argument, however, it should be remembered that the appeal to expert opinion is open to critical questioning. The phrase "beyond any reasonable doubt that we have no evidence" comes across very smoothly as a polished phrase. It is not perhaps likely to be noticed, challenged, or seen for what it is as a very aggressive combination of the argument from ignorance and appeal to expert opinion in one abbreviated crisp phrase. In a televised interview, such a phrase can zip by quickly without much attention being paid to it. Yet it has a convincing effect on viewers, and sounds authoritative. The combination of the *ad ignorantiam* and *ad verecundiam* is a dovetailing tactic that is rhetorically effective.

This factor was prominent in the silicone breast implants controversy as well: the basis of the judgment of the physicians that there was no "scientific evidence" for the harmfulness of the implants was a claim based on medical expertise, and medical standards of acceptable evidence. One problem here, however, is that "scientific evidence" and "evidence" in some broader (unqualified) sense, may not be the same thing.

Of course, as shown in Chapter 2, the mere fact that an argument from ignorance is based on an appeal to expert opinion does not (by itself) make it fallacious. Many common arguments from ignorance that are quite reasonable are based on an expert's knowledge of a database in her field of expertise.

What must be noted is that the two types of tactics so well defined by Locke, the *ad ignorantiam* and the *ad verecundiam* can often be used together, the one piggybacking on the other. This can make both more powerful, and the potential faults or errors in their use harder to spot. Curiously, the third Lockean type of argument, the *ad hominem*, can also be involved.

Combining with *Ad Hominem*

A case study presented by Blair (1988, 96) gives an example of an argument that combines the *ad ignorantiam, ad verecundiam,* and *ad hominem,* all in the same case. The case is a full-page advertisement run in 1985 in *Life* magazine by the R. J. Reynolds Tobacco Company. In this advertisement, Reynolds argued that the attack citing the dangers of secondhand smoke as a health hazard is really a disguised attack on smoking. The ad claimed, "Many independent experts believe the scientific evidence on passive smoking is questionable." This appeal to expert opinion was followed by the segment of the ad quoted by Blair (96), repeated below.

Case 4.13

> But a zealous group of anti-smokers are using this issue in their campaign against tobacco as if the claims were established scientific fact.
>
> We deplore the actions of those who try to manipulate public opinion through scare tactics . . .
>
> We are not ignoring the fact that cigarette smoke can be bothersome to many non-smokers. But we believe this problem is best solved not by governments but by individuals, not with more rhetoric but more common sense and courtesy . . .

Following the part of text cited above, the ad quoted Dr. H. Russell Fisher as a respected pathologist who, it is alleged, has said that there is no proof of harm from "atmospheric tobacco smoke," and who suggested that fear of secondhand smoke may be a "social problem" that might lead to medical problems. The first part of this argument is clearly a species of *argumentum ad ignorantiam,* arguing that no proof of harm indicates that there is no harm. And most interestingly, the *ad ignorantiam* argument is based on an appeal to expertise. If Dr. Fisher is an expert, and he says there is no harm to be found, then the conclusion is that there is good reason to believe that, since he knows whether such proof would be there to be found or not, we may conclude that there is good reason to accept the conclusion that no proof exists.

But it is not this *ad ignorantiam cum ad verecundiam* aspect of the argument that Blair comments on; his concern is to criticize the bias he contends is in the ad. According to Blair, "zealotry" is excessive enthusiasm, "manipulation" is improper influence, "scare tactics" are substitutes for good reasons, and "rhetoric" is commonly taken to be empty, unsubstantiated persuasion. The evidence presented by the ad is not sufficient to support this extreme language, according to Blair. Therefore he concludes that the language of the Reynolds ad is biased.

Now note that it would be easy to attack the argument of the ad by pointing out that R. J. Reynolds is in the tobacco business, and that therefore they want to promote smoking, and stand to lose if people start to think that smoking is unhealthy in any way, or if people impose more restrictions on smoking in public places. Therefore, it would be easy to utilize an *ad hominem* attack to accuse Reynolds of bias in advancing this argument.

But that is not Blair's contention. Bypassing the possibility of this simple kind of criticism, Blair takes a much more subtle and carefully substantiated point of view, contending that it is the language of the specific wording of the ad that makes it open to a criticism of bias.

Blair contends (96) that the language of the Reynolds ad is biased and that "as a result, the ad as a whole contains a subtly biased message that the opposition to secondhand smoke is not responsible." Blair concludes that this charge of bias implies that the ad misrepresents the position of their adversaries in the argument about secondhand smoke in a way that violates norms of fairness and honesty in dialogue. In effect, Blair is saying that the ad contains a subtle form of *ad hominem* argumentation. The ad is biased because it suggests, more or less subtly in its wording at various points, that the opposition to secondhand smoking are not responsible people; instead, it suggests that they are enthusiastic zealots who use scare tactics and other emotional kinds of rhetoric, instead of good evidence. To provide contrast, the ad cites the evidence of scientific, expert opinion, and even uses this appeal to expertise to suggest that opposers of secondhand smoking may be verging on mental illness or instability of some sort: they have "social problems" that might lead to "medical problems." This is a not so subtle *ad hominem* attack on the opposition.

Another somewhat different kind of case, below, also combines the use of *ad hominem, ad verecundiam,* and *ad ignorantiam* tactics in the same argumentation. In the following case, the proponent is arguing for the non-existence of ESP.

Case 4.14

> No intelligent and informed person could be ignorant of the well-known fact that no serious and respectable scientific evidence for the existence of extrasensory perception has ever been established. You are an intelligent person. Therefore, of course, you must accept the fact that extrasensory perception does not exist.

The tactic of the proponent of this argument is to try to put pressure on the respondent by presenting the argument in such a manner that if the respondent does not accept it, he is an unintelligent and ignorant person who is unaware of well-known, serious, and respectable evidence. The argument is heavily stacked against the respondent in favor of an affirmative reply, or acquiescence. By disagreeing with the argument, the respondent appears to be put in a position where he is damaging his own credibility as someone capable of taking part in intelligent argumentation. Indeed, this case verges on the *argumentum ad hominem* in its attack on the respondent in order to force a certain conclusion.

Case 4.14 exhibits the underlying fault of the aggressive or attacking *argumentum ad ignorantiam*. Instead of giving the evidence to back up his contention that ESP does not exist, the arguer is attacking the respondent's presumed lack of proof for ESP by browbeating him.

The context of dialogue in this case appears to be that of a critical discussion of the dispute type where one party is arguing for the existence of ESP and the other party (the speaker of the discourse given in the case) opposes the thesis of the existence of ESP. The internal evidence of the text of discourse indicates how the proponent (the second party) is aggressively trying to force closure of the dialogue by using the terms "intelligent person," "informed person," "respectable scientific evidence," and "must accept the fact" to load a positive presumption to one side of the argument. The presumption of analysis (itself a kind of *ad ignorantiam* argument) is that the proponent is using these terms in place of giving positive evidence of the state of current scientific investigations on the subject of ESP.

However, at a secondary level of analysis, the inquiry is also partially involved in this case. The proponent purports to appeal to the current findings of scientific investigations into ESP, and claims that no "serious and respectable" evidence has been established by the scientific community of investigators. A kind of appeal to the authority of expert opinion could also be involved in this type of argument.

Thus in this case, although it is primarily a critical discussion, both contexts of dialogue are involved. What is common to them both however is the fallacy of the *argumentum ad ignorantiam* as a tactic by the proponent to prevail on the assent of the respondent in order to force closure in the proponent's favor by pressing more weight on his heavily loaded presumptions than the evidence given in his argument can really bear.

It is quite common for the *ad hominem* and *ad ignorantiam* arguments to overlap in this way, as used in everyday argumentation. The *ad hominem* is so often such a powerful tactic precisely because it is put forward on a basis of suggestion or innuendo, instead of solid evidence. And the tactic is to try to use the innuendo to shift the burden of proof to the other side. If serious evidence were to be required to back up these *ad hominem* attacks, the argument would be easily perceived as weak and unconvincing. Yet typically, *ad hominem* attacks are quite powerful, particularly in political debates, for example (D. Walton, 1985). It seems that the explanation of this puzzle is that the *ad hominem* attack is combined with an *ad ignorantiam* argument that shifts the burden of proof.

Innuendo

Among the most striking kinds of cases where the argument from ignorance is powerful are those where it is used to create doubt and suspicion by innuendo. An illustrative case of this sort is given by Weddle (1978, 26–27).

Case 4.15

> The story which appeared last month in these pages documenting the governor's extramarital liaisons raised considerable protest. We were accused of being "greedy scandalmongers who would publish doubtfully authentic photos of the state's highest official."
>
> Well, it's been several weeks since our story appeared. If the Governor's Office can manage to respond overnight to a little girl who wants to complete her autograph collection, surely it could muster the vast resources at its disposal to deny the allegation contained in our story. The fact that it has not done so speaks for itself.

The failure to respond to these allegations by the governor's office is understandable, because as Weddle (27) puts it, "To respond to them would be to dignify them." It would also give more publicity to them. And then there is the danger that a response might be interpreted by the public as a sign of defensiveness or guilt. Thus here the failure to respond is not necessarily, as the argument of the case implies, a sign that the allegation is true. It is not hard to see how this use of the argument from ignorance is a very common and effective tactic of exploiting innuendo.

An account of how this type of tactic of appeal to ignorance generally works is given by Waller (1988, 36).

Case 4.16

> The sensationalist tabloids have a field day with the appeal to igno-rance. They publish scandalous accusations concerning the lives and loves of movie stars and politicians and then—in *support* of those stories—they point out that: "Two weeks ago we published an exclu-sive story about Ima Starr's torrid love affair with the Ambassador to Rutabaga; if it's not true, they should deny it, but since they haven't denied it, much less offered any proof that it is false, then it must be true." But Ima Starr and the Ambassador are caught in a bind: If they ignore the story, a few people will believe it, but most will ignore it and it will soon pass, since none of the major newspa-pers or television networks will consider the story reliable. However, if they deny the story then *that* is news—whenever a film star and an Ambassador issue statements, the press considers it newswor-thy—and those denials (along with the *charges* being denied) will receive national news coverage, and the story will not blow over quickly. So even if there is not a grain of truth to the charges, it's unlikely that a denial will be issued. And more to the point, it's not up to them to prove the charges *false* (think for a moment of how difficult it would be to *prove* that you did not have a secret love affair with someone); the burden of proof rests on those making the charges.

Charges of this kind put the accused party in a bind. If she denies them too vigorously, then observers may conclude, "Where there's smoke, there's fire." Giving evidence to prove one is innocent may appear to concede guilt. On the other hand, saying nothing at all may suggest acceptance of the claim made in the charge. Another alternative is to attack the party who made the charge. But as Waller points out, any attempt at rebuttal may just have the effect of giving more publicity to the charges.

The problem basically is one of burden of proof. The accuser who made the charge in the first place has the burden of proving it, on the principle that whoever makes an assertion is obliged to give evidence to support it, if questioned. But here too, things can get very shifty. Typically what the sensationalist tabloids do in a case like this is to say that they are just reporting what someone else said. So they don't have the burden of proof—they may even claim that they don't believe the accusation at all. They can claim that they are just reporting what was said, "according to a source." Nevertheless, once such a charge appears in print, it tends to take on a certain credibility. The tabloid has to have a source, but that source could be anybody, even somebody who has no possessions that could be subject to the danger of a lawsuit for slander or libel damages. In reality then, the responsibility for burden of proof can be minimal.

It seems to be in cases like this where there is the most danger of the *argumentum ad ignorantiam* being used fallaciously. In cases where it is clear exactly what constitutes evidence, and there is a clear and appropriate burden of proof set for evidence, then the *ad ignorantiam* is much less likely to go wrong. It is just to avoid fallacious use of arguments from ignorance that rules of evidence are clearly formulated in legal trials, and standards of burden of proof are set for both sides, in advance of the proceedings.

In these tabloid cases, however, the notion of evidence required to back up a claim is very thin. The "source" does not have to be an expert, does not have to justify on oath, and does not even have to be named. Reporting rumors, gossip, and the like is accepted practice. As long as everyone knows what to expect in these tabloids, presumably nobody takes them seriously anyway. Yet they do cause harm because once such a rumor is voiced, it can damage someone's reputation.

The worst case scenario is the witch-hunt type of case, typified by the Salem witchcraft trials. In this type of case, the normal weighting of burden of proof that would be imposed in a criminal trial is reversed: the accused person has to prove herself innocent. But the worst aspect of such a proceeding can be—as we saw both in the witchcraft trials and in the Alger Hiss case—that it is actually impossible for the accused person to succeed in fulfilling this burden of proof. In the Salem trials, this was made impossible by the nature of the proceedings itself—the spectral evidence and the wailing of the accusers made for a format designed only to "prove" guilt. In the Hiss case, the accused person was never able to clear his name in the court of public opinion, once the news media had prominently featured him as a spy, or suspected spy who had been convicted of something in court.

The heart of the problem in the McCarthy and Salem tribunals was a wave of public zeal or hysteria to prosecute "Communists" or "witches" that was so overpowering that any accused person was almost certain to be convicted. Anyone who disagreed would themselves be perceived as a "Communist sympathizer" or "in league with Satan." Thus there was a widespread and justified fear that if you spoke out against this trend, you too could be "fingered." And once charged, by innuendo you would be guilty of the same perceived offense, and have no chance to prove otherwise, or defend yourself. As we saw in the Hiss case, even long after the hysteria passes, the stigma of the accusation can still linger.

5
———————— Forms of the *Argumentum ad Ignorantiam*

Among the types of argumentation associated with the various traditional informal fallacies, the *argumentum ad ignorantiam* is one of the subtler. It is not so easy to identify, in many cases, as it is used in everyday argumentation. It often operates under the surface of one of the arguments associated with the other traditional fallacies, under an *ad hominem* or an *ad verecundiam* argument, for example (as noted in Chapter 4).

The *argumentum ad ignorantiam,* as we saw in Chapter 2, is not just any appeal to ignorance, or attempt to exploit another party's ignorance in a discussion. It is a distinctive type of argument that has a characteristic negative logic—absence of proof that a particular proposition is true (false) is taken as proof that it is false (true). It is a sort of flip-flop argument that starts from a negative premise, and goes to an opposite conclusion. By double negation, one infers that the conclusion is a positive claim that a proposition is true.

This, however, is only a rough and incomplete sketch of the logic of the *argumentum ad ignorantiam.* In this chapter, I shall abstract further from the various cases already studied, to see that it has several distinctive logical forms. At least, I shall try to offer a good enough account so that we will be in a better position to identify the *argumentum ad ignorantiam* when it occurs in a text of discourse. Learning how to use these forms to evaluate instances of the *argumentum ad ignorantiam* as reasonable or fallacious will come later. Here I presume an underlying general distinction between the two tasks of argument identification and argument evaluation.

Identifying the *Argumentum ad Ignorantiam*

A problem is the difficulty, in many cases, of distinguishing between absence of proof that something is true, has taken place, or exists (ignorance), on the one hand; and the presence of proof that the thing in question is false, or has not taken place, or does not exist (knowledge of something negative). The problem here is posed by the possibility that a failure to find something can count as a kind of knowledge, in some cases. Copi (1982, 102), after considering the case (case 4.5) where a serious security investigation has failed to find any evidence at all that Mr. X is a foreign agent, comments, "it would be wrong to conclude that their research has left us ignorant." Rather, we have positive knowledge here that if something had occurred it would be known. Hence, according to Copi, the case of Mr. X is not really an *argumentum ad ignorantiam,* after all. It is not a fallacious argument at all, but rather a knowledge-based argument with a negative conclusion. It is not fallacious, according to Copi, because it does not really qualify as an argument from ignorance, despite its initial appearance of being an argument of this type. The same kind of argument used to dismiss the ostensibly nonfallacious cases of *argumentum ad ignorantiam* is used by Kahane (1992, 64) (see also Chapter 9, "The Basic Fallacy").

This type of case is a serious identification problem, because it raises the question of whether the failure of the investigation to find any evidence that Mr. X is a spy is really "positive proof" (knowledge) or "absence of proof" (ignorance). It seems to be partly both. The problem here is analogous to the ancient philosophical problems of whether there can be "negative facts," or whether you can have positive knowledge of something nonexistent. It's like the difference between the optimist, who sees a glass of water as "half full," and the pessimist, who sees the same glass of water as "half empty." This is a problem of identifying the *argumentum ad ignorantiam* as a distinctive species of argument.

Ad ignorantiam arguments are tricky; they can often be redescribed in a positive way that makes them seem not to be arguments from ignorance at all. This redescription or transformation turns an argument from ignorance into a more positive-appearing kind of argumentation using *modus tollens,* and an implicit conditional assumption of a kind we have found so often characteristic of cases classified as arguments from ignorance (see Chapters 2 and 4). The transformation is based on the conditional that if you have looked for something, and clearly it is not there, then this observation can count as a kind of positive evidence that it is not there. This transformation will form the basis of our analysis of the structure of the *argumentum ad ignorantiam* as a distinctive type of argument given in Chapter 8.

Another example will help to illustrate this transformation.

Case 5.1

> Rob asks Frans whether his umbrella is on the coat rack in the doorway. Frans shouts from the doorway, "I do not see it here."

In this case, Frans has looked at the coat rack in the doorway and reported that he does not see Rob's umbrella there. Rob draws the conclusion, "My umbrella is not on the coat rack." While this inference has a negative conclusion, it does seem to be based on a premise derived from an actual observation, which would seem to be, in some sense, empirical evidence and not merely lack of knowledge. It is negative evidence, in the sense of Chapter 3, but at the same time it seems acceptable to define it as positive knowledge.

This positive aspect of the sequence of argumentation involved in case 5.1 can be brought out more clearly by transforming the sequence as follows:

> If the umbrella were there, Frans would see it. Frans [looked and reported that he] did not see it. Therefore, the umbrella is not there.

This *modus tollens* sequence does have a negative conclusion, but in some ways it seems to be a definite and non-negative piece of knowledge, as opposed to a case of not knowing whether something is true or not. The second premise seems to be more appropriately described as "knowledge" rather than "ignorance."

If case 5.1 were modified somewhat, so that Frans reported his observation in a more emphatic way, saying that the umbrella is not there, the argument would seem even less like an *ad ignorantiam.*

Case 5.2

> Rob asks Frans whether his umbrella is on the coat rack in the door-
> way. Frans shouts from the doorway, "It is not here."

The implicit premises are that Frans looked for the umbrella in the coat-
rack area, and did not find it there. His proposition asserted is supposedly
the conclusion drawn from these premises. Here, the argument involved
seems even less like an *ad ignorantiam* than that of case 5.1, because the
premise is not a report of lack of knowledge so much as a report of definite
knowledge that the umbrella is not there (positive knowledge of a negative finding).

But cases 5.1 and 5.2 do not seem all that different. In case 5.2, Frans is
just being slightly more emphatic in reporting what he saw on the coat rack.
Thus there seems to be a range from a mixture of less knowledge/more
ignorance to more knowledge/less ignorance. Neither is a case of absolute
ignorance or absolute knowledge.

Cases like these could even lead skeptics to conclude that there is really
no *argumentum ad ignorantiam* as a distinct species of argumentation, because all apparent arguments from ignorance can be transformed into arguments that are positive to some degree. And there is some wisdom in this
philosophical point of view, because we have found it characteristic of the
arguments classified as *ad ignorantiam* in Chapters 2 and 3 that they involve
searching through a given knowledge base. In some of these cases, failure
to find an item, once a complete search has been made through a (finite)
knowledge base, may result in definite knowledge that the item is not there.
This is the conclusive type of argument from ignorance.

However, it is stretching a point too far to say that all *ad ignorantiam*
arguments are based on premises that can be described as complete
searches through fixed and well-circumscribed knowledge bases. What is
revealed, rather, is that knowledge can be negative (ignorance) in one respect, while it is also positive (knowledge that something is the case) in
another respect. One only has to remember, for example, that to have Socratic wisdom on a subject is to know that you don't know something about
that subject. In other words, being aware of one's limitations can be a positive kind of knowledge, despite its negative character in another respect.
As we saw in Chapter 4 this iterated type of epistemic structure of the form
"she knows that she does not know *A*" is partly knowledge and partly lack
of knowledge.

What one does have to do here is to be aware that in many cases traditionally classified as arguments from ignorance, the argument is based partly on ignorance, and at the same time, based also partly on positive items of knowledge. In other words, many arguments from ignorance are not totally arguments from ignorance, but they are nevertheless arguments based on ignorance in a less rigorous or exclusive sense. In fact, the kind of *modus tollens* transformation shown in case 5.1 above indicates that many arguments are based on collections of premises linked together, where some of these premises are positive items of knowledge and others are propositions expressing lack of knowledge or absence of findings.

In case 5.2, you could argue that the argumentation is not really an *ad ignorantiam,* because it is based on positive knowledge that Frans has gathered, based on his observations of the coat-rack area. But in another respect, the argumentation is based on absence of knowledge—on a negative rather than a positive finding—because Frans looked for the umbrella, but failed to find it. Perhaps we could say that the argumentation in this type of case is a mixed form of reasoning, partially based on ignorance (not finding something), and partially based on positive observations that represent findings that can be better described as knowledge than ignorance.

A somewhat similar type of knowledge-based reasoning also appears to be an argument from ignorance, but is perhaps even more questionable as being identified in this category. The following example concerns a search through a computer directory.

Case 5.3

> When I am ready to print a document, the directory comes on my computer screen, and it is divided into two columns of file names. I know that the word processing program always puts the file names in one column or the other, but with a newly created file, I never know in advance which column the file name will be in. Quickly I scan down the left column (alphabetically) and see that the file name I am searching for (*Lipman*) is not there. Before even looking in the second column, I switch the cursor from the head of the first column to the head of the second column, and begin working it down to where the *L* section (for *Lipman* would be there).

Now in this case, I could look directly into the second column to see if *Lipman* is there, before moving the cursor to the second column. But it is faster to reason by *ad ignorantiam:* since I know that *Lipman* must be in the second column, because I have already found it is *not* in the first column, I act right away on the presumption that it is in the second column.

The *ad ignorantiam* argument in this case has the form of a disjunctive syllogism: *Lipman* is either in the first column or the second column; *Lipman* is not in the first column; therefore, *Lipman* is in the second column. The argument seems conclusive because it is deductively valid. But the conclusion is also directly verifiable: I shall confirm that the conclusion is true when I finally do run my eye down the second column.

There is a key difference between this case and case 3.5, Reiter's case of the airline database giving stops in a flight to different cities. In this case, if a city is not listed, then the presumption is that the flight does not stop there. The reason is the convention, presumed to obtain, that all stops are listed on the monitor. But in case 5.3, when I see *Lipman* not listed in the first column, I know this file name has to be in the second column because I know that I just filed this document, and therefore I know that the file name must be either in the first or the second column. This inference is not based on a conversational postulate to the effect that any item not mentioned is false, or not included in the database. It is based on my confidence that once I file a document, it is kept, and its file name is listed somewhere in the directory.

Thus you could argue that the inference in the *Lipman* case is not really an argument from ignorance, in the same way the inference in the airline database case is. Instead, the inference in the *Lipman* case is a knowledge-based argument taking the form of the disjunctive syllogism in propositional logic. In other words, the suggestion is that it is an argument from knowledge, not an argument from ignorance.

There are pros and cons to this case. On the one hand, it does have the negative logic characteristic of the *argumentum ad ignorantiam.* On the other hand, the premises and the conclusion seem to be so definite, and so highly verified, that it does not seem appropriate to categorize the inference as a genuine argument from ignorance. For one thing, it seems like case 5.2, because it seems appropriate to say (positively) that I know that *Lipman* is not in the left column. For another thing, it seems also like case 3.5, because the closed world assumption seems to apply. At any rate, we can see now that in some cases, it seems difficult to say absolutely whether the argument is an argument from ignorance or an argument from knowledge (or observation). In many cases, it seems that ignorance and knowledge tend to be mixed together, and to depend on each other in framing the logic of the argument.

In the nonfallacious cases of the *argumentum ad ignorantiam* discussed in Chapter 3, none of these arguments were based on pure ignorance. In none of these cases, was *mere* lack of knowledge that a proposition *A* is true, all by itself, being claimed to provide evidential support for *not-A*. In these cases, there was antecedent reason to believe that if *A* is the case, then we will discover evidence for it, subsequent upon a certain sort of investigation. This fact conjoined with the knowledge that we carried out the investigation and not discovered such evidence yields a *modus tollens* type of argument for the conclusion *not-A*.

In these cases then, it is incorrect to say that there was no evidence for *A* at all, or that the argument for *not-A* was purely or solely based on ignorance. Instead, the premise was that an inquiry or investigation was carried out, to some greater or lesser degree of completeness, and the inquiry yielded no evidence for *A*. Presuming the inquiry was a good and successful one, at least to some degree, it would have turned up some evidence for *A* if the evidence were there. Hence, at least indirectly, it can be reasonable to conclude that this failure to find something is a kind of evidence that *A* is not true. It is a kind of negative evidence, but that is different from being no evidence at all. Thus we could say that even negative evidence is not totally negative, but really a kind of mixed evidence.

Hence defining the argument from ignorance is trickier than one may have initially thought. Such an argument is never an argument from total ignorance (a complete absence of all knowledge), but is always a mixture of knowledge and ignorance. This is a significant practical problem, because arguments from ignorance can be implicit in a text of discourse, and are often mixed in with other types of arguments. But it is also a theoretical problem of defining what ignorance is.

Defining Ignorance

Ignorance is not an easy concept to define adequately and precisely. Basically, ignorance is absence, or negation of knowledge: we are ignorant of a proposition, or set of propositions, when we don't know that proposition, or set of propositions.

But as noted above, it is unclear that ignorance and knowledge are entirely distinct. If I know that I don't know something, then that ignorance is a kind of knowledge. Socratic ignorance is a species of this type of ignorance, when Socrates claimed to be a wise man only in the sense that he knew that he did not really know certain things that other people claimed confidently to know (Plato, *Apology* 21b–21e). This is really a mixture of knowledge and ignorance.

An everyday example of this sort of ignorance mixed with knowledge is the following case. Marylin is an architect, hired by Charles to build a house for his family. They get into a complex discussion of the slope of the land in discussing how the house should best be set at a particular level.

Case 5.4

Charles: Well, I don't really understand these complicated technical matters very well. I'm just trying to grasp what the house will look like so it will suit my personal requirements.

Marylin: You are much better off than some people I deal with, who *think* they know all about these things.

Here, Marylin is suggesting that Charles is doing well in trying to grapple with a subject he does not know much about, because he is admitting his limitations. In doing so, he is not being overconfident, or pretending he knows more than he does, and is avoiding errors that can result from this pretense. This kind of case could be described by the phrase "he knows what he doesn't know." Thus it combines positive knowledge with negative knowledge (or ignorance).

Another problematic type of case to define is that of *negative evidence,* the kind of situation studied in Chapter 3, where a thorough investigation has been made for something, and turned up no positive evidence of it. The more thorough the search has been, the more we can say that the outcome is no longer just ignorance, but positive knowledge that the thing does not exist. But in many cases, in the middle regions, it could be hard to say whether what we have is ignorance or (positive) knowledge. It often seems that it is partly both. The difference here, once again, is between not knowing that something is true versus knowing that it is false. The first is a kind of ignorance, but the second is a kind of knowledge.

Three different types of ignorance have been recognized by M. H. Witte,

A. Kerwin, and C. L. Witte (1988, 793), in their Curriculum in Medical Ignorance: "The curriculum consists of seminars and hands-on clinical and laboratory experiences dealing with 'what we know we don't know, what we don't know we don't know, and what we think we know but don't.'" These three subtypes could be called, respectively, *known ignorance,* or ignorance we are aware of, *unknown ignorance,* or ignorance we are not aware of, and *pseudoknowledge* (or ignorance that appears to be knowledge, to some person or group, at some time, but is not). It appears then that there can be different types of ignorance, depending on how it is mixed with knowledge, or the appearance of knowledge.

When we say then that ignorance is absence or negation of knowledge then, we do not mean total absence of all knowledge. Instead, it means we do not know enough about some particular proposition to say that we know it is true, or we know it is false. If we wish to define ignorance more precisely than this, by using some formal system of epistemic (or autoepistemic logic) there are also some problems that arise. The immediate problem is how to define negation.

Some Buddhist and idealist philosophers have in fact advocated defining negation as an absence of knowledge, in a way that makes negation virtually identical with the *argumentum ad ignorantiam* itself. According to this analysis of negation, a proposition like "There is no jar on this spot." (taken to be the simplest case of negation), would be analyzed as a conditional inference having the form of *modus tollens:* "if a jar would have been present on this spot, it would have been perceived, but since it is not perceived, we can deny its presence" (Stcherbatsky, 1962, 392). According to Stcherbatsky (392), both the European idealist Sigwart and the Indian philosopher Dharmakirti advocated what amounts to this same analysis of the meaning of negation.

> If we compare with this statement of Sigwart the theory of Dharmakirti, we cannot but find the similarity striking. The Buddhist philosopher begins, we have seen, by dividing all cognition in direct and indirect. Negation is referred to the indirect class, to what he calls inferential cognition. Even the simplest case of negation, the judgment of the pattern "there is here no jar" is treated not as a variety of perception, but as an indirect cognition, as an inferential nonperception. The full meaning of such a judgment is the following one. "Since all conditions of normal perceptibility are intact, the jar,

had it been present on this spot, would have been perceived; but it is not actually perceived, therefore we must conclude that it is absent."

Here negation is treated not as a perception, but as a kind of inference, or indirect finding. There is a striking similarity between this definition and the recent idea in computer science of defining negation as failure in a knowledge base.

The *negation as failure rule* in logic programming in computer science is defined as follows (Sterling and Shapiro (1986, 88): a proposition ¬A is assumed to be a consequence of a program if A is not a consequence of the program. A *program* is a "collection of facts and rules describing what is true" (Sterling and Shapiro, 1986, 88). Thus a program can be thought of as a knowledge base, and one way of structuring it, as done in PROLOG, is to think of it as a *search tree*, in which the rules are applied to the facts, generating all the propositions possible. However, a search tree contains only positive (non-negated) propositions. To find whether a negation proposition like ¬A is contained in it, you have to search through all the nodes in the tree, and then ¬A is said to be "implied" by the program if A is not found.

What this amounts to is that negation is seen as a species of inference, or implied conclusion, generated on the basis of a search, and on not finding something. In other words, negation is really defined as being the same kind of reasoning as the *argumentum ad ignorantiam,* just as it is by Dharmakirti and Sigwart. This problem is significant, if we want to define ignorance as absence or negation of knowledge, because we are presuming that "negation" can be defined independently of "ignorance." This route to defining the *argumentum ad ignorantiam* presupposes that we can define negation in some clear way, independently of the argument from ignorance. Otherwise our definition will be circular. A circular definition is not necessarily fallacious or unenlightening, but it certainly can be confusing if we are not aware that it is circular. And generally, noncircular definitions tend to be preferable, if they are available (D. Walton, 1991a, 276–79).

Hence, it might seem better, in trying to define the logical form of the *argumentum ad ignorantiam* to start by using a concept of *classical negation,* where ¬A (*not-A*) is defined as having the opposite truth-value of A. Then the concept of knowledge can be defined in a way that is independent from the concept of negation. It is to this approach that we now turn.

Three Types of Arguments from Ignorance

According to the analysis of the *ad ignorantiam* fallacy given in Woods and Walton (1978b), there are three basic types of arguments involved: an epistemic type, an inductive type, and a dialectical type. The form of the epistemic type of *ad ignorantiam* argument is exhibited through the use of the symbol $\neg$ for classical negation, and a modal expression KA of the form "It is known that A" where A is a proposition. Then the fallacious pair of *ad ignorantiam* inferences on the left can be explained as unlicensed shifts of the negation sign from the valid inferences on the right (92).

$$(\text{F}_1) \quad \frac{\neg KA}{\neg A} \qquad\qquad (\text{V}_1) \quad \frac{K\neg A}{\neg A}$$

$$(\text{F}_2) \quad \frac{\neg K\neg A}{A} \qquad\qquad (\text{V}_2) \quad \frac{K\neg\neg A}{A}$$

However, no exact analysis of the meaning of the K-operator is given by Woods and Walton, and therefore the precise meaning of "valid," in which (V_1) and (V_2) are said to be valid inferences, is not given, apart from mentioning Hintikka's system (1962). However, in an appendix (96–99) it is shown how the K-operator can be defined semantically in the Kripke (1965) semantics for intuitionistic logic, therefore modeling *ad ignorantiam* reasoning formally in an interesting way. But it is not clear that this is the only way that the meaning of the expression "It is known that A" can be reasonably interpreted, with respect to *ad ignorantiam* arguments. Moreover, negation remains something of a problem, because there are two different ways negation could be expressed in the Kripke model (Woods and Walton, 1978b, 99). So there remain open questions about the exact meaning of the forms (V_1), (V_2), (F_1), and (F_2) as arguments.

The inductive type of *ad ignorantiam* fallacy is represented in Woods and Walton (1978b, 91) by presuming a tripartite partitioning of three types of testable scientific hypotheses (H): confirmed, unconfirmed, and disconfirmed. Then the valid forms of inference on the right can be compared to the fallacious forms on the left.

(F_1) *H* is not disconfirmed (V_1) *H* is not disconfirmed
    H is confirmed   *H* is confirmed or unconfirmed

(F_2) $\dfrac{H \text{ is not confirmed}}{H \text{ is disconfirmed}}$ (V_2) $\dfrac{H \text{ is not confirmed}}{H \text{ is disconfirmed or unconfirmed}}$

The pair on the left are fallacies because the conclusion fails to properly take both alternatives into account, as shown in the valid forms on the right.

The inductive type of *ad ignorantiam* argument represents the kind of reasoning used in the verification of a scientific hypothesis. As we saw in Chapter 3, negative evidence can be acceptable in scientific research, at least in some cases, provided it is not overrated, or taken as a stronger form of argument than it really is. So it is important to recognize that the inductive type is a distinctive type of *ad ignorantiam* argument in its own right, and is inherently less conclusive in nature than the epistemic type. For as we saw in Chapter 3, the epistemic type of *ad ignorantiam* can be conclusive under certain conditions. However, the inductive type of *ad ignorantiam* argument tends, by its nature, to generally be nonconclusive.

In case 3.5 for example, suppose we definitely know that all the Air Canada flights from any city to any other city are explicitly represented in the given database. Then, say, if a Vancouver-Toulouse flight is not in that database, we can conclude that it is false that Air Canada has a flight connecting Vancouver and Toulouse. The inference is conclusive, provided that the database is complete; that is, that the closed world assumption is met. The inference is valid because we know that if there were an Air Canada Vancouver-Toulouse flight, it would be in the database. Since it is not in the database, we can conclude, by *modus tollens,* that there is no Air Canada Vancouver-Toulouse flight.

In many cases, however, the argument from ignorance is not a conclusive type of argument like the one in case 3.5. The following case is an inductive type of argument from ignorance.

Case 5.5

>   Suppose you have a box full of marbles, and you have good reason to think that the marbles in the box are mixed homogeneously with respect to color. You take out a large handful of marbles containing a reasonable proportion of the marbles in the box, and no marble in your hand is green. Using the handful of marbles as a sample, you could conclude that the hypothesis that there are no green marbles

in the box is confirmed, or made probable, to some degree. This kind of argument is of a kind that would not be judged fallacious in every case by statistical criteria of reasoning. Yet it does seem to be an *argumentum ad ignorantiam* of the following form: you have not found a green marble in the box, therefore it is (probably) false that there is a green marble in the box. In this case, it does seem that the absence of evidence, for the claim "There is a green marble in the box." does count as legitimate grounds for drawing the conclusion that the claim is false.

The basis for reasoned acceptance of the conclusion in the case above is probabilistic in nature, rather than conclusive. But consider another type of case. Suppose you examined the color of every marble in the box, and found no green ones. You might now reason more confidently: I have not found a green marble in the box, therefore the proposition that there is a green marble in the box is false. In this case, the closed world assumption applies, and therefore the negative answer to the query can be given with justifiable confidence: we can rightly say that the argument is conclusive (relative to the assumption of epistemic closure).

The third type of *ad ignorantiam* argument identified by Woods and Walton (1978b, 93) is presumptive in nature, and has to do with shifts of the burden of proof in a dialogue exchange of argumentation. The formal model of dialogue in which this type of argument is modeled by Woods and Walton (94) is the Hamblin (1970, 265) "Why-Because-System-with-Questions." In this system of dialogue, a why-question is interpreted as a request for the other party to justify a particular proposition by backing it up with some kind of argument. Hamblin (265) formulates the following rule of his system, requiring that a respondent must either indicate his lack of commitment to a proposition A, when asked "Why A?" or else justify A in one of two ways.

Rule S3

"Why A?" must be followed by
    (a) "Statement $\neg A$"
or (b) "No commitment A"
or (c) "Statement B, where B is equivalent to A"
or (d) "Statements 'B, $B \supset A$,' for any B."

Rule $S3$ bars the dialogue-sequence below, which is characteristic of an attempt to unfairly shift the burden of proof to the other party.

Profile 5.1

Speaker: Why *A?*
Respondent: Why $\neg A?$

The problem with this type of dialogue exchange is that it could go on indefinitely, without either party having to bring forth any real arguments to support its side. For example, the speaker could continue the dialogue by replying at her next move, "Why $\neg\neg A$?" and the respondent could then reply, "Why $\neg\neg\neg A$?" and so forth. This profile is the formal structure of the *ad ignorantiam* tug-of-war in case 4.11.

Note however that the type of dialogue modeled by profile 5.1 is similar to, but not exactly the same thing as the Lockean forking tactic, "You must accept my contention unless you can give a better argument against it than I have given for it." The former seems to be part of the structure of dialogue underlying the latter. Nor perhaps do we want to say that the dialogue fragment in profile 5.1 is identical to the presumptive type of *ad ignorantiam* fallacy. Yet clearly, it is part of the underlying basis of that as well.

At any rate, we can see now that the presumptive type of *ad ignorantiam* argument, already well illustrated as a type in Chapter 3 does have a form that could possibly be modeled by some sort of formal structure or system of dialogue rules.

Knowledge-Based Forms

The attempts to give an account of the logical form of the *argumentum ad ignorantiam* (outlined in Chapter 2, "Burden of Proof") as well as the account given by Woods and Walton (1978b) have not adequately addressed the issue raised earlier in this chapter: that, generally, arguments from ignorance are not arguments purely from ignorance, but are partly knowledge-based arguments as well. This fact was already implicit in many of the case studies examined so far. The reasoning in these cases is based on a key premise to the effect that if such-and-such were the case, then we would know it (because a search has already been made, or we have some relevant knowledge). Such a conditional premise was notably relevant in cases 2.4, 2.5, 2.26, 2.30, 3.2, 4.5, and 5. 1. What is missing in these earlier attempts to give an account of the logical form of the *argumentum ad ignorantiam* is an additional principle in the reasoning that links the given state of knowledge conditionally to the opposite of the conclusion to be derived.

The basic principle at work in this kind of case is what de Cornulier (1988, 182) calls *epistemic closure:* the principle, "If it were true, I would know it."

> *Epistemic Closure:* If one knows that it cannot be the case that *A* without his knowing it, then, if *not-A,* he can infer that *not-A.*

An example given by de Cornulier (182) is the following inference: "If it were raining, I would know it; now, it is not the case that I know it is raining; therefore, it is not raining." In outline, this type of argument has the form of *modus tollens:* if *A* then *B;* not *B;* therefore not *A.* It seems, at least in some cases, to be a correct kind of reasoning: once a knowledge base is definitely closed (complete), then if a given proposition is not included in it, we can say (correctly) that this proposition may be taken to be false. This kind of reasoning would seem to be very common in everyday argumentation in natural conversations, as we have seen in many cases, (e.g., case 3.5).

In conclusive knowledge-based (epistemic) reasoning, this type of argument from ignorance has the form represented in the argumentation scheme (KBS) below, according to the analysis given in D. Walton (1992a, 385). Let **D** be a domain of knowledge, and **K** be a knowledge base in that domain. To the extent that we know a knowledge base **K** is closed (i.e., complete), in the sense of containing all the relevant information in some well-circumscribed subpart of **D,** we can infer that if a proposition *A* is not found in **K,** then *A* is false.

(KBS) All the true propositions in domain **D** of knowledge are contained in **K.**
A is in **D.**
A is not in **K.**
For all *A* in **D,** *A* is either true or false.

Therefore, *A* is false.

The form of argument (KBS) is said to be deductively valid in **D.** Walton (1992a, 386). To the extent that it can be established that **K** is closed, one is entitled to infer that it follows that A is false (provided all four premises of [KBS] above are true) in a given case.

But what about the nonconclusive type of case, like case 3.6, where the closed world assumption does not hold? Here, the computer program SCHOLAR reasons on the basis that it knows a lot about the major rubber producers in South America. Guyana is not included in its knowledge base as a major rubber producer. It is a reasonable presumption to infer that Guyana is not a major rubber producer in South America, but that conclusion is not conclusively implied by what is known. The conclusion that Guyana is not a major rubber producer is, in this case, based on presumptive reasoning, and not on a deductively valid type of inference.

In such a case, outlined in case 5.6 below, the computer can reason presumptively as follows, selecting one or the other of two possible responses, depending on its depth of knowledge.

Case 5.6

   ▷   Proposition A is not in my knowledge base.
   ▷   I am asked: is A true?

Alternative Response 1
   ▷   Suppose I know my knowledge base is fairly extensive and deep in the domain of A (even though it is not closed).
   ▷   *Hence,* if A were true, it would be in my knowledge base (presumably), because A would be prominent (if true) in that knowledge base.
   ▷   Therefore, I conclude by replying: A is presumably not true.

Alternative Response 2
   ▷   Suppose I know my knowledge base is incomplete and shallow in the domain of A.
   ▷   *Hence,* even if A were true, I might (presumably) not know about it.
   ▷   Therefore, I conclude by replying: I don't know.

In either alternative response, the computer could also reply by saying, "A is not true, *as far as I know.*" But this response does not distinguish between alternatives 1 and 2 above. It is not so informative as one or the other of these might be, if one of them was appropriate, given the knowledge base of the expert system. Under the right conditions, the balance should tilt toward the reasonableness of the first response, even though the inference on which that response is based is not deductively closed. It represents a different type of *ad ignorantiam* argumentation than the kind of inference represented by the form (KBS).

In the first inference (alternative response 1), the first premise does not imply the closed world assumption. But even so, the *ad ignorantiam* argument holds, to the degree that a certain weight of presumption is justified: that if true, *A* would be known to be true.

The general conclusion to be derived from these nonconclusive kinds of *lack-of-knowledge* inferences found useful in AI is that a nonconclusive, presumptive *ad ignorantiam* can be a correct and useful form of reasoning given the right premises holding. However, it is an intrinsically knowledge-based kind of reasoning; at the same time, it is characteristically a kind of presumptive reasoning. The lack-of-knowledge inferences used by SCHOLAR in case 3.6 are always relative to presumptions about the depth of SCHOLAR's knowledge on a subject. Most typically, such *ad ignorantiam* reasoning is useful and appropriate where the computer reasons on an open-world basis of what it would presumably know. Whether such *ad ignorantiam* arguments are reasonable or erroneous depends on presumptions about the depth of knowledge in the domain of the queried proposition.

In cases like 5.6, the kind of reasoning involved is weaker than that of deductive or even inductive inference. It is a plausible or presumptive type of nonmonotonic reasoning that rests on a major premise postulating how things can *usually* or *normally* be expected to go in a typical situation, subject to exceptions. The argumentation scheme for the type of reasoning involved in cases 3.6 and 5.4 has the following form (D. Walton, 1992a, 386). **D** is a domain of knowledge, and **K** is a knowledge base in **D**.

(PPS)   It has not been established that all the true propositions in **D** are contained in **K**.

A is a special type of proposition such that if *A* were true, *A* would normally or usually be expected to be in **K**.

A is in **D**.

A is not in **K**.

For all *A* in **D**, *A* is either true or false.

Therefore, it is plausible to presume that *A* is false (subject to further investigations in **D**).

To back up the second premise of an argument of the form (PPS), various kinds of evidence can be used. One is that *A* is such a prominent type of item of knowledge in **D** that, if it were true, it would be known to be true by an expert in **D.** This kind of argumentation often pertains to the nature of expert knowledge in a domain of expertise, and is therefore closely related to the type of argumentation at work in *ad verecundiam* arguments.

The two forms (KBS) and (PPS) represent what Woods and Walton (1978b) called the epistemic type of *ad ignorantiam* argument. Here we propose calling it the knowledge-based type of *ad ignorantiam* argument. And here we have shown that it is not a purely deductive type of argumentation. It can have a deductive form (KBS), as well as a presumptive form (PPS). Although (PPS) is clearly a presumptive type of *ad ignorantiam* argument, based on normal expectations (subject to known exceptions), it could also be possible to have an inductive variant of this same kind of knowledge-based reasoning. In this type of *ad ignorantiam* argument, the depth of knowledge could be estimated by some inductive measure of probable closure of the knowledge base. Case 5.5 is an example, where the probable conclusion that there are no green marbles in the box could be arrived at on a basis of the number of marbles sampled, the number of marbles estimated in the box, and other numerical parameters. (I have not yet attempted to determine the conditions under which the *ad ignorantiam* argument is a fallacy, or becomes fallacious. Note clearly that the forms [KBS] and [PPS] in this section are meant to represent reasonable, i.e. nonfallacious types of argumentation.)

In other words, so far I have only analyzed the form of the knowledge-based type of *ad ignorantiam* argument, even though one subtype is presumptive in nature. I turn now to an analysis of the logical form of the presumptive type of *ad ignorantiam* characterized by the shift of a burden of proof in a dialogue.

Profiles of Dialogue

When it comes to identifying the logical structure of the presumptive type of *ad ignorantiam* argument, the form of argument can no longer be modeled as a conclusion drawn autoepistemically by a single reasoner from her own knowledge base. Instead we must look at the argument as a sequence of exchanges in a dialogue between two parties who are reasoning together. In such a case, the form is modeled by a *profile of dialogue:* a sequence of moves, or types of moves, in a rule-governed dialectical exchange between two participants engaged in some conventionalized type of dialogue.[1] In other words, as Reiter (1987) already suggested in connection with case 3.18, tacit conventions of politeness and implicature as conversational postulates licensing certain kinds of inferences need to be taken into account. The form of an argument is no longer just a set of propositions, premises, and a conclusion, in the traditional or semantic sense. Instead, the form needs to be modeled as an account of the use of the argument in a context of dialogue for some communicative purpose (see also Walton and Krabbe 1994).

Let us recall the account of the *argumentum ad ignorantiam* given by Ruby (1950, 136).

Profile 2.1

Speaker:	*A* is true.
Respondent:	Why?
Speaker:	Because you can't disprove it.

This account seems quite similar to Locke's description of the *argumentum ad ignorantiam,* which could perhaps be profiled as follows.

Profile 5.2

Speaker:	Here is my proof of *A: B,* therefore *A.*
Respondent:	That is a supporting argument for *A,* but not strong enough to require me to concede *A* as a commitment.
Speaker:	Can you produce a stronger argument that proves $\neg A$?
Respondent:	No, not right now.
Speaker:	Therefore, you must concede *A* as a commitment, right now.

The exact formal structure and rules for the dialogues in profiles 2.1 and 5.2 are not given. But certain general features are evident.

The speaker and the respondent are engaged in a critical discussion (van Eemeren and Grootendorst, 1984) or persuasion dialogue (D. Walton, 1984). That is, the speaker, in these instances, has the aim of trying to per-

---

1. These profiles of dialogue were first used as a tool for analyzing the structure of the fallacy of many questions in D. Walton (1989b, 37–38, 68–69), as noted by Krabbe (1992, 277).

suade or convince the respondent to accept or concede (Locke uses the term "admit") that a particular proposition is true, or is a commitment he is willing to incur (see also the discussion at the end of this chapter). The speaker and the respondent are taking turns asking questions, and replying to them. Both parties have a set of commitments (Hamblin, 1970, 257–258), and at each move, propositions can be inserted into, or deleted from their respective commitment sets (Walton and Krabbe, 1994). Also, presumably, in this type of dialogue, there is a rule defining the requirements of the kind of successful argument (proof) needed to make a participant concede a particular proposition as a commitment. Furthermore, there should ideally be some level of strength required for such an argument (i.e., a burden of proof).

Now, in this light, let us look at profiles 2.1 and 5.2 and ask whether they represent fallacious or reasonable patterns of argumentation, in context. Profile 2.1 would be a fallacious type of argumentation if in fact the speaker never gave any argument at all, in the previous moves in the dialogue, to support A. If neither party has proved or disproved A, then neither party has to accept A either as a commitment (unless there was some other reason for someone's accepting A; e.g., if A was the designated thesis of one party). Thus profile 2.1 could be a fallacious argument, but is not necessarily so. It depends on burden of proof, and on prior moves that may or may not have given support to A.

Profile 5.2 is more interesting, and is a special instance of profile 2.1 where the speaker has already, at the first move, given an argument in support of A. The question then is whether that argument is sufficient, or is strong enough to compel the respondent to admit A as a commitment. At the respondent's first move, it is made clear that it is not strong enough to fulfill this objective. Presumably, this means that the speaker's argument for A was not strong enough to meet the burden or strength of proof required by the agreements made by the participants at the opening stage of the dialogue.

Given this situation, what can we say about the speaker's next moves, when he tries to get the respondent to concede A on the grounds that the respondent cannot give any stronger argument against A? Is this a fallacy? Remember that Locke does not say that it is fallacious per se, but he does indicate that it is suspicious, or could be used in a fallacious way. To dig a little deeper into the fallacy implicit in this profile, we should first note that the problem is that the speaker seems to be forcing the issue. He can be seen to be putting pressure on the respondent to accept A "right now," without leaving room for considering further argumentation for or against A.

This general type of fallacious move has been recognized by Perelman and Olbrechts-Tyteca (1969, 238) as a species of dilemma tactic that attempts to reduce everything to two alternatives only and then force the issue.

> A somewhat different technique consists in presenting a thesis as the answer to the problem, all other hypotheses being tossed aside *en bloc*. Only the thesis which the speaker is developing is made present. Sometimes, after having set it forth, he asks his hearers if they have a better solution to offer. This appeal, known classically as the *argumentum ad ignorantiam*, derives its force essentially from its very urgency, for it excludes the possibility of pausing for thought: the debate is limited to the thesis that has been offered and to what might possibly be opposed to it immediately. Thus this argument, to be useful, places the interlocutors in a limited framework which recalls that of the dilemma.

In this tactic, Perelman and Olbrechts-Tyteca (238) note, negation plays an essential role: "it is negation that seems to guarantee that the division is exhaustive." But in profile 5.2, it is not just the exhaustive division between A and $\neg A$ that is the crux of the fallacy that seems implicit in this type of dialogue exchange; it is the forcing of an immediate choice between them on the basis of the strongest argument for one or the other, at that particular point in dialogue. This forcing of choice could be called the *Lockean forking tactic*.

The problem exhibited by profile 5.2 in context is that, presumably, the dialogue is not finished yet (closure of the argumentation stage). Hence the respondent should be given room to build up further sequences of argumentation that may ultimately prove $\neg A$. Even if the dialogue is just at the closure point, still the respondent should not have to accept A if the speaker's argument for A is not strong enough to meet the requirements of burden of proof laid down at the opening stage.[2] Given such placings of the profile in a larger context of dialogue, the speaker's *argumentum ad igno-*

2. See also the comments at the end of this chapter, showing that there are also possible interpretations of profile 5.2 that make it seem to be nonfallacious as a sequence of argumentation.

rantiam can be seen as a kind of preemptive strike that tries to force acceptance prematurely. The "urgency" aspect of the fallacy is modeled by placing profile 5.2 in a larger context of dialogue, and making a normative judgment about how the profile, as one segment, or bit of subargument, fits into the larger dialogue of which it is (presumably) a part. It is a question then, of identifying the implicit conversational structure and rules surrounding the profile.

Suspension of Commitment

The problem with the Lockean forking tactic displayed by profile 5.2 is that the respondent is left no room for temporary suspension of commitment, one way or the other. But in real cases of discourse where the argument from ignorance is used, it may be, in some cases, appropriate to suspend judgment. In other cases (as in the second half of Chapter 3), it may be necessary to not suspend one's commitment to some sort of action, and to act on a presumption, even if it is not proved true, or based on knowledge that would meet a high burden of proof. On the other hand, in some of the fallacious cases studied in Chapter 4, the fallacy arose because of an attempt to advocate commitment, even in the lack of enough knowledge or verification to prove or disprove a hypothesis, on the very basis of this lack of evidence to refute the hypothesis.

The kind of case so often featured in the discussions of *ad ignorantiam* arguments in the textbooks is one where there is no evidence, one way or the other, on whether a proposition is true or false. Such cases often arise where, for some reason it is very difficult to get evidence to support or refute a proposition, or even difficult to know or decide what might constitute such evidence. These are the cases about ESP, telepathy, the existence of God, paranormal phenomena, and the like. What is it rational to do in such a case—to suspend acceptance either way, or to put it in the category of nonacceptance?

Case 5.7

> Take a proposition like "Hannibal wore a beard on the day of the battle at Lake Trasimeno." We know very little about Hannibal's appearance, and no likeness of him survives. Let's say then that, as far

as we know, many Carthaginians of the time wore beards, but many were also clean-shaven. Let's say further that in fact we have no real evidence whether Hannibal wore a beard on this particular day or not. What stance should we take then? Should we not accept it as true that Hannibal wore a beard on that day? Or even more strongly, should we dismiss it; that is, should we accept that it is not true that he wore a beard on that day? Or should we suspend acceptance; that is, say that we cannot accept that he did, and cannot accept that he did not?

One thing to note is that if we accept it as not true that Hannibal wore a beard that day, then it follows that we are accepting the opposite proposition as true. That is, we are accepting the proposition that he did not wear a beard that day; that is, that he was clean-shaven. So despite what may appear to be the case, we are in fact admitting the truth of some proposition here.

What about nonacceptance of his wearing a beard on that day? This is a little trickier. If we say we do not accept it, this seems to imply we are, in some sense, against it, as a true proposition. But not necessarily; not accepting it does not necessarily imply rejecting it. We are not conceding that it is true that he did not wear a beard on that day; we are only saying that we aren't committed to his wearing a beard on that day, which doesn't mean that we are committed to his being clean-shaven on that day. It only means we are withholding commitment from the proposition that he wore a beard that day.

In this case, it would be best for a historian writing about the battle at Lake Trasimeno to make no presumption one way or the other, on whether Hannibal wore a beard on the day of that battle. There is little evidence one way or the other, and no practical need to make a presumption. The best option is what we could call *suspension of commitment,* defined by Sextus Empiricus in the *Outlines of Pyrrhonism* (I.10.10) as "a state of mental rest owing to which we neither deny nor affirm anything." Instead of defining commitment, or absence of commitment as mental states, however, Hamblin (1970, 257) defined it as a log or set of propositions, kept track of in a game of dialogue. So defined, commitment is a kind of normative model of what one ought to be rationally committed to (or not), given one's past moves in a sequence of dialogue exchanges in which an argument is taking place. *Acceptance* of a proposition is the act of conceding it as a commitment in a dialogue. What could be fallacious about the Lockean

forking tactic in such a given context of dialogue is that it does not allow
for suspension of commitment, in a context of dialogue where suspension
would be appropriate.

Nonacceptance and Suspension

According to the Lockean forking tactic, the respondent is asked to accept
A or disprove it. This type of choice could be represented by Figure 5.1.
Here the *opposite* of A is its contradictory or negation, $\neg A$. However, this
could be a false or premature dichotomization of the alternatives, depending on the particulars of the case. A prior, and more reasonable sequence of how the alternatives should be presented is given in Figure 5.2,
in many cases.

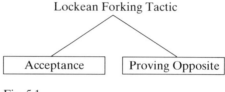

Fig. 5.1

This dichotomy is more reasonable than the previous one, but is still too
simplistic for many cases. The respondent should not always be "torn" between accepting A and accepting $\neg A$. This form of negation is too strong
for many dialogues. Instead, there may be many profiles of reasonable dialogue where the respondent should have to choose only between accepting
A and not accepting A (Fig. 5.3). Acceptance of $\neg A$ would then be a subsequent choice possibly following from nonacceptance of A. The alternative
would be suspension, that is, neither acceptance of A nor of $\neg A$. But some
would say that even this order of choices is too restrictive in some cases,
on the grounds that nonacceptance is compatible with acceptance of the
opposite. Acceptance of the opposite is a subspecies of nonacceptance, and
is therefore compatible with it. From this perspective a third alternative
(suspension) is immediately needed, which is separate from either acceptance or nonacceptance. This framework is shown in Figure 5.4. Here, sus-

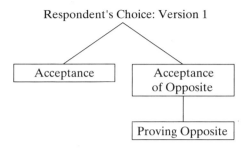

Fig. 5.2

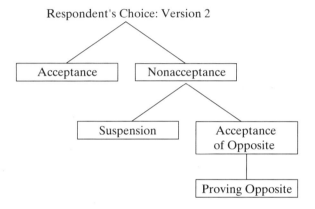

Fig. 5.3

pension, as noted in the previous section, means neither acceptance nor nonacceptance.

The differences between versions 1, 2, and 3 raise a question. What should one do if there is no evidence either for or against a proposition *A* (or very little evidence)? Should one have an attitude of nonacceptance toward *A,* or should one suspend acceptance; that is, have no attitude of acceptance or nonacceptance toward *A* or not-*A?* There seem to be two different philosophical points of view on this question. Some, like Sextus, would say that if there is no evidence one way or the other, you ought to suspend commitment. Others would say that if there is no evidence one way or the other, you ought to be on the side of nonacceptance.

An extreme form of this second point of view says that if there is no

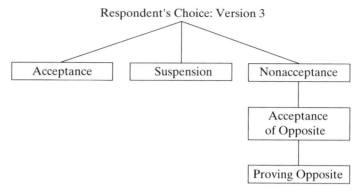

Fig. 5.4

evidence either way, you ought to reject the proposition in question. Here "reject" means, presume that it is false. Halverson (1984, 63) adopts this point of view when he writes that the *argumentum ad ignorantiam* is "always fallacious," except that there is a practical principle that "modifies" the general rule against arguing from ignorance. He calls this principle *the presumption of falsity with respect to unsupported statements of fact* (63), and illustrates it with the following example.

Case 5.8

> According to this principle, in the absence of any evidence one way or the other, a statement affirming some alleged matter of fact is presumed to be false. For example: I am aware of no evidence that would indicate either that there is or that there is not at this moment a group of evil men plotting to kill me within the next thirty days. According to the principle just stated, under these circumstances I am justified in assuming that the assertion that there is such a group is false.

In the case cited, it seems reasonable to presume that the proposition, "There is a group of evil men plotting to kill me within the next thirty days." is false, because it would be very unusual (let's say, in the given case) for this proposition to be true. The assumption that such a plot exists is highly implausible; the situation it describes (let's say, in this case) would be highly unusual and unexpected. Therefore, in the absence of evidence to the contrary, the presumption is, reasonably enough, that it is false. In a case where the given weight of presumption is more evenly balanced, however, like case 5.5, Halverson's rule does not work so well.

But even the statement or such a principle in such a strong form indicates the existence of a tendency to take a version 2 point of view, inclining one toward nonacceptance rather than merely suspension (as indicated by version 3). According to this tendency, in a case where there is no real evidence for or against a proposition, the presumption is for nonacceptance—a negative as opposed to a neutral attitude.

What seems to be the problem with the Lockean forking tactic is that it is too restrictive to fit all possible contexts of dialogue. On the other hand, when we try to liberalize it by expanding it to any of the four structures of choice for the respondent represented by Figures 5.1 through 5.4, the problem is that no single structure among this set of four appears to be the one that perfectly fits the right profile for all types of dialogue.

The range of differences in this respect is quite apparent from the cases already studied. In a case of practical reasoning, like the gun safety case (case 3.14), unless you can prove that the gun is not loaded (prove the opposite), then it is right to accept the proposition that the gun is loaded, or at least to act on that presumption (by not waving it around, etc.). On the other hand, if the context of dialogue is that of a scientific inquiry, then it might be best to suspend judgment (as in Fig. 5.4), if you do not have sufficient evidence to verify or falsify the hypothesis, based on the results you have.

Presumptions and Assertions

Whether an *ad ignorantiam* argument is correct or not depends very much on whether the proposition put forward as the conclusion is meant to be a presumption or an assertion. This analysis at first seems very odd, because it makes the evaluation hinge on what kind of speech act is performed, and not on whether the premises lend support to the conclusion. However, our analysis construes the task of evaluation as pragmatic: the structure used to evaluate the argument is the profile of dialogue, not just the form of argument in abstraction from the context of use.

When a proposition is put forward as an assertion, then normally there is a burden of proof attached to its having been put forward. This means that if the respondent questions the proposition, the proponent is obliged to provide some other proposition(s) that can function as a premise (premises) to back up, or support the original one. This is the so-called probative function of an argument, meaning that the premise is being used to give support to the conclusion. It means that the premise is a proposition of a kind that, if true, would support the claim of the conclusion to be true.

When an argument is put forward by a proponent in this fashion, in a critical discussion, it doesn't mean that the respondent has to accept the conclusion. He has the right to criticize it; that is, to ask appropriate critical questions that would throw doubt on it. However, in a critical discussion, the respondent's rights are limited. He has basically only two options: he can either raise critical questions, or he must accept the argument. That is, unless he questions the premises, or the argument, he must accept the conclusion. That is, if he accepts the premises, and he accepts the argument, then he must accept the conclusion as a commitment. But to question the premises or the argument, he does not need to find even stronger arguments against them than the ones put forth by the proponent. In general, that would be too strong a requirement.

This is where the *ad ignorantiam* can be revealed as a type of fallacy, in fact. If the proponent insists, in the Lockean fashion, that the respondent must either accept the proposition or find a stronger argument against it than the one that was given for it, she is committing the *ad ignorantiam* fallacy (unless [a] there is already a presumption in place in favor of the argument, or [b] the argument is at the closing stage; see Chapter 8 on these two factors).

Now contrast this whole framework of rights and obligations with the case where the proposition was put forward as a presumption. A presumption has no burden of proof attached to it. It can be put forward for any practical reason, even as a mere assumption that might facilitate the dialogue, if explored. But although there is no burden of proof on the proponent when a presumption is brought forward, there is a burden of disproof on the respondent.[3] That is, if the respondent does not wish to accept the presumption, he must give some evidence against it. In the case of presumption, as opposed to assertion, the burden of proof shifts to the other side, and becomes a burden of disproof.

In the case of presumption then the proponent really does have the right

---

3. This way of defining presumption will be further explored in Chapter 7.

to say to the respondent, "Here, accept this proposition, unless you can give a good enough argument against it." The proponent can use the Lockean forking tactic of declaring, "You must accept it unless you can refute it." In the case of presumption, this type of move is generally correct and appropriate, whereas in the case of assertion, it would be an *ad ignorantiam* fallacy.

The following profile may seem very similar to the Lockean profile, but in fact it is quite different, because the speaker is putting *A* forward explicitly as a presumption in the dialogue.

Profile 5.3

Speaker:	I am putting forward *A* as a presumption in the dialogue.
Respondent:	I don't accept *A* as a presumption.
Speaker:	You must either accept *A,* right now, or give some good reason for not accepting *A.*

This profile of dialogue is a reasonable sequence of dialogue, and instances of it are not generally fallacious. The reason has to do with the nature of presumption, as a way of putting a proposition forward in argumentation in a dialogue exchange.

Our conclusion so far is that it is possible to identify forms of *argumentum ad ignorantiam*—argumentation schemes and profiles of dialogue—to determine, however, whether the form of argument is used reasonably or fallaciously in a given case, you have to fit the scheme or profile in a larger context.

Evidence from the Context of Dialogue

In order to take a given text of discourse where an *argumentum ad ignorantiam* appears to, or is alleged to exist, and go ahead with the job of evaluating the argument as fallacious or reasonable, it is necessary to reconstruct the context of dialogue. Several factors may be especially critical, as indicated by the following questions. (1) What type of dialogue is it? (2) Where does the global burden of proof lie—on which party? (3) How heavy should the burden of proof be? (4) What are the premises of the argument? (5) What is the (local) conclusion? (6) What is the local form of move in the dialogue, and what does that tell us about the relevant local presumptions? (7) What is the knowledge base (or commitment) of the proponent of the argument, and of the respondent to it?

Typically, the *argumentum ad ignorantiam* is not an argument from total ignorance, but rather an argument for partial ignorance where the problem is that not enough is known to conclusively decide between a conclusion *A* and its opposite *not-A*. These are cases where there is reason to believe that if *A* is true, a particular sort of investigation will discover evidence for it, but the investigation has been carried out and not found the evidence. Or they may be cases where there was an antecedent burden of proof in favor of *A*. Then *A* is challenged by someone who argues for *not-A*. But then it is shown that there is no evidence for *not-A*, and argued that the burden remains in favor of *A*. But this is not based purely on our ignorance on how to prove *not-A* as the only basis for moving to the conclusion *A*. For the burden in favor of *A* was there all along.

To decide whether such cases are fallacious or nonfallacious instances of the *argumentum ad ignorantiam*, we cannot just look at the propositions that make up the premises and conclusion, apart from the context of dialogue in which they are set. We have to look at what stage the dialogue is in, how far the investigation has gone, and what the requirements of burden of proof are at that stage. We have to look at the sequence of argumentation in the profile of dialogue where it occurs.

Problems with the *argumentum ad ignorantiam* often occur in the form of a question that is asked. According to R. Robinson (1971, 100), the following question is a fallacious *argumentum ad ignorantiam*.

Case 5.9

What reason could anyone have for forging them?

Robinson argues that this is a fallacious *argumentum ad ignorantiam* of the following form: "You do not know they are forged; therefore, they are genuine." But is it fair to attribute either this premise or conclusion to anyone who asks this question? The problem is that the question could occur in different contexts of dialogue, which shift the interpretation of it as an *argumentum ad ignorantiam* one way or the other.

First, consider the following sequence of dialogue.

Case 5.10

Mavis: I think somebody forged them.
Rod: What reason could anyone have for forging them?
Mavis: There was a lot of money to be made.

Here, Rod is not concluding that the items in question are genuine (not forged). He is raising the question, or the possibility that they might not be forged. But he could well be convinced by Mavis's reply that money was the motive for forgery, and therefore concluding, as well, that the items were (or probably, or plausibly) were forged. In this case, it would not be justified to conclude that Rod has committed a fallacious *argumentum ad ignorantiam*.

In another, context of dialogue, the conclusion indicated by the given evidence of the text of discourse might be quite different.

Case 5.11

Rita: Why do you think they are genuine?
Morris: What reason could anyone have for forging them?

In this case, instead of answering Rita's question by offering evidence for the items being genuine, and not forged, Morris tries to evade answering by shifting the burden of proof back to Rita's side.[4] The local evidence of dialogue given in this text could more easily substantiate the criticism that Morris's question amounts to a fallacious use of the *argumentum ad ignorantiam*.

However, it depends on what the "they" are, on whether the existing presumption is in favor of their being genuine or forged, and what the prior sequence of dialogue indicated on these matters of commitment and presumption.

The problem with many cases of argument that show a superficial appearance of being an instance of the fallacious *argumentum ad ignorantiam* is that it is not clear whether the conclusion asserted by the arguer in question is an assertion that a proposition is false, or proved, or known not to be true, or whether it is merely a disclaimer that the proposition is known

4. These cases are also discussed in D. Walton (1989b, 268–69).

to be true, or has been proved by the available evidence. In such cases, a hard look at the wording of the text of discourse, and other relevant factors of the context of dialogue, is the only way to sort out a dispute.

For example, what might one make of a claim like "No evidence brought in from the Soviet Union has ever been found inaccurate in American courts." Is the conclusion that all Soviet evidence is accurate, or is the proponent only saying that Soviet evidence is less unreliable than the conventional wisdom in the United States typically takes it to be? Who knows? The claim appears to be a strong one, but until we know how it is being used in a context of dialogue, we are in no position to say whether it is a fallacious *argumentum ad ignorantiam* or not.

Indicator words attached to the conclusion of an argument in the text of discourse of the argument can be a key factor in evaluating whether an *ad ignorantiam* argument is erroneous or not. The very strong indicator words "established," "beyond doubt," "with absolute certainty," and so forth, are often key items to observe, especially in relation to a claim made that is not susceptible to conclusive verification. We have already seen, in the various cases of UFOs and the like in Chapter 2, how the *argumentum ad ignorantiam* can become especially weak or fallacious when the kind of evidence required to support it may be difficult—even in principle—to come by.

One thing to watch for then is a mismatch between a highly confident conclusion, expressed in language of certainty or absence of doubt, and a premise that could be difficult, or even impossible to verify, without doubt. But judging such questions of burden of proof is a matter of the type of dialogue involved. What is sufficient evidence to prove a chain in one type of dialogue could be highly insufficient in another.

Frameworks of Evidence

What constitutes sufficient proof for a conclusion? This seems to be the central question. But answering this question about burden of proof is very much a relative matter of what type of dialogue is involved in a given case. The standards for a scientific inquiry may be very different from those of a legal trial. Standards appropriate for practical reasoning in everyday deliberations may in turn be quite different from either of these two contexts. Here, we may often have to depend on presumptions, as a basis for action; and going into a scientific research inquiry, while it might eventually yield the relevant knowledge, might be far too costly and delaying to be appropriate. Even building up a case "beyond reasonable doubt" could be far too costly and time-consuming to be of practical use.

The following case graphically illustrates the variability of different standards of sufficient proof in different types of dialogue. In 1951, two British Secret Service agents, Guy Burgess and Donald Maclean, fled to the Soviet Union with just hours to spare, after being exposed as Soviet double agents. Kim Philby, the principal British intelligence liaison officer in Washington, who had been a student with Burgess at Trinity College, Cambridge, was so strongly suspected of being the third "mole" in this spy ring that he was fired from the British Secret Intelligence Service; but at that time there was not enough evidence to prove that Philby was guilty. The situation in 1951 is described by West (1987, 24).

Case 5.12

> Philby was strongly suspected of having sent Maclean a secret warning via their mutual friend Burgess, but there was no definite proof. Those who had attended Philby's interrogation conducted at MI5's headquarters in London in November 1951, after his recall from Washington, by a leading barrister and former wartime MI5 officer, Helenus "Buster" Milmo, had no doubt of his guilt. But guilt is a legal term and in the espionage world binding or "smoking gun" evidence is notoriously difficult to find. There was no direct proof of Philby's complicity with Burgess or Maclean which could be presented in a court of law, and those who witnessed his performance knew that he would produce an equally impressive turn before any Old Bailey jury. Hence, four years later, when Philby's name was first mentioned in a Parliamentary Question as the possible "third man," Eden's Foreign Secretary, Harold Macmillan, was obliged to clear him.

Although the counterespionage branch of MI5 had investigated Philby, by 1955 they concluded in a White Paper (West, 24), "there was no reason to conclude that Mr. Philby has at any time betrayed the interests of this country or to identify him with the so-called 'third man' if indeed there was one." As a consequence of this report, the director-general of the Security Service was "obliged" to advise the prime minister that "the government had no choice but to clear Philby" (West, 1987, 24). Even as late as 1961, when a defecting KGB officer named Philby as a Soviet spy of long standing, his evidence was "third-hand" and therefore "not admissible in court" (West, 24). It wasn't until 1963 that Philby was confronted with enough evidence that he was forced to flee to the Soviet Union to avoid arrest.

In this case, you could say that from a legal point of view, the argument from ignorance was reasonable: because there was insufficient evidence to prove Philby guilty in a court of law, the government was obliged to clear him. On the other hand, from a more practical point of view of Philby's usefulness as an intelligence officer, there was certainly enough evidence against him to warrant his dismissal. Thus it seems that in this case, there are two distinct types of evidence involved. One is legal evidence, and here the question is whether it is sufficient to prove guilt in a court of law. The other is the type of evidence required to prove compromise or complicity in the espionage world. As West put it, "binding" or "smoking gun" evidence is notoriously hard to find in the espionage world. This is no doubt because the whole purpose of espionage is to conceal this evidence from those who are looking for it, in order to be a successful spy. And because of the very great danger to national security of a spy, a strong suspicion would be enough to warrant no longer trusting that person with secret information.

Case 5.12 reveals a very interesting ambiguity in the concept of evidence, and in the nature and weight of evidence required to prove a conclusion on the basis of an argument from ignorance. The difference seems to be a contextual one, relating to the type of investigation and proof appropriate for a particular framework. The legal framework is quite different from the espionage framework in the kind and level of evidence needed to support a conclusion as a basis for action. The type of evidence, and the type of investigation needed to find it, are quite different in the two frameworks.

To sum up the findings of this chapter then, there are two types of forms of the *argumentum ad ignorantiam*. The knowledge-based type of form, or argumentation scheme, depends for its evaluation on what stage the search for evidence has progressed to, so that we can answer the question, "If A were true, would we know it was true, as a result of our investigation?" The presumptive type of form, or profile 5.2, also depends on what stage of the dialogue has been reached. If we are in the opening or middle stages of the dialogue, then the respondent has a right to ask critical questions about the speaker's argument, "B, therefore A," and hence the respondent need not concede A immediately. Also, the respondent has the right to develop new lines of argument of his own that may ultimately yield a proof of $\neg A$

that is stronger than the speaker's argument for A. On the other hand, if we are at the closing stage of the dialogue in evaluating profile 5.2, and the respondent has now exhausted all these alternatives without either refuting the speaker's argument for A, or himself proving $\neg A$, then he should concede A, as requested by the speaker. In such a case, the speaker's final move in profile 5.2 would be nonfallacious.

In short then, the problem of evaluating the forms of the *argumentum ad ignorantiam* now identified, remains. The forms need to be set in a context of dialogue appropriate for a given case.

6

Normative Models of Dialogue

Starting out in this book, I based my approach on the methods used traditionally in logic, whereby evaluation of the argument from ignorance concentrated on the reasoning in the argument and the propositional form of the argument (the premises and conclusion), a kind of local-level analysis. But I saw more and more, especially in Chapter 5, that the focus needs to be over a longer sequence of dialogue interchanges, judging an argument in relation to its contribution to some stage of a dialogue. Several normative models of dialogue that are useful for this purpose have been set out by D. Walton (1989a; 1991a; 1992c) and Walton and Krabbe (1995). The purpose of this chapter will be to describe their relevant features, as applied to the evaluation of the *argumentum ad ignorantiam.*

An exception to tradition was the work of Grice (1975), who studied the structure of a conversation as a whole. But lacking here was an account of the different types of conversations (dialogues) specific enough to lead to a systematic study of the various kinds of conversational structures in which arguments are put forward by speakers and hearers in an organized interpersonal exchange.

A step forward from Grice was the work of van Eemeren and Grootendorst (1984), which began to evaluate fallacies as moves in argumentation that violate a normative model of dialogue called the *critical discussion* (see also van Eemeren and Grootendorst, 1992; and Schiffrin, 1990). Here we began to see the evaluation of argumentation as having a normative and a practical element. Evaluation of the argument focused on its use in a context of dialogue.

The normative element is the general structure of dialogue needed to frame the concept of the argument from ignorance, a use of a technique of argumentation to shift a burden of proof in a dialogue (Chapter 7 will also deal with burden of proof). What we need for the evaluation of the *argumentum ad ignorantiam* is a way of putting an argumentation scheme or a profile of dialogue into a wider context of enveloping dialogue in which that scheme or profile is a functioning part. This could give us a method of argument analysis that can be applied to a text of discourse in a particular case. In general, models of dialogue have to at least make sense, as possible developments for informal logic, in order for our argumentation schemes and profiles of dialogue to be useful as part of a method of argument evaluation.

Pragmatic and Semantic Approaches

The structure of a dialogue is one ingredient enabling a critic of an argumentative discourse to reconstruct the dialogue context of a given utterance that is contentious or problematic as an instance of, or part of an instance of, a criticism at issue. The analysis of an utterance alleged to be an instance of a "fallacy," to have committed an error, or to be the focus of some critical comment or evaluation, requires the theoretical construct of dialogue. This brings out the role of the context of the surrounding speech acts for organizing a "rational" sequence of multiple speech acts into which the original argument fits. The sequence of dialogue is derived from the given discourse by the critic's knowledge of the goals of the speaker and hearer in relation to a particular type of dialogue, and by judging the expectations of the speaker and hearer appropriate for that context. To the extent that the would-be critic can extract dialogue rules from the evidence offered by the context of discourse of an argument presented or criticized by a speaker, the would-be critic can make out a "reasoned" or "logical" basis for his criticism.

The terms "reasoned" and "logical" are put in quotation marks because their use in this context departs from the widespread and widely accepted current preconception that identifies logic with the semantic analysis of propositions and truth-values (e.g., classical first-order logic). The use of the dialogue concept to analyze a sequence of multisentence units in an interactive argumentation between two speakers is a radical departure from these previously dominant semantic traditions in logic. The pragmatic approach of using models of dialogue as the tool to arbitrate what is rational or logical, to use these terms in the pragmatic sense now, without quotation marks, calls for different methods. Instead of only looking to the analysis of the core propositions that make up an argument, we must examine questions and other speech acts, and look at single stages of premises and conclusions as part of a larger sequence or chain of arguments directed toward resolving an issue of contention. This task is in some ways more ambitious than the narrower kind of task set by the semantic approach, for it involves judging the goals of a speaker and hearer, and filling in missing parts of a sequence of argumentation that are not explicitly stated by an arguer. This task involves judgments of what can be reasonably taken for granted in an argument, giving a speaker the benefit of a fair hearing. Thus qualities of empathy and interpretation in studying a text of discourse, goals once cultivated in the traditional humanities curriculum, become very important.

However, a critic should not be given carte blanche too generously to deconstruct an argument any way that suits his moods or purposes. The concept of dialogue gives a structure to these judgments that can make them "reasonable" or "logical" if they are backed up in the right manner by good evidence from the text of discourse. Although pragmatic analysis of an argument does depend on expectations of what is plausible or implausible, which is in a sense "subjective," it also depends on rules of dialogue that can be stated in a clear and precise form. Therefore an "objective" element is involved which justifies a critic in backing up his criticism of an argument as "logical" or "reasonable." But pragmatic analysis of an argument is not exclusively concerned with truth-values and deductive validity like the semantic approach. It is also concerned with techniques like the use of presumption, burden of proof, tactics of questioning, appeals to authority, circular argumentation, and other phenomena of argument usually associated with the domain of informal fallacies.

The basic problem with the traditional accounts of informal fallacies however, is that they have been treated in a mock semantic fashion as one-utterance events that exemplify arguments gone badly and decisively wrong ("howlers"); (Hamblin, 1970). In fact, however, many of the kinds of arguments labeled as "fallacious" types turn out to be reasonable arguments (see D. Walton, 1989a). Others are weak in a certain respect, or subject to criticism, as falling short in a particular respect. In any event, it has become clear that each case cited as a potential fallacy needs to be evaluated on its merits. And this characteristically means bringing in considerations of the context of a discussion, and evaluating the sequence of dialogue using pragmatic methods. It turns out then that the Standard Treatment usage of the term "fallacies" is at once too crude and exaggerated to be very useful (Hamblin, 1970). Most often, the language of replies, objections, challenges, and criticisms is far more helpful and accurate, reserving the term "fallacy" for the extreme cases (see D. Walton, 1989a).

When conducting a pragmatic analysis of an argument, it is appropriate to speak of "games" of dialogue when referring to the dialogue structure of a given sequence of argument. The concept of game is appropriate because neither participant is pursuing his goal of dialogue alone: each requires the other to interact in a prearranged type of pattern of move and response in order to reach his own goal (Barth and Krabbe, 1982). There are conventions or rules that underlie the orderliness of these sequences of interactive moves (Hamblin, 1971). The reasoning advanced by each side only gives the other side an opportunity to take part in the discussion in virtue of the cooperative other-directed nature of each single move in a larger process.

Dialogue Structures and Stages

Because it is a sequence of cooperative moves where each participant has a distinctive goal that may be realized or not, dialogue is classified as having the structure of a game. Like many games, dialogues can involve conflict, disputes, and competition to win. But this adversarial quality is a matter of degree. Some games of dialogue are more cooperative than others, and all games of dialogue require an element of cooperative action by virtue of the rules that underlie conventions of communication.

A goal of dialogue is normally set by the participant who is obliged to realize it to be successful in his argumentation. But it is not always so. In some cases, goals can be set by a third party external to the dialogue, and then agreed-upon to be taken up by a proponent. In any event, there is an element of cooperation and agreement in setting goals of dialogue. A proponent may set out a certain thesis as his goal of argument to be proved, but it may be that nobody takes up the challenge to dispute his claim, or is interested in discussing the subject. To agree to discuss a subject is to take up a stance that engages one as a participant in a dialogue. So engaging in dialogue requires a kind of agreement to enter into discussion by both parties. This point is what van Eemeren and Grootendorst (1984) call the opening stage of a discussion.

The critical discussion is a special type of persuasion dialogue, and the latter has four stages, like those of the critical discussion: the opening stage, the confrontation stage, the argumentation stage, and the closing stage. In the opening stage of a persuasion dialogue, the participants fix on what type of dialogue they will be engaged in. This stage determines what type of dialogue the participants are supposed to be engaged in. Hence the fixing of this stage enables us to determine when a dialectical shift to another type of dialogue has taken place. Either the participants agree that they will be taking part in such-and-such a type of dialogue, or the context indicates that they are supposed to be engaging in a particular type of dialogue.

In the confrontation stage of a persuasion dialogue, the participants identify the thesis (a proposition) which is to be the subject of the argumentation, and they also give some indications of the attitudes or stances they will take up toward this proposition (e.g., pro, contra, doubtful of its truth, doubtful of its falsity). Essentially, this means that the participants must formulate and take upon themselves a burden of proof, by initially indicating their basic commitment toward the proposition at issue. Are they for it, against it, undecided? These declarations of level of commitment set the goals to determine what degree or weight of persuasiveness their arguments in the dialogue will have to attain (Walton and Krabbe, 1995).

In the argumentation stage, each participant has the opportunity to fulfill his goal by trying to extract commitments from the other side that can be used as premises to prove his own conclusion. What "prove" means here depends on the prior two stages; it depends on the kind of dialogue involved (including the specifics of the given speech event, which may involve institutional rules and requirements of various sorts in relation to the given situation), and on the levels for burden of proof on each side (van Eemeren and Grootendorst, 1984; 1992).

In the closing stage, the argument is brought to a close in a polite and fair way which presumes that both sides have had a reasonable opportunity to bring forward their best arguments. Here it is important that there not be an illicit shift to another type of dialogue that prematurely blocks off the persuasion dialogue. However, in some cases, a persuasion dialogue may be licitly closed off, even though neither participant has been success-ful in fulfilling his goal in the dialogue (van Eemeren and Grootendorst, 1984; 1992).

The sequence of four stages—opening, confrontation, argumentation, and closing—is a general format that can be applied to all the types of dialogue (the negotiation, the quarrel, and so forth) that are appropriate contexts of argumentation. The various kinds of dialectical shifts in argu-mentation can occur at any one of the four stages. And it is always im-portant to determine at which stage in the original dialogue the shift has occurred, when evaluating a particular case where a fallacy has allegedly been committed.

In a *negotiation* type of dialogue, the goal of each participant is to max-imize gains and minimize losses. The goal of negotiation dialogue is per-sonal (or group) self-interest. The initial situation of a negotiation dialogue is a shortage of desired goods that results in a conflict of interests; not everybody can have everything he wants. The modus operandi of negotia-tion dialogue is a give-and-take procedure where compromises are argued out and agreed upon (Donohue, 1978; 1981).

In an *inquiry,* the goal is to build on established propositions, known securely to be true by both participants. Then by drawing inferences from what is known and agreed to, the goal is to work toward establishing new knowledge (see below, this chapter, "Components of Dialogue"). Science is often portrayed by its exponents as a cumulative inquiry of this sort (see Chapter 1). However, philosophers of science differ on whether such an interpretation of scientific dialogue can be sustained, or to what extent it is an accurate account of scientific practices.

The goal of the inquiry is to prove that a particular proposition is true or false, or to show that it cannot be proved as true or false, in relation to the evidence that it is possible to collect. The beginning stage of the inquiry is the collection of relevant evidence. Then there is a discovery stage of formulating hypotheses that can be verified or falsified by this evidence. Finally, there is a presentation of evidence stage at the closure of the in-quiry, where the results of the inquiry are communicated to a wider audi-ence. In a scientific inquiry, this last stage might take the form of publication of research results in a journal.

Another type of inquiry is the empirical public inquiry into problems like an air disaster, or the question of how AIDS was transmitted through the blood supply system. A commonsense type of inquiry in everyday delibera-tions would occur in the kind of case where I try to determine the reason why my bicycle has a flat tire. I hypothesize that the problem might be a puncture, for example, so I look for evidence of a cut in the tire. In this type of case the inquiry is joined to a deliberation type of reasoning once I turn to the problem of how to fix the puncture, once I have discovered it.

The key characteristic of the inquiry is that it is supposed to be a *cumulative* type of dialogue framework of argument, meaning that once this proposition is established (verified), there should be no need to retract it, at a later point, as a commitment. In contrast to the inquiry, the persuasion type of dialogue is noncumulative in nature, because participants need to change their minds frequently and retract commitments (e.g., when confronted with an inconsistency in their commitment sets). And this should be a rational and permissible move in some instances. However, in the inquiry the goal is to argue from only well-established premises, in order to minimize, or even try to eliminate retractions.

When a critic is confronted with a given text of argumentative discourse, and has the job of evaluating the arguments in it as weak or strong, the first question to be asked is, What type of dialogue is it? In some cases, a criticism can only be understood if a *dialectical shift,* from one type of dialogue to another, is detected (D. Walton, 1992c). For example, what occurs in many cases of *ad hominem* argumentation is that a participant in a persuasion dialogue is attacked for having allegedly made the dialogue into an unannounced and unilateral negotiation, based on self-interested bargaining rather than reasoned persuasion (D. Walton, 1992c).

Every dialogue has *rules of procedure (dialogue rules)* of four types: turn-taking rules, locution rules, commitment rules, and strategic rules (Barth and Krabbe, 1982). A problem is that, in practice, these rules may not be specifically agreed to, articulated, or expressed at the opening stages. Very often the rules are implicit in the conventional context of dialogue, and it requires skills of discourse analysis to elicit evidence concerning the form, existence, and applicability of the rule. Ideally, however, the best time to articulate, or agree upon, rules is at the opening stages of a dialogue.

From the foregoing analysis of the requirements of argument analysis, it is evident that this skill, as a branch of logic (practical, or applied logic), requires the introduction of a framework of regulated dialogue as a model of orderly interpersonal exchange of argument moves. Not only single arguments, but also sequences of argumentation could properly then come under pragmatic methods of logical evaluation. However, this possibility immediately presents a problem. By which set of rules should a dialogue be regulated?

Already in the literature, several different formal systems of dialogue have been advocated: see Hamblin (1970; 1971), Rescher (1977), Hintikka and Saarinen (1979), Hintikka (1981), Mackenzie (1981; 1989), Barth and Krabbe (1982), and D. Walton (1984; 1992c). Which set of rules is the right way of regulating a dialogue? The answer appears to be that no *one* set is exactly right for every situation of argument, and that there are several different contexts of dialogue, with different rules for each of these contexts. This relativism of dialogue to a context need not be a cause of despair. It is simply an indication that dialogue is a flexible structure that can be used in different ways to regulate different kinds of discussions with somewhat different goals and methods.

Although different formal systems or representations of the structure of dialogue are possible, this whole network of systems needs to be put in perspective by examining the nature of dialogue as a whole, with reference to its different contexts. By this means, a philosophical perspective on the nature of dialogue as a framework for argumentation can be achieved, in which the concept of fallacy can be set. Once philosophically set in this pragma-dialectical framework, the concept of fallacy can then be implemented by empirical disciplines as a useful tool of the analysis and evaluation of argumentation.

Every argument occurs in the context of a dialogue, a bilateral interactive communication between two arguers who have undertaken to pursue a goal of argument together. At least this is the assumption. But in the practical job of evaluating argumentation in a given case, judging from a text of discourse, it may be quite difficult (or even impossible, in some cases) to determine what type of dialogue the arguer may rightly be supposed to be taking part in.

Argument Interpretation

In interpreting any argument prior to its evaluation, the first step should be to identify the conclusion being argued for. Once the conclusion is identified, the second step is to identify the premises being advanced in support of the conclusion. In some cases, the premises and conclusion of an argument are clearly stated and can easily be identified. But in other cases, the question What is the argument? cannot be answered adequately without evaluating evidence from the corpus that indicates the context of dialogue.

Interpretation of an Item of Text of Argument

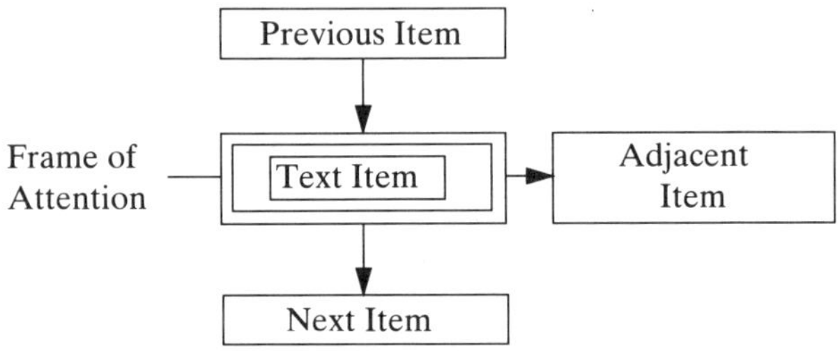

Fig. 6.1

Ideally the context of dialogue should indicate what the issue of the dialogue is supposed to be. The issue is the pair of propositions set as the conclusion (thesis) of each participant, the proponent and the respondent. But the problem of identifying the conclusion is by no means trivial in many cases. The participants in the argument should be clear on what their conclusions are, but sometimes in realistic argumentation, the participants are not even clear on what they are arguing about (see Fig. 6.1).

The interpretation of an argumentative text of discourse typically begins by focusing on a particular assertion or question that is singled out as a candidate for possible criticism or query. Once singled out, this item becomes subject to interpretation. The process of interpretation involves mapping the item onto a structure of dialogue by initially relating it to an adjacency item, a previous item, or a next item in the sequence of dialogue.

For example, if the text item in the frame of attention is a question, inferences may be drawn about the previous questions or replies that led to the question. At the same time the range of possible and permissible replies to the question may be considered (the adjacent item) as a subject of interpretation. Third, possible further questions or subsequent items consequent on the reply may be conjectured or inferred. By initiating this type of process of interpretation, the original item comes to be placed in a wider sequence of dialogue within which it can be comprehended as part of an argument. There are different kinds of inferences whereby these three kinds of consequences are drawn out.

The process of critical evaluation of a given text of argument discourse rests on the twin assumptions that (i) there is a context of dialogue rich enough to yield some dialogue rules, and (ii) the dialogue has a goal. Of course, in actual cases of argument discourse, it may be that neither requirement is met, because the critic is not given enough information to determine (i) or (ii) from the available discourse. Even so, the theoretical presumption remains that to evaluate the argument normatively as good or bad, strong or weak, correct or fallacious, a goal and context of dialogue must exist. The problem then, in the case of incomplete information, is to try to determine a goal and context on the basis of the given evidence. This is a second-order task of argument evaluation, a task of reconstructing the argument, according to van Eemeren (1986).

The basic type of task of argument evaluation is to evaluate whether, or to what extent, a given argument fulfills the goal appropriate for the context of dialogue. But if that goal has not been clearly identified, the critic has a second-order task of trying to establish what this goal of dialogue is, or should be. Sometimes further dialogue is the best way to find out. But if this option is not available, a critic may have to go by whatever evidence is given in the text, even if it is subject to possible corrections or uncertainties. Indeed, at this second-order level of dialogue, disputes can arise among the proponents of a position on what their goal of dialogue should be (Jacobs and Jackson, 1983a).

The question of how issues are selected and formulated by candidates for political office is an interesting question of metadialogue. Issues are presumably chosen by a candidate on the basis of what the candidate feels is important in relation to her position in relation to particular events of the day. This would seem to be a presumption of democratic systems generally (D. Walton, 1992b). However, this account by itself is too simple, because in fact issues seem to be formulated in a way that will be in tune with what the voters will accept, as a candidate sees it. Thus issues as voiced by a particular political group are in a continual process of change and refinement, as public opinions are perceived to change.

Case 6.1

> It was reported that at a meeting of the National Women's Political Caucus in Portland, Oregon, in August 1987, there was very little discussion of issues such as "liberation" and "reproductive freedom" that had previously been prominent issues. It was reported that the Equal Rights Amendment, once a subject of chanting and shouting at the caucus, was now an issue that lacked emotional intensity ("Women: A New Politics," Tamar Jacoby, Howard Fineman, Sue

Hutchison and Michael Reese, *Newsweek,* September 7, 1987, 20–
21). The change in the caucus, and in other speeches, was away from
"feminist" issues to so-called gender-neutral issues like defense
spending, and international alliances. According to Geraldine Fer-
raro, however, this change did not mean an abandonment of the
original feminist concerns, but a rephrasing of the older issues of
freedom and equality into "more concrete, prosaic terms" such as
"day care," "parental leave," "pay equity," and the like (21). According to another speaker, the new trend was to pose issues in such
a way that there should be no longer a clear demarcation between
women's issues and other political issues that affect everyone alike.

What these and similar subtleties of actual cases of argumentation show
is that, in fact, the metadialogue goals and rules of argument may not be
unalterably fixed; they may be subject to change and evolution even as an
argument proceeds. This instability and change at both levels of dialogue
simultaneously is a cause for deep concern to the critical evaluator of an
argument. It involves a kind of reflexivity or vicious circularity between the
metadialogue level and the interdialogue level of argumentation similar in
kind to the paradoxes of dialogue identified in D. Walton (1991a).

Quite generally then, it is a theoretical requirement of the critical evaluation of an actual specimen of argument discourse that the goal and context
of the dialogue (including locution rules, dialogue rules, commitment rules,
and win-loss rules) be regarded as given hypotheses. Then, relative to these
premises or assumptions, conclusions can be drawn about the worth of the
argumentation in relation to what is required to carry out goals of argument
by the appropriate moves in dialogue. This requirement brings out the necessity of making a clear theoretical distinction between the metadialogue
level (confrontation stage) and the first-order level (argumentation stage).

Something often noticed is that there characteristically seems to be an
adversarial or competitive aspect to dialogue on contentious issues. It is a
perennial question whether this negative or "attacking the opponent" aspect of dialogue on contestable opinions, or questions of values, is essential,
or whether it is merely an accidental feature of dialogue that can be overcome. Sometimes, it is felt that this negative aspect, the goal of trying to
refute or "shoot down" the other participant, is a harmful aspect of dialogue that should be overcome. The feeling is that good dialogue is constructive and cooperative, and therefore the negative or attacking, adversarial type of dialogue is a degenerative or bad phase of dialogue that ought

to be overcome and phased out in the higher and more productive types of dialogue.

Quite the contrary, however: it is possible to make out a case for the contention that adversarial argument is built into the essential structure of any critical discussion on contentious issues (see below, this chapter, "Types of Dialogue"). The reasoning behind this case has to do with the concepts of presumption and burden of proof. Without burden of proof, dialogue could continue indefinitely, and never resolve a controversial issue, one way or the other. Burden of proof sets a reasonable standard for the weight of presumption in a plausible argument required to alter one's commitments on the issue. Open, adversarial argumentation, according to rules of reasonable dialogue can provide the testing ground for the contending theses that represent both sides of the issue. This testing to determine the stronger and weaker arguments in persuasion dialogue is analogous to the testing of a scientific hypothesis by subjecting it to the experimental evidence produced in an inquiry.

Persuasion dialogue combines a collaborative aspect with an antagonistic aspect. The key to understanding the nature of fallacies, as we shall see in subsequent chapters, lies in the balancing of these two aspects. But persuasion dialogue is not the only type of dialogue needed to be used to analyze fallacies. Some of the fallacies we shall analyze, in fact, will turn out to be illicit types of shifts from one context of dialogue to another.

The reader will by now be beginning to get the picture that argument interpretation is no trivial matter. By the standards of the new pragmatic theory, many cases traditionally classified as "fallacious arguments" will have to be reclassified as "incomplete arguments." Thus in many instances, a finding of an argument as fallacious should be regarded as conditional upon the interpretation of the given evidence of the text, as far as it is known. Most important, the finding of an argument as fallacious should be regarded as relative to the type of dialogue the speaker and hearer were originally supposed to be engaged in, as far as this is known in a given case.

Dialogue: What Is It?

From a point of view of logic and the analysis of argumentation, the focus of interest has tended to be on certain aspects of dialogue, and certain types of dialogue, especially persuasion dialogue. But the concept of dialogue is more general than this focus might suggest (see, for example, van Eemeren and Grootendorst, 1984). Generally, *dialogue* may be defined as a two-way interactive communication by a series of back-and-forth messages that are steps toward fulfilling a goal. At least this is a basic or minimal definition. Derivatively, it is also possible to have many-person dialogue, as in a group dialogue, like a conference.

In the definition given above, the basic unit is that of the message. A *message* is a move or speech act, in a dialogue, that contains a piece of information (i.e., a proposition), but that also has a pragmatic element (Harrah, 1971; 1976). For example, a message may be an assertion, a question, or a request for action. It is also essential to the concept of message that it goes from one participant (the source) toward another participant (the receiver) (Harrah, 1971; 1976). Given the concept of message, seven requirements of the concept of dialogue can be identified and set out.

The first requirement is that there should be two participants, **a** and **b,** and each of these participants has a commitment set that contains a set of propositions. This set of propositions is the commitment-set of the participant, but in many characteristic contexts of dialogue, this set also represents the internal knowledge or strategy of the participant.

The second requirement is that **a** sends out a message, M_a, to **b** (see Fig. 6.2). The third requirement is that **b** receives the message M_a and sends a message M_b back to **a.** The fourth requirement is that **b** comprehends the message, and his sending back M_b is based on some internal knowledge or strategy that **b** has. The fifth requirement is that **b**'s sending out M_b was influenced (partially determined) by his receipt of the message M_a.

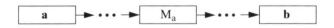

Fig. 6.2

These last three requirements might be considered fairly strong conditions, implying that the dialogue is intelligent and genuinely communicative. But unless these requirements are met in a particular instance of transmission of a message, it should not truly be considered a dialogue in the full sense of the word. For otherwise the sending of the message could be merely a mechanical signal that does not represent informed communication characteristic of real dialogue.

Respondent's Significant Reply in Dialogue

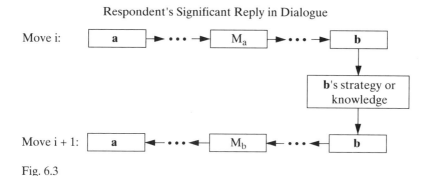

Fig. 6.3

Generally speaking then, as indicated in Figure 6.3, dialogue requires that the respondent's reply be based on his receipt of the message and on some sort of "intelligent" reaction to it (Jacobs and Jackson, 1983a; 1983b; 1989; see also Owen, 1987). Of course, exactly how we are to interpret the expressions "intelligent," "strategy," and "knowledge" depends very much on the particular context of dialogue. At its weakest, these terms can refer to a commitment-set that has no special conditions imposed on it. But as special conditions are added, commitment can become strategy or knowledge. The sixth requirement is that extended dialogue generally involves a sequence of messages in a certain order (Harrah, 1976). The seventh requirement is that the sequence of messages must move toward some final stage or goal.

Thus the general idea is that dialogue is a sequence of moves, messages (message-events), locutions, or speech acts that can be placed in some sort of order so that it can be seen as moving toward some final move or event that makes the sequence complete or successful (Harrah, 1976). When the term "move" is used, it emphasizes the game-like character of dialogue. When the term "message" is used, it implies communication between the participants (Harrah, 1976). When the term "speech act" is used, the goal-oriented nature of dialogue as a kind of directed, joint activity is emphasized. A dialogue is a series of back-and-forth, connected sequence of speech acts formed into an ordered profile that points in a certain direction. Thus dialogue is essentially a form of directive, interactive activity.

However, the units of dialogue are primarily thought of as verbal actions (speech acts) or signals (messages) rather than more purely physical actions or reactions. For example, we would not normally be inclined to describe a game of tennis as a dialogue. For the same reason, we would not normally be inclined to describe a game of chess as a dialogue. But if you think about it, chess could actually be described quite insightfully as a species of dialogue. However, chess would seem more like a dialogue when played by electronic transmission of verbally dictated moves registered on a televised screen by satellite transmission.

Even here there is an artificial quality to the use of the term "dialogue," perhaps because we often associate dialogue with natural language communication by means of certain speech acts. However, this association is not total. Coded communications or even abstract mathematical game-like interactions with strict and precise win-loss rules can quite rightly be considered species of dialogue. Although certain contexts of dialogue are much more familiar than others in common experience, new forms of dialogue can be encountered in fields like artificial intelligence.

The user interface between a computer program and a user of the system is a species of dialogue. This kind of dialogue is carried on in an artificial language that has a specific purpose, like PROLOG or LISP, to cite two well-known languages. However, such languages often incorporate words and phrases from a natural language like English, in order to make the system "user friendly." A sequence of messages in the form of a dialogue between a person and a computer program is therefore a special type of dialogue. It is a legitimate kind of dialogue in its own right, and comes under the concept of dialogue outlined below.

Components of Dialogue

Dialogue is made up of five components. First, there is a set of participants. In the basic case, there are two participants, usually called the proponent and the respondent, or some equivalent names. We do not have to read in too much to the concept of a participant. For purposes of theory, a participant can be thought of as a set of propositions, or a repository of propositions that can be enlarged or diminished by adding propositions or deleting propositions from the set.

The second component is a sequence of moves or speech acts that the participants advance. Usually, the participants take turns making these moves. These moves typically take the form of questions or assertions, but many other kinds of speech acts can also be involved in different types of dialogue (Jacobs, 1989). Also, it is worth noting that these various speech acts typically contain propositions or presuppose propositions in a variety of ways.

The third component in a dialogue is the commitment-set attached to each of the participants. As the sequence of moves in a dialogue progresses, a record must be kept of the set of commitments of each participant at each point in the sequence. Commitments are propositions. At each move, a participant can incur commitments, or in some instances, a participant can retract previous commitments.

A commitment-set is like a knowledge base or database in AI. It provides a collection of premises, a pool of data for information retrieval.

One basic rule of commitment is that whenever a participant advances an assertion, he becomes committed to the proposition or propositions contained in the assertion (Hamblin, 1970). However, commitments need not arise conclusively through moves in a dialogue. They can be presumptions already included in a participant's commitment-set prior to any moves in a dialogue (D. Walton, 1989b).

The rules are the fourth component of dialogue. There are four types of rules. The locution rules define the forms of speech act permissible at the moves. The dialogue rules define turn-taking, and which type of move can follow which. The commitment rules define which commitments are inserted or deleted from a player's commitment-set at each type of move (Walton and Krabbe, 1995). The strategic rules define what counts as a "win" or "loss" of the dialogue, what counts as a successful realization of the goal of the dialogue.

The fifth component is the *goal* of the dialogue, the final state toward which the sequence moves. The goal could be to prove a proposition, to explain a proposition, to obtain advice on a problem, to solicit help to carry out an action, or to obtain information. There is a wide variety of different possible goals of dialogue. The goal of dialogue is the most important factor in determining the type of dialogue and the nature of the other four components of dialogue (Moore, Levin, and Mann, 1977).

The goal is the end-point of a dialogue, the commitment-set is the initial point or basis of the dialogue, and the moves provide the connecting sequence that bridges the gap between the initial point and the end-point.

The five basic components of dialogue are summarized below.

1. *Participants.* There can be any number of participants in a dialogue. But characteristically, a dialogue reduces to two leading participants, the *pro* and *con* parties.

2. *Moves.* Each participant must take his turn making a move, in a sequence of pairs of moves (see also Sacks, Schlegloff, and Jefferson, 1974). Normally, each move is either a question or a reply to a question which can take the form of an assertion.

3. *Commitments.* Attached to each side is a set of propositions called a *commitment-set.* At each move, propositions may be inserted into or removed from a participant's commitment-set (position). This set characteristically changes during the sequence of the dialogue, reflecting a participant's changes of position.

4. *Rules of Procedure.* The function of the rules is to define the conditions under which moves are required, allowed, or forbidden during the course of the game at each characteristic type of move-situation. These rules should ideally be set and agreed upon during the opening moves, or prior to the initiation of the sequence of dialogue.

5. *Goal of Dialogue.* The dialogue must have some specific goal or criterion of success, so that a particular type of sequence of moves, according to the rules, counts as a successful culmination or resolution of the dialogue.

When each of these components has been defined in a clear and nonambiguous manner, so that the dialogue has an abstract structure, we have what Hamblin (1970, 256) calls a *formal dialectical structure.*

When these five components have been clearly defined, it is possible to classify the dialogue as a certain type of dialogue. Traditionally, most attention seems to have been paid to dialogues where the purpose is proof or persuasion, where the goal of the one participant is to prove something to the other one, usually on the basis of the opposing participant's concessions (commitments). However, dialogue is by no means confined to this persuasive type of goal and format. In some instances of dialogue, proof is not involved, or only marginally involved.

The abstract structure of the set of rules for a dialogue is like a game, and Hamblin called such a set a *game of dialogue.* This type of structure provides a model of "good" or "reasoned" dialogue, according to the rules defined in the structure. Hence van Eemeren and Grootendorst (1992, 5) call such a structure a *normative model of dialogue,* meaning that it is a kind of ideal that can be constructed or implicitly inferred from dialogue exchanges in discourse of argumentative discussions (speech events), and it provides a model of dialogue to evaluate this discourse.

When we say that argumentation is based on a game of dialogue, we do not mean *game* in the sense of something frivolous, played for entertainment. Rather, we mean that it is a two-person, or many-person organized, interactive, goal-directed activity with a sequence of moves, where each party takes a turn to move, and the moves are governed by rules of procedure. In this sense, a game of dialogue has a structure, and it has a set of rules.

It is a sort of logical ideal that the rules of dialogue should be precisely formulated and explicitly stated before the sequence of moves is initiated. But in fact, this ideal is often far from met. In some contexts of dialogue, rules of procedure are explicitly set out in advance, but most often these rules do not cover every eventuality. In other contexts of dialogue, there are stated rules, but they are vague, and require skill and judgment to be fairly interpreted. In still other contexts of dialogue, rules are not explicitly stated, but are tacit expectations or implicatures. And finally, in some cases, rules are lacking, and may have to be proposed and agreed upon by the participants, during the course of the dialogue itself. In some instances the rules themselves can be subject to argumentative dialogue. In short, finding out what the rules are or should be, and interpreting them to apply to particular moves, can be a nontrivial exercise, in many instances of "real-life" dialogue.

In the simplest type of case, there are only two participants in a dialogue, and these two participants communicate back and forth on the same level. However, if the rules of dialogue require judgment and interpretation in order for the goal of dialogue to be facilitated, a third party may enter the picture. In some instances, there may be a referee, judge, moderator, mediator, or chairman of dialogue who makes rulings on the legitimacy or acceptability of the moves of the other participants. This third party is, in a way, external to the dialogue. She presides over it, so to speak. Her function is to shape and enforce the rules as they apply to the moves of the participants affected by the rules. The judge or referee is not a direct participant per se in the sequence of moves. She is a kind of overseer who regulates the sequence from a higher level. Accordingly, we could say that this third party is not a part of, or component of the dialogue itself. Rather she functions at the metadialogue level. The referee takes the structure of dialogue as a whole and implements it in a practical form to steer the participants toward the goal of the dialogue, if possible.

As mentioned earlier, there are basically two participants in a dialogue, called the proponent and respondent, or some equivalent names. There may be an external third party, and there may be more than two participants in a dialogue. But characteristically, the dialogue can be reduced to two sides, and the actual speakers in the text of discourse can then be viewed as representing the one side or the other. In many instances of dialogue, the speech-acts can be paired as question-reply argumentation. In this type of dialogue, the participants take turns asking and replying to questions.

Another important characteristic of dialogue is that there is a sequence of moves (messages) in a certain order. In argumentative dialogue, chains of arguments are linked together, and at the local level of dialogue, there are subarguments. The sequence of arguments moves toward a final stage or outcome of the dialogue called a *goal*. The goal defines a successful outcome of good dialogue. Every dialogue starts from an initial situation (initial position) and, according to rules of procedure agreed to by the participants, moves from the initial position through a sequence of moves toward the goal or outcome. Shorter sequences of rule-governed moves can in some cases be shown to be instances of the use of argumentation techniques. The uses of these techniques are woven through the thread of argumentation that holds a dialogue together as a coherent discourse.

Types of Dialogue

There are many different types of dialogue, but three types—persuasion, negotiation, and inquiry—are of primary importance: In a *persuasion dialogue,* the goal of each participant is to persuade the other participant of his own thesis (conclusion) by inferences drawn exclusively from premises that are commitments of the other participant. Thus the proponent must prove his own thesis from propositions conceded by the respondent. And the respondent must prove his thesis from propositions conceded by the proponent. In a persuasion dialogue, each participant has a commitment-set, which is a set of propositions indexed to a specific participant. The rules of procedure define how propositions are inserted into or deleted from commitment-sets as each move is made.

The model of the critical discussion outlined in van Eemeren and Grootendorst (1984) is complex, detailed, and thorough in its stipulation of the actual rules for the four stages of discussion. It is so detailed and precise, indeed, that it would be too exacting as a model to describe exactly the realistic conduct of argumentation in everyday discussions in the normal conversational setting. Of course, the critical discussion, with its various rules, as outlined by van Eemeren and Grootendorst, is not meant to be a description of ordinary conversation. It is meant to be a normative model that gives structured guidelines to tell you which arguments in actual conversations are correct, or correct in relation to the model.

However, because of the detailed, specialized, and precisely formulated rules of the critical discussion as postulated by van Eemeren and Grootendorst, it is helpful to see the critical discussion as a special case or subspecies of a more general type of dialogue called persuasion dialogue. In a persuasion dialogue, according to D. Walton (1984; 1989a), the aim of each participant is to persuade the other participant that his (the first participant's) thesis is true, using only premises that the other participant (the second participant) is committed to. Generally, the persuasion dialogue is less rigid and strict than the critical discussion. The rules are more flexible and open to exceptions. Hence persuasion dialogue, as a more general category of dialogue, is a more natural model of the kinds of argument moves that take place in everyday conversation.

According to van Eemeren and Grootendorst (1984; 1992), fallacies are violations of the rules of a critical discussion. But using the persuasion dialogue model, a fallacy is not simply the breaking of one of the specific rules of conduct for a critical discussion. A fallacy is now conceived of as the use of an argumentation tactic or sequence of reasoning that could plausibly be appropriate in one type of dialogue, but is not correct or helpful in relation to the goals of the type of dialogue the participants are supposed to be engaged in. Accordingly, fallacies in the functional way of looking at them, are characteristically dialectical shifts from one context of dialogue to another. Shifts from one type of dialogue to another in arguments are sometimes acceptable, and even helpful or constructive in supporting goals of an original dialogue (Walton and Krabbe, 1995). In other cases, however, such shifts actually undermine or hinder the goals of the dialogue the participants are supposed to be engaged in. Such shifting arguments often seem nonetheless plausible and convincing precisely because this kind of argumentation move would be appropriate for the other type of dialogue involved. This is exactly the kind of case in which a fallacy occurs, according to the broader point of view whereby the persuasion dialogue can be seen as shifting to other types of dialogue in argumentation.

The basic situation that leads to the persuasion type of dialogue is a conflict of opinions on some issue of controversy where each side takes up a position on the issue that reflects its underlying values. Thus each side wants the other side to see the issue from his own point of view. Accordingly, the type of argumentation involved in persuasion dialogue is other-directed. The goal of each participant is to prove his own conclusion based on premises drawn exclusively from commitments of the other side. Hence this type of dialogue requires a sensitive empathy, an insight into the other party's position on the issue, and an understanding of what the other party would be prepared to accept as a reasonable presumption in the argument.

In the type of dialogue called the *persuasion dialogue* (D. Walton, 1984, 120) or the subspecies of it called the *critical discussion* (van Eemeren and Grootendorst, 1984, 60), there are two participants, and each participant has a well-defined task (burden, role, point of view). In a *simple conflict of opinion,* one participant has the burden of defending a designated proposition, called his *thesis,* while the other participant has the burden of throwing doubt on that thesis (asking critical questions about it). In a *dispute,* which is a symmetrical type of game of dialogue, both participants have a thesis to be proved, and the one thesis is the opposite (negation) of the other. In both these types of persuasion dialogue, the goal is for the one participant to prove his thesis exclusively from the commitments of the other participant, by means of argumentation schemes allowed by the rules.

Some games of dialogue are basically *eristic,* meaning that the goal is to attack or "hit out" verbally at the other party, while others are basically *collaborative.* The persuasion dialogue, on the surface, appears to be primarily adversarial in nature, but closer inspection reveals that it has strong collaborative aspects as well. Persuasion dialogue is based on the burden of proof concept, meaning that a participant's objective is to produce a more convincing argument than the other party, showing that his own argument fulfills the burden and that, therefore, the other party's does not. If one side meets the burden, the other must not. Hence persuasion dialogue is (to some degree) inherently adversarial in nature.

However, persuasion dialogue also has a collaborative or constructive aspect as well. Participants must adhere to the rules: in order to find persuasive arguments they must not only come to know the commitments of the other party; they must also probe into, reveal, and anticipate the commitments of the other party. This process of probing by asking sequences of questions, and gaining concessions, has a maieutic function of helping both parties to discover not only their opponent's underlying position, but their own as well. The skill required is to persuade successfully by producing strong arguments based on empathy and insight into the depths of the other's position. Thus collaborative elements are involved, and positive gains of insight and knowledge are side-benefits. Above all, an arguer must have an "open" attitude of conceding the other party's arguments when they are strong, and generally being open to defeat. By contrast, the quarrel is characterized by a "closed" attitude of refusing to budge, even in the face of a good point (Flowers, McGuire, and Birnbaum, 1982).

There are many kinds of games of dialogue other than persuasion dialogue, however, as indicated in Figure 6.4. In *negotiation dialogue,* the goal of the dialogue is to "make a deal," to reach agreement on how to share scarce resources by interest-based bargaining. In an *inquiry,* the goal is for a collaborative group of participants to prove a particular proposition by inferring it from well-established premises. The inquiry is basically similar to what Aristotle called a *demonstration* in its goals and methods.

Negotiation dialogue as a normative model of argumentation is well described by C. W. Moore (1986) and Donohue (1978; 1981). It is a normative structure with well-defined rules and tactics. Each side makes concessions to the other side in order to get the other side to make concessions that are of value as acquisitions. The concept of the inquiry is similar to Aristotle's conception of the *demonstration,* a kind of argument where a conclusion is based on evidentially prior and better known premises. In recent times, the epistemology of the inquiry is called *foundationalism,* often identified with Descartes's quest for premises that are indubitable as starting points for argument (see Chapter 1, "Foundationalism and Scientific Reasoning"). However, there are various philosophical approaches to defining the inquiry, or setting standards for the premises of an inquiry. While it is clear that the inquiry seeks to be based on knowledge, there is room for dispute about exactly what ought to constitute knowledge, to accord with the purposes and standards of an inquiry.

While the persuasion dialogue has a personal, subjective, or position-centered quality, compared to the inquiry, the negotiation dialogue is even more person-centered. The goal of negotiation has nothing directly to do with finding the truth, or with defending or maintaining one's principles. It is outright self-interest. The goal of interest-based negotiation is to maximize one's personal gains. The setting of negotiation dialogue is a situation where there are not enough available goods to be shared without someone losing. It is a case of "my loss is your gain" (and vice versa). Therefore the goal of each participant in the dialogue is to get as much as he can while getting the others to settle for the remainder. This type of dialogue, perhaps even more than the persuasion dialogue, characteristically has a strongly adversarial cast.

Ten Basic Types of Dialogue

	Type of Dialogue	Initial Situation	Goal	Benefits
1.	Persuasion	Conflict of Opinion	To Persuade Other Party	Understand Positions
2.	Debate	Adversarial Contest	Persuade Third Party	Display of Rhetorical Skills
3.	Inquiry	Need to Establish a Finding	Prove or Disprove Conjecture	Obtain Knowledge
4.	Negotiation	Conflict of Interest	Minimize Gains (Self-Interest)	Settlement and Consensus
5.	Planning Committee	Collective Action Required	Joint Plan or Decision	Airing of Objections
6.	Pedagogical	Ignorance of One Party	Teaching and Learning	Reverse Transfer
7.	Deliberation	Practical Problem of Action	Solution to Problem of Action	Goals Are Articulated
8.	Quarrel	Unstated Grudge	To Defeat Opponent	Reveal Hidden Feelings
9.	Interview	Curiosity about Position	Develop Subject's Position	Spread of Information
10.	Expert Consultation	Need For Expert Advice	Decision for Action	Second-Hand Knowledge

Fig. 6.4

However, the negotiation as a type of dialogue exhibits several subtypes, according to the analysis of Walton and McKersie (1965). The zero-sum game, characteristic of the "my loss is your gain," property, is most definitely typified by *distributive bargaining,* where one party wins some commodity or interest if, and only if, the other party loses it (4). In the *attitudinal structuring* type of negotiation dialogue, the issue concerns relationships, and not just money or commodities. In *intraorganizational bargaining,* the goal is to bring goals and expectations together within a team. In these latter two types of negotiation dialogue, opposition of interests is less sharp, and the dialogue is more collaborative in nature.

In negotiation, participants often form into groups. Therefore, in effect, each side of the two sides participating, is a group of individuals. The classic example is the union-management negotiation in a strike. There are many participants involved, but there are essentially two sides to the bargaining table.

The most outstanding difference between the persuasion and inquiry dialogues and the negotiation dialogue is that in the former, the issue is whether a certain proposition is, or should be held to be, true or false. By contrast, in the negotiation dialogue, the issue is who will get goods, property, money, or the claim to these goods. Hence negotiation is the ultimate in subjective dialogue in the sense that the pursuit of truth or objective knowledge is nonessential, and often peripheral to the goal of the dialogue. An argument that shows a zealous concern for the truth of a proposition could be quite correct and appropriate in a critical discussion, yet be a fallacy of irrelevance in the context of a negotiation.

Expert Consultation Dialogue

The expert consultation dialogue also has a subjective aspect, because the user of the sought knowledge is acting, or making a decision, based on secondhand knowledge. The user is going on the say-so of the source, instead of conducting his own independent inquiry into the domain of knowledge relevant to his problem. On the other hand, the user of the advice must have reason to presume that the other participant is a genuine source of high-grade knowledge in the domain of the question to be decided on, in order for the appeal to his opinion to be a basis for reasonable argument. Hence even though this form of argument is subjective, from the point of view of the user, and based on plausible rather than inductive or deductive reasoning, it can still be a knowledge-based, and therefore not exclusively person-centered, type of dialogue.

The expert consultation is a species of advice-giving dialogue. But there can also be cases of advice-giving dialogue (often combined with means-end reasoning) that are not, strictly speaking, instances of expert consultation.

Case 6.2

> A typical type of case of non-expertise-based, advice-giving dialogue might occur where a stranger to a city needs to find the location of the Central Train Station, and asks a passerby for this information. If the passerby knows the city, he may be in a position to supply the stranger with the required information in the form of a set of directions for arriving at the Central Station.

In this type of case, we would not be very strongly inclined to say that the supplier of information is an "expert" on locations of sites in the city. For example, he may not be a cartographer, or an expert in urban geography. Instead, we say that he is in a *position to know* about these things, since he is familiar with the city as someone who has lived there for some time, or at least is more familiar with the city than the person who has queried him.

However, one of the most prominent and interesting kinds of advice-giving dialogue, in relation to the study of fallacies, is the expert consultation. In this type of dialogue, the one party is an expert in a particular domain of knowledge, and the other is a user who is trying to get answers to questions on how to proceed with a decision, problem, or action related to this special domain of expertise. A familiar type of case is the type of physician-patient dialogue where a patient who is not very knowledgeable about medical matters goes to a physician for advice on how to deal with a particular problem in an area of medicine where this physician is a specialist. The physician bases his answers, and his questions, in this type of dialogue, on his knowledge base of the field, acquired from his studies and experience. Since the patient is not an expert, it may not be easy for him to extract the information he requires in order to make an intelligent decision about the best course of treatment for his special problem. And in fact the success of the treatment often depends significantly on the quality of the dialogue that takes place in this type of encounter.

It is worth emphasizing that although the expert consultation is a very important and interesting kind of dialogue in its own right, nevertheless properly it is a subclass of advice-giving dialogues. To have an advice-giving dialogue, it is not necessary that the one participant be an expert in a domain of knowledge.

As a distinctive type of dialogue, the expert consultation dialogue has two major characteristics. First, it is an inherently *asymmetrical* type of dialogue: the consulted party is an expert in a particular domain and the party seeking advice is characteristically a layperson in that domain. The two parties are not equals. Thus there is a strong burden on the advice-seeking party to try to probe the expert, asking for clarification, and trying to get the expert to explain his advice in layman's terms. Also, there is a burden on the expert to answer questions put to him by the other party as fully and clearly as possible. These burdens are of a different nature, hence this type of dialogue is markedly asymmetrical in nature.

Second, expert consultation dialogue is an essentially collaborative type of dialogue, where each party is trying (ideally) to help the other. The expert tries to help the other party by giving out accurate, useful, and clear advice to help solve a problem. The advice-seeking party wants to get this information or advice to solve his problem, so he must cooperate by asking the expert the right questions, and asking for clarifications if he does not understand the answers given. Expert consultations can become adversarial—for example, in a courtroom setting—but often this is because the expert consultation dialogue is set in a larger context of a trial, which represents a very different type of dialogue. Basically then, the expert consultation should, ideally, be collaborative, rather than adversarial, in its goals and methods.

The advice-giving dialogue and the inquiry dialogue can overlap in particular cases. However, one key difference is that the inquiry seeks to be objective in a way that the knowledge elicitation dialogue cannot aspire to be. In the knowledge elicitation dialogue, the user is not seeking direct access to knowledge, but is always taking the say-so of the source as reliable or authoritative advice. Hence the kind of information received by the user is always inherently subjective, and is based on plausible reasoning.

By contrast, the inquiry aspires to objective proof or knowledge of a proposition. The basis of the distinction between these two types of dialogue is brought out very well by a distinction made by Hintikka and Saarinen (1979) who described the inquiry type of dialogue as a kind of dialogue where the source can be Nature. What this indicates is that the inquiry type of dialogue purports to be based on "the facts." It is often portrayed as a cumulative investigation based on experimental findings that have been carefully documented or verified by repeated trials. By contrast, the knowledge elicitation dialogue can at best achieve what might be called *second-hand knowledge,* a kind of conclusion that is not based on the user's direct knowledge, because he is not in a position to have direct knowledge concerning the proposition he asks about.

Eristic Dialogue

The quarrel sometimes seems to be a kind of critical discussion because participants will criticize each other's arguments, saying things like "You are inconsistent." or "That does not follow from your premises." But this is not a genuine critical discussion, because the arguer is not really open to conceding defeat. What is characteristic here is a tightened-up kind of apparent critical-discussion dialogue best described by the popular terms "quibbling" or "logic-chopping." The participants seize on the particular wording or phrasing of their opponent's concessions and, in a very literal-minded way, draw out logical implications of what was said in order to use these propositions to attack the opponent's commitments as "illogical." The problem is that these alleged commitments don't really represent the deeper (dark side) commitments of the opponent at all, and hence the dialogue typically degenerates into trivial attacks and defenses. It is not a real critical discussion at all, but a kind of quarrel, a species of eristic dialogue.

In cases like this, a person may find himself defending a kind of position he would normally not be inclined to accept at all. But in the heat of argument and in the zeal of attacking the other person, he doesn't think about this at all. The main object has become the attack on the opponent, and it no longer seems to matter what position one adopts as long as it is arguable. What is uppermost in the attacker's mind is to humiliate the opponent for being "illogical."

The lack of a real openness to defeat is an important characteristic of the quarrel which marks it off clearly from the critical discussion as a type of dialogue, according to Flowers, McGuire, and Birnbaum (1982). This element reveals a systematic aspect of duplicity in the quarrel. The participant in the quarrel makes a great show of willingness to be reasonable, open-minded, and following rules of logical reasoning, but in fact this apparent attitude is really part of a systematic attempt to make the opponent appear to be unreasonable and illogical. The attempt is to put oneself on the high ground, making the other side look like the perpetrator, the one who is sustaining the quarrel by continuing to be emotional and unreasonable.

It is characteristic of the quarrel that when a participant is presented with a reasonable argument that he would normally concede in a critical discussion, he pounces on it and tries to find any weakness in it, using it as an instance of his opponent's illogical and unreasonable approach. He grasps at any counterargument, and tries to use it as the basis of an *ad hominem* attack by claiming that it shows the typical "bad reasoning" of his opponent.

Another characteristic of the quarrel is excess. The quarrel takes place in an emotionally heightened atmosphere of blaming and counterblaming where every charge must be quashed with a strong response. Every attack imputes heavy guilt, and not to respond with an equally powerful defense would be, in effect, to concede guilt. Hence the quarrel has a way of escalating, perhaps from some trivial incident, and then reaching a peak of sustained emotional outbursts and excessive laying of serious charges and countercharges by both sides. It seems to both sides that they can't let their guard down, and that they have to keep attacking and to match the emotional level of outrage evoked by the other side. Appearing to back off from this heavy exchange too early gives an appearance of being "licked" or shameful, of conceding defeat and humiliation. A serious problem with the argumentation stage of the quarrel is that once started into it, you can't then back off to try to get out of it by not responding, or by trying to de-escalate, because you will appear to be conceding defeat. And appearances mean a lot in the quarrel. If you appear to have lost, then you have lost the quarrel.

A good closing stage binds up the wounds that have been opened during the argumentation stage of the quarrel. There should be not only apologies, but also assurances that a participant will make serious efforts to change the habits or actions that the other party has expressed strong feelings about. A good outcome is that a stressful and unpleasant exchange has been undergone in order to cement a deeper bond in future relationships. A quarrel can go either way. It can lead to a deeper rift or a stronger bond. A personal relationship can either break or strengthen as a result of a quarrel.

It is easy to condemn the quarrel, because the participants are in a highly emotional stage, and therefore they seem to have abandoned rational argument altogether. Moreover, if they were originally supposed to be engaged in some other type of dialogue, such as a critical discussion or negotiation, the quarrel is rightly seen as a dialectical shift that may be illicit and unproductive. Another basis for condemnation is that the positions taken by the participants in a quarrel are often exaggerated or thoughtless, because they have arisen out of a need to attack and humiliate the other party.

Although the quarrel is often a bad sign of dialogue that is degenerating, we should not be dogmatically negative about the quarrel as a type of dialogue. The best attitude is to be wary of the quarrel, especially where conditions are not appropriate for this type of dialogue, but also to have a degree of tolerance for the quarrel. It can be a type of dialogue that has beneficial results in some cases. True, it is a type of dialogue in which logic does not matter much—it generates more heat than light. But it can have a valuable function of allowing powerful emotions to be expressed that might otherwise be bottled up and foster resentment and bad feeling that could find worse forms of expression.

From a point of view of critical argumentation, the quarrel most often needs to be evaluated negatively when there has been an illicit shift from another type of dialogue during the course of an argumentative exchange (Walton and Krabbe, 1995).

There is typically a kind of duplicity inherent in the quarrel, and eristic dialogue generally. The participants may be clearly engaged in a quarrel, yet each one may criticize the other for being "illogical"—for failing to meet standards of good dialogue appropriate for a critical discussion. This pretense that the dialogue is a sort of critical discussion enables a participant to lay blame on his opponent for being a bad and unreliable person, for being so quarrelsome instead of keeping to the rules of critical discussion. But of course, such an attack is hypocritical if the participants are both clearly engaged in a quarrel, and neither of them supposed from the beginning that the dialogue was a critical discussion.

Case 6.3

> For example, one participant in a quarrel may say to another, "You can never stay on the topic. Your arguments are always so irrelevant."

This criticism presumes that the dialogue is an exchange like a critical discussion, where relevance to the issue of the discussion is very important for the argumentation. But in a quarrel, relevance does not matter, and the quarrel typically skips from one issue of grievance or blame to another, where topical relevance of the issues is of little or no real importance.

This type of duplicity suggests that people often think that the quarrel is inherently bad, so it is always acceptable to criticize someone for quarreling. But it is based on a dubious assumption. For if the dialogue is overtly a quarrel, and was not supposed to be anything else at the outset, then it is not fair to attack the other party for failing to be engaged in some other type of dialogue.

In the argumentation stage, the quarrel sustains great shifts to topical relevance, often leaping from one issue to another issue that appears to be completely unrelated in subject matter. In this it is quite different from the critical discussion and the debate, where criticisms of irrelevance are much more serious.

Typically, some trivial incident "sparks" a quarrel, and then some apparently unrelated issue is suddenly brought forward as a grievance by one participant.

Case 6.4

> For example, a domestic quarrel may start over a trivial dispute about who was supposed to take out the garbage, but forgot. Then as emotions heighten in the dispute, suddenly one participant may bring forward some serious accusation or grievance, totally unrelated to the garbage issue: "I saw you drink all that beer at the barbecue party. Then you tried to do a cartwheel and fell on the grass. Your behavior made me disgusted and ashamed. You made a fool of yourself in front of the whole department."

What started out as a conflict about the garbage duty suddenly shifted to a different issue of personal blame for acting foolishly at a barbecue. Suddenly, a serious grievance has come out, and one side is in danger of humiliation unless some defensive response to the charge is forthcoming.

In the quarrel, once the heavy emotional stage of the serious argumentation is reached, a grievance surfaces and is expressed. From there, the other side is likely to respond with an equally serious grievance, "What about the time you ... " One grievance brings out another, but the subjects of the grievances may be unrelated.

During the argumentation stage of the quarrel, a number of tender issues or grievances are opened up for discussion and feelings are vented. During this phase the quarrel typically exceeds the bounds of propriety. This process is painful; it is like opening up a wound that has become infected.

In the closing stage, ideally the quarrel should be "made up." The excesses need to be apologized for, and recriminations need to be put in a balanced perspective. A participant needs to acknowledge feelings expressed as being important by the other side. No further mention of the issue may be made, but a participant needs to make it clear that he has got the message.

Goals, Commitments, and Presumptions in Dialogue

The most basic and essential characteristic of the structure of dialogue is its goal-directed nature. In any particular case, the first question to ask is: "What is the purpose of the dialogue?" The *goal* of a dialogue is a particular state or proposition that is the final stage or intended outcome toward which the sequence of dialogue should move. Each type of dialogue has its characteristic type of goal. For example, in a persuasion dialogue, the goal of each participant is to prove a proposition designated as his *conclusion* or *thesis,* from the commitments of the other participant. The *issue* is the pair of propositions to be proved by the two participants in the persuasion dialogue. And so, resolving the issue by argument is the goal of a persuasion dialogue.

The goal defines the global structure of a dialogue and enables an observer to understand the strategies of the participants in the dialogue and the reasons they make the moves they do. Every dialogue starts from an *initial situation (initial position),* and the rules of dialogue chart the permissible sequences of moves that take the dialogue from the initial position to the goal.

The following structure of dialogue represents a normative ideal, for dialogue, in practice, may fail to realize its goal. Reaching its goal is a characteristic of "good" or "successful" dialogue. Many actual cases of debates and arguments in dialogue are in fact notoriously unsuccessful, in relation to the proper goal of each particular case.

The global goal of each dialogue leads to and defines the formulation of subgoals of dialogue (Moore, Levin, and Mann, 1977) at particular, local moves, or sets of moves, in the sequence of moves. For example, in a persua-

Global Structure of Dialogue

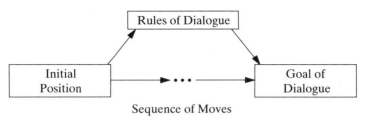

Fig. 6.5

sion dialogue, it may be strategically necessary or useful for a participant to attempt to persuade his opponent of a certain proposition in order to subsequently prove his global thesis (see Fig. 6.5). Goals can also be complex in other ways. A goal can be a negative proposition, a conjunctive proposition, a disjunctive proposition, or a conditional proposition. Strategy may be dictated by the structure of the goal. For example, if the proposition to be proved is a (weakly) disjunctive proposition, then if you are having a hard time proving the one disjunct, it may make sense to temporarily give up, and try instead to prove the other disjunct (see Barth and Krabbe, 1982).

In general, a goal of dialogue can be any description of a state or set of states of the world that can be articulated, expressed, or conceded as a commitment by a participant in the dialogue. Very often, however, a participant's goal is not clearly or expressly articulated to other participants or observers of a dialogue. It is then left up to an interpreter or critic of the dialogue to reconstruct a plausible set of goals that the participant can reasonably construe from the evidence given by the traces of goal pursuit in the given text of discourse. This process of plausible interpretation is one of argument reconstruction of a particular corpus or given body of discourse.

Goals of dialogue are set at an external or metadialogue level where the game of dialogue is fixed as a cooperative, joint undertaking. However, in fact, participants do dispute, in some cases, about what the proper goals of a discussion should be. Goals are ideally determined at the confrontation stage of the dialogue, according to van Eemeren and Grootendorst (1984), where the framework of the discussion is set up and agreed upon by the participants, ideally, prior to the argumentation stage of the dialogue. Thus goals are external to the argumentation stage of a dialogue, and ideally

should be agreed upon by the participants at an earlier stage where procedural questions are clarified.

Once a goal is set, the process of reasoning whereby moves in a dialogue
contribute toward the realization of a goal is inherently teleological in nature. Teleological (goal-directed, practical) reasoning is a process of searching through a set of propositions that represents the knowledge base or
position of one or more of the participants in a dialogue, to find a sequence
of inferences that links up the goal-proposition to some subset of this given
set of propositions.

In traditional logic, an argument was defined as an arbitrarily designated
set of propositions called *premises,* and a proposition called a *conclusion*
that follows from the premises by a deductively valid rule (form) of inference. With the advent of artificial intelligence, a new conception of argument has been introduced which is knowledge-based and goal-directed. A
knowledge base (already defined in Chapter 3) is a set of propositions (both
facts and rules) that represent a domain of knowledge, skill, or experience
relative to a particular problem or question. A *goal* is a description of a
state (proposition) that represents the answer to a question or solution to
a problem. An *argument* is a sequence of inferences along a path or line of
inquiry from the knowledge base to the goal. Thus the argument moves
toward the goal from the initial situation given by the knowledge base.
This conception of argument is implicit in programming languages for AI
like PROLOG.

In traditional logic, the length of the proof did not matter, although the
shorter proof was generally held to be aesthetically preferable. In the newer
conception of argument, the reasoning should encompass all possible lines
of argument from the initial situation to the goal. How you get there matters. For some lines of reasoning may be more efficient than others. For
example, a circular path may loop endlessly, and therefore not be a practical
solution to a problem (D. Walton, 1991a).

In traditional logic, the argument was said to be *valid* where it is impossible for the premises to be true and the conclusion false. A circular argument, of the form "A, therefore A" clearly fulfills this requirement, given
the law of excluded middle. For if A is true, it is impossible for A to be
false. Hence in traditional deductive logic, a circular argument is as good
an argument as you could require by deductive standards.

But in knowledge-based reasoning, a circular argument may be less desirable than a noncircular path of argument that goes to the same goal. Here,
whether an argument is circular or not may make a difference to the worth

of the argument (D. Walton, 1991a). Knowledge-based reasoning uses rules of inference to extrapolate paths of argument from a given knowledge situation in order to reach a conclusion, or goal to be established (see Heidorn, 1986).

The goal is a particular proposition which is in question and which is required to be proved. Knowledge-based reasoning starts by exploring different ways of attempting to reach the desired conclusion. Each step of reasoning is linked to a next step, and therefore a chain of inferences takes the form of a path of argument. However, generally there can be more than one path diverging from the same point. Hence there can be different lines of argument all leading toward the same conclusion. Generally, knowledge-based reasoning will try to explore all possible paths that seem to lead toward the goal. But in some cases, there may be an overabundance of different paths available; in these cases, part of the reasoning is the job of cutting down the options by selecting more promising lines of argument.

An arguer's *position* may be defined as the whole set of that arguer's commitments. As dialogue proceeds, propositions are inserted into, or deleted from a participant's set of commitments. Ideally, a record of these assertions and retractions should be kept. This record of commitments defines an arguer's position. Distorting or unfairly representing your opponent's position in a dialogue is the basis of the straw man fallacy.

Commitment-sets are not generally required to be internally consistent (see Hamblin, 1970, 263). But if one participant finds an inconsistency, or plausible evidence of an inconsistency, in the position of another participant, then this finding can be strong grounds for challenging the tenability of the position of the second participant in argument (Krabbe, 1990). In many instances, the basis of this type of challenge is not logical inconsistency per se, but *pragmatic (practical) inconsistency,* where one commitment is contrary to another in a practical way. Practical inconsistency is defined in terms of practical reasoning.

Characteristically, in contentious dialogues like political debates, each participant may not know what the other participant's position is. Most often, something is known about an arguer's position, but many aspects of it may be unknown or untested by debate, at any particular juncture of a dialogue. From the point of view of one arguer, it may be said that the position of another arguer has a light side, referring to all the known commitments of the second arguer. And it may be said that the position of this other arguer also has a dark side, a set of commitments that are definitely contained in the position of that other arguer, but that are not known to be contained therein by the first arguer. Typically on a new issue that has not previously been discussed in depth, we may know something about a politician's stand on the issue, but we may not know what his stand is on many specific propositions related to it (D. Walton, 1984; Walton and Krabbe, 1995).

Another typical characteristic of position in dialogue is that we may know certain general principles in an arguer's position, but we may not know the specific propositions that arguer will accept on a specific issue.

Case 6.5

> For example, if you know that someone is a conservative in his political views generally, then you may plausibly expect him to take a certain sort of position on some specific issue. But there is scope for exceptions and surprises. For one thing, there are different degrees of conservatism, and different kinds of conservatives. And it is possible for an arguer to defend a kind of position where he is conservative on some issues, yet liberal on other issues.

Generally speaking, a position is a kind of balance between more general commitments (principles) and an arguer's actions or other specific commitments on a particular issue or question. The more general commitments are usually expressed as an arguer's goals, while the more specific commitments are often expressed by an arguer's actions.

Serious questions of interpreting and criticizing argumentative discourse are posed by the fact that in most cases there is not an exact fit or a clear clash between an action and a goal. Instead, particular actions are related to other actions of a more general description that are in turn related to subgoals of a more general goal. Thus an apparent conflict between an action and a goal may require an analysis of a hierarchical sequence of propositions in an arguer's position, in order for a critic of that position to sort out a criticism of practical inconsistency.

An arguer's position is *coherent* if the propositions contained in it fit together in a sequence so that the goals and the actions mesh. Any failure to fit can be questioned by a critic. There are many kinds of criticisms of an arguer's position, but the most powerful criticism is posed by an allegation of pragmatic inconsistency. If an arguer's position is demonstrably pragmatically inconsistent, there is often a presumption that the arguer is a *hypocrite,* someone whose real position (often revealed or betrayed by his actions) is inconsistent with his professed position (often expressed in general principles). It is not necessarily the case that an arguer whose position is pragmatically inconsistent is a hypocrite. However, the presumption that such a person may be arguing hypocritically makes criticisms of practical inconsistency highly dangerous as refutations, especially in political argumentation. Criticisms of practical inconsistency are associated with the *argumentum ad hominem* of the logic texts (D. N. Walton, 1989a).

Ad hominem criticisms are characteristically problematic for a critic to pin down as a tight refutation because there should be a certain flexibility and openness to exceptions inherent in position reasoning. Positional argumentation is based on principles and generalizations that are subject to exceptions in particular situations. These generalizations are plausible rather than certain or probable. They require only a provisional, presumptive kind of commitment that may arguably be withdrawn or overruled in a special case (D. Walton, 1992c).

Indeed, an arguer who adheres too rigidly to his position without conceding exceptions to it or uncertainties in defending it can be accused of being dogmatic. In more severe criticisms of extreme cases of this sort, an arguer may even be accused of being fanatical (see Flowers, McGuire, and Birnbaum, 1982). The term "fanatic" however, is such a strong form of criticism and condemnation of an arguer that it is usually reserved for extreme cases. Characteristically, this term is used by a critic against a position which the critic strongly opposes. In wartime for example, our troops are "determined" or "courageous" whereas the soldiers of the enemy are "fanatical."

Politicians who respond too reflexively to opinion polls and other indexes of popular opinion, especially if their collective responses show little consistency, may be suspected of political opportunism precisely because of the presumption that their position lacks coherence. The suspicion is that such a person is not deeply enough committed to some set of general principles to have a deeply thought out or reasoned position as a basis for intelligent political action. A position that is too vague or too flexible can be just as severe a basis for criticism as a position too tight or dogmatic.

An arguer's position must be tight and consistent, yet at the same time loose and flexible. This right degree of tautness and balance in an argument requires sensitivity and judgment. When this balance gets out of line, an arguer may be criticized as exhibiting bias. This form of criticism is studied in D. Walton (1991b). Bias may involve not only a lack of dialogue coherence, but also an allegation that an arguer has shifted from one type of dialogue to another.

Dialectical Relevance

Every dialogue has a goal. A sequence of moves (represented by a profile) in the dialogue that *facilitates* the goal moves toward realizing the goal, or is part of a longer sequence that moves toward realizing the goal. Any particular move or speech act is dialectically relevant in the context of dialogue in which it occurs if the move is one member of a sequence of moves in the dialogue where the sequence facilitates the goal of dialogue. A sequence of moves *obstructs* a goal of dialogue if it moves away from the goal, or is part of a sequence that moves away from realizing the goal. A particular speech act or move is *compatible with the context of dialogue* in which it occurs if it does not obstruct a goal of the dialogue.

Rules of dialogue are said to be good (reasonable, appropriate, acceptable) rules to the extent that they facilitate the goal of a particular dialogue. However, some rules can facilitate a goal of dialogue better than others. And in actual debates or discussions, rules that participants in a dialogue accept may, in fact, not facilitate the goal of the dialogue. Therefore, it is possible in a real discussion that a move could be compatible with the rules of a dialogue, but not compatible with the goal of the dialogue (and vice versa). The point to be taken is that rules of dialogue can themselves be independently evaluated as favorable or unfavorable.

A move in dialogue can be compatible with the rules, and it is then a *permitted move*. Relative to a set of rules, moves can also be *required* or *forbidden*. In a set of rules, some rules can be permissive while others are of an obligatory nature. Some rules can pertain to burdens of proof, or other kinds of burdens that do not strictly require certain types of moves in every situation. These rules impose a conditional obligation to make a move in a certain type of situation.

A move can be compatible with the context of dialogue in which it occurs and still be criticized, quite reasonably, as an irrelevant move in the dialogue. A particular move or speech act that is one member of a sequence of moves that does not facilitate a goal of dialogue may be criticized as a *dialectically irrelevant* move in the context of dialogue (Berg, 1991). More generally, any move that is not coherent with the context of a dialogue will be perceived as *not dialectically relevant* in that context of dialogue. Such a move will be said to be a "red herring" or a *non sequitur*. Failure of dialogue coherence is the basis for criticisms of failure of dialectical relevance in dialogue (see Berg, 1991).

It is well to emphasize that a move in dialogue can be compatible with the context of dialogue yet fail to be dialectically relevant with that context of dialogue. To be relevant, a move must fit into the sequence of dialogue, in the sense of facilitating the goal of the dialogue. An irrelevant move (i.e., one that is not coherent with the context of dialogue in which it has occurred) may nevertheless be compatible with that context, meaning that it does not positively obstruct the goal of dialogue. Irrelevant moves are delaying or distracting maneuvers in argument, as opposed to direct obstructions to a line of argument.

Among types of criticisms of arguments then, an important distinction should be made between irrelevant moves in argument and obstructive moves in argument. For example, the *ad baculum* move (argument from appeal to fear, or to a threat) has been classified by van Eemeren and Grootendorst (1984, 182) as an obstruction to argument because it typically is an attempt to close off the possibility of further argument. In some instances, (the *ad populum* type of move also has this character, where a speaker says, in effect: "If you don't agree with our group position, then you are an outsider, and your point of view is worthless." This type of move attempts to close off or block any possibility of further meaningful argument.)*Ad hominem* arguments are sometimes also of this type.

By contrast, moves in argument that are said to be irrelevant are very often moves that are not positively obstructive to the line of argument. They are moves that are perceived as wandering away from the line of argument (D. Walton, 1989b).

In short, the obstructive type of error in argument can be said to be a more serious type of transgression of dialogue than the error of irrelevance. Irrelevance does not cancel out or stop dialogue altogether, but it does pose a threat of delay or distraction. In any particular instance of dialogue, coherence of a move must be evaluated by determining the goal of the dialogue, and then seeing how this particular move fits into a sequence of argument that is designed to move towards that goal. Determining the goal of dialogue characteristically involves finding out what type of dialogue the participants are ostensibly engaged in. Then evaluating the sequence of argumentation in relation to the goal involves the hierarchical fitting together of subsequences into longer sequences of argumentation. Thus coherence must be judged, in a particular case, from the available information given from the corpus of discourse of the dialogue. Similarly with incoherence (irrelevance), a critic must judge the line of argument from the discourse given and the context of dialogue. If the speaker has not yet finished his argument, the would-be critic of irrelevance must judge what use the speaker could conceivably make of this particular move in developing a line of argument that makes some contribution to the goal of a dialogue. Thus criticisms of irrelevance are often more like challenges than refutations. A speaker should have a right to reply to a criticism of irrelevance if he can. He may be able to justify his questioned move as having some function in his line of argument, as he sees it.

This is not to say, however, that irrelevance in an argument cannot, at the same time, also be an obstruction to the line of argument. Clearly, in some cases, it can.

Case 6.6

> The classic case is that of the filibuster, where a prolonged speech on some completely irrelevant matter is used to block the other party from speaking. According to *Webster's Third International Dictionary* (1966), a *filibuster* is "the use of extreme dilatory tactics (as speaking merely to consume time) by an individual or group in an attempt to delay or prevent action by the majority in a legislative or deliberative assembly."

Even more generally a filibuster could be defined as a violation of fair turntaking in dialogue by making a move that is so long or complex that it effectively prevents the other party from making a next move.

In the case of the filibuster, it is not simply the irrelevance of the time-consuming speech that is objectionable, however. It is the length of the speech that performs the function of blocking the other party from advancing his side of the argument. Not all tactics of irrelevance have this blocking effect or function. And in principle, there is a distinction between mere irrelevance in argumentation, and worse abuses, which may include prolonged irrelevance, that block off the other participant from participating at all.

The first rule of argumentation listed by van Eemeren and Grootendorst (1984, 23; 1987, 284), is to the effect that participants in an argument must not obstruct each other in advancing points of view or doubt. Besides the *ad baculum* (mentioned above), van Eemeren and Grootendorst also cite the *argumentum ad misericordiam* (27) and the *argumentum ad hominem* (28) in this connection. An *ad misericordiam* argument is one that uses pity or compassion to get a respondent to accept a conclusion.

In this regard, it is useful to classify instances of informal fallacies or other abuses of argumentation into two categories: (1) irrelevant moves of arguments that fail to advance the main goal of an argument, or deflect the line of argumentation away from the real goal of the dialogue; and (2) even more serious kinds of tactics or abuses that are designed to prevent or block off the sequence of argument.

7

Presumption and Burden of Proof

In this chapter I shall show presumption to be a distinctive kind of speech act halfway between assertion and (mere) assumption (supposition). The distinction among these three important types of speech act is analyzed within the structure of dialogue as a framework of argumentation (outlined in Chapter 6) in which there are two participants, usually called a proponent and a respondent, who take turns reasoning with each other. In such a normative framework of dialogue, different types of speech acts are employed by the participants, in their moves, in a goal-directed sequence of exchanges. A key part of the framework is the burden of proof, a concept previously introduced, but more precisely defined in this chapter.

Searle (1979) makes no room specifically for presumptions in his taxonomy of speech acts: presumably, however, they would come under the heading of *assertives,* the point of the members of this class being "to commit the speaker (in varying degrees) to something's being the case" (12). Much depends here, however, on what is meant by "commitment." Presumption requires a notion of provisional commitment, not characterized by an obligation to defend the proposition in question, if challenged.

Vanderveken (1990, 180) does not mention presumption either, in his classification of assertives. However, he does leave a little room for possibly including presumption in or around his categories of "suggest," "guess," and "hypothesize." Although it is misleading to call presumption an "assertive" speech act, that is where it fits in, according to the current taxonomies of speech acts.

One puzzling question concerning presumptions is the nature of their relation to evidence in argumentation. It seems that presumptions can go forward in an argument without being based on evidence sufficient to prove them. This appears to make them suspicious, from a logical point of view. If they can extend beyond the evidence, doesn't that mean that argumentation based on them can become rampant, even empty speculation—mere conjecture, perhaps masquerading as argumentation that compels rational acceptance? This suspicion is at the basis of the traditional tendency to think of the *argumentum ad ignorantiam*—a kind of argument, as we have seen, often based on presumption—as being a fallacy.

Moreover, if critical discussion, as a type of dialogue, is typically built on presumptions—prima facie cases and plausible assumptions that are generally accepted but cannot be definitively proved—does it not suggest that critical discussion does not ever really prove anything? Isn't the subjective character of critical discussion a dubious way of proving something using adversarial arguments based on a burden of proof? These very general questions and worries are at the heart of our concern with the concept of presumption in this chapter. Nevertheless, I shall show that presumptive reasoning is a distinctive and legitimate kind of reasoning in its own right, one that has a valuable pragmatic function in argumentation, and has specific dialogical characteristics as a kind of speech act.

The Practical Nature of Presumption

Presumption, as characterized in this chapter, is an essentially pragmatic notion that enables a discussion or action to go ahead on a rational, even if provisional basis, where access to evidence that would definitively resolve a question is lacking. Even if the evidence is insufficient, there may be enough of it to indicate the wisdom of a provisional course of action, in given circumstances. Such a procedure can be rationally justified, if, for practical but good reasons, a burden of proof can be set to tilt the resolution of the issue in one direction or the other.

For example, in a potentially hazardous situation, it may be prudent to tilt the burden of proof in the direction of safety. The principle behind this way of proceeding is called *tutiorism,* sticking to the safest known way of proceeding where there is doubt, or lack of knowledge on how best to proceed in a given set of circumstances. The maxim is to "err on the side of safety," where doubt creates the potential for danger.

A simple example is the accepted procedure for handling weapons on a firing range, illustrated in case 3.14. The principle is always to assume a weapon is loaded (or at least, to act on that presumption by forbearing from waving it around, or pointing it at someone), unless you are sure that it is not loaded. The test of whether you are sure of this is that you have, just before, inspected the chamber and perceived clearly that it is empty.

The *ad ignorantiam* nature of this type of presumptive reasoning is quite clear. If you do not know the weapon is unloaded, then you infer that it is loaded. Or at least, you operate on this presumption, by acting as though it is a loaded weapon.

The same kind of example, in case 3.15, showed also, however, how tied to the specifics of a context or situation this kind of reasoning is. Suppose you are a soldier in wartime getting ready to defend your position against an imminent enemy assault. Here, reasoning again on practical grounds of safety or self-preservation, you act on the presumption that your weapon may be empty, by checking to see that it is not empty. It is the same kind of *ad ignorantiam* inference as the one in the firing range case above, but turned around in this new situation to reason in the opposite direction.

Presumptive reasoning is far more common in everyday life than you might think until you begin to reflect on it. It has many uses, and many practical justifications. One of the most common uses is to facilitate practical actions in situations where a commitment must be acted upon or implemented, even in the absence of hard evidence sufficient to resolve an issue in time to be of use. Practical reasoning, in such cases, often rests on general presumptions based on routine or customary ways of doing something. Such practices are often justified because they have been found to be successful in the past by practitioners skilled in this type of task.

It is quite common for presumptions to be based on expert opinion where the person who acts on the presumption—not being an expert himself—is not in a position to verify the proposition by basing it on hard evidence within the field of expertise in question. Such secondhand knowledge is, from the point of view of the user, really based on presumption.

Customs and fashions, popularly accepted ways of doing things, are another important source of presumptions. With many choices of how to do things in life, in the absence of knowledge that one way of doing something is any better or more harmful than another, people often tend to act on the presumption that the way to do something is the popularly accepted way of doing it.

Manners and conventions of polite behavior are sources of presumptions that enable business and social activities to proceed smoothly, expedited by tolerance and cooperation. These are the sorts of nonexplicit presumptions that we take for granted so often in daily, practical affairs, without really thinking about how important they are.

The following case is a good example of how a nonexplicit presumption functions as part of a sequence of practical reasoning in the context of a discussion of a practical problem.

Case 7.1

> Bob is an astronaut, in orbit in a space capsule, and he is suffering from acute life-threatening symptoms of nausea, breathing difficulty, and dizziness. He has a certain medication, M, aboard the capsule, which he could take, but he does not know it is on board. But he has a rare genetic condition, X, which would make this medication fatal for him to take. Bob's physician says to Bob's mother, Alice, "We know that your husband, Henry, has condition X, and that condition X is genetically linked from fathers to sons, therefore we should not tell Bob to take the M." Alice replies, "I have never told anyone this, but Henry is not Bob's father." Alice goes on to tell the physician the true circumstances of how Bob came to be conceived, while Henry was on military service overseas.

In this case, the whole sequence of practical reasoning initially went forward on the basis of the unstated presumption that Henry is Bob's father. Normally, we would have no reason to doubt or challenge this presumption. However, in this case, Alice brings forward new evidence relating to the special circumstances of the case. The doctor would have no reason not to accept what she says as reliable, since she is Bob's mother, and Bob's life is at stake.

We can represent, in outline, the sequence of practical reasoning involved, as follows.

1. The usual treatment for someone who has symptoms like those of Bob, is to take *M*.
2. The exception is the kind of case where the patient has condition *X*.
3. But, as far as we know, Bob does not have condition *X*.
4. Therefore, Bob should take *M*.
5. But, if Bob's father has condition *X*, Bob should not take *M*, because *X* is sex-linked, and taking *M* is fatal for patients with condition *X*.
6. We know that Henry has condition *X*.
7. And we presume, or take it for granted, that Henry is Bob's father, because Henry is the husband of Alice, and Alice is Bob's mother.

This last step in the sequence of reasoning contains a key inference explicitly represented below.

Henry is Alice's husband.
Bob is Alice's son.
Therefore, Henry is the father of Bob.

The physician accepted this presumptive inference, knowing that the premises are true. In the face of having no evidence to the contrary, he drew the inference (implicitly) from the premises to accepting the conclusion. However, Alice's introduction of new evidence overturned the presumptive inference from going forward in this case. Why? Because normally one presumes that a woman's husband is the father of her child, until paternity is rebutted or disproved by the circumstances known in a particular case. In this case, presuming that Alice was giving credible evidence to rebut this presumption, the conclusion of the inference has to be withdrawn.

In this case, there is a practical problem that is urgent: Should Bob be told to take the *M* or not? The problem is argued out in a kind of expert consultation dialogue between the physician and Bob's mother. What should they do? Implicit in their reasoning was the presumption that Henry is Bob's father. Such a presumption would normally go forward unchallenged. But in this case, once rebutted, it changed the outcome of the sequence of reasoning entirely. One can clearly see the nonmonotonic basis of this sequence of reasoning. Normally *M* would be the medication for Bob's systems. But once we find that Henry has condition *X*, this normal generalization is defeated. But then a second default inference occurs when we find that, once again contrary to normal presumption, Henry is not Bob's father.

Here we have a series of arguments from ignorance, each one being defeated, by default, as new information relevant to the case comes in. But each argument is reasonable, when taken as a presumptive inference, relative to the knowledge base, or set of commitments in the dialogue, at that given point. Presumptive reasoning is tentative, and is by its very nature, based on a profile of dialogue that is an *argumentum ad ignorantiam* in its structure. But does that make it fallacious? To explore the question, the concept of presumption needs to be defined precisely in a framework of dialogue.

Received Views of Presumption

According to Lewis and Short (1969, 1433) the meaning of *praesumptio*, the Latin root term of the English word "presumption," is "a taking up and answering in advance, an anticipation of possible or suspected objections." This explication of the Latin term is very revealing, because it is premised on the key concepts of (i) a sequence of questions and answers in an extended chain of argumentation running through an ongoing dialogue, (ii) an order in the sequence, and (iii) a set of "possible or suspected objections" or critical questions put forward by a respondent, at some appropriate point in the sequence of dialogue, to match an argument or speech act put forward by a proponent. The phrase *in advance* is very important here.

The idea seems to be that a presumption does meet a burden of proof, but in a manner different from an assertion or argument that is nonpresumptive. The presumption somehow takes up its meeting of this burden before any actual objection is made to it in a dialogue. How this is done, or why it is useful, is not made clear, however.

Whately (1846; 1963) described presumption using the metaphor of preoccupation of a ground, based on the idea of two parties alternately occupying and contesting a piece of terrain; it seems to be a kind of military metaphor suggesting a two-party adversarial exchange or relationship (compare case 2.8). The one party occupies the ground until the other can bring forward a sufficient weight or force to dislodge it, and then the second party occupies the ground.

This engaging metaphor was backed up by Whately by phrasing it in terms of burden of proof, a concept already recognized in legal argumentation. Whately wrote (170) that when a presumption exists in favor of the proponent of an argument, "the burden of proof lies on the side of him who would dispute it." For example, in a criminal trial, there is a "presumption of innocence" (171) until guilt is established by the trial.

Although Whately's account succeeded in linking the concept of presumption with its partner concept of burden of proof, he left open basic questions about the exact nature of this relationship and how it works in practice.

A continuing controversy (Reinard, 1991, 252) is whether presumption is relevant only at the beginning of a discussion, or whether it continues to be important throughout the dialogue. The same kind of controversy surrounds the notion of burden of proof. Is it set at the initial stage of a dialogue once and for all, until the issue is resolved or the dialogue ends, or does it vary (shifting back and forth) as the dialogue proceeds? Indeed, given the lack of any rigorous analytical explication of the concepts of presumption and burden of proof, it is hard to distinguish between the two notions, or to show clearly where the difference lies.

Whately also brought forward the idea that there is a legitimate weight of presumption in argumentation in favor of existing institutions and practices (e.g., the Anglican Church). Naturally, this idea turned out to be very controversial. However, Whately's idea was backed up by an analysis of presumption offered by Perelman and Olbrechts-Tyteca (1969, 71) which linked it with degree of risk in practical reasoning designed to conclude toward a prudent course of action. According to Perelman and Olbrechts-Tyteca (1969), current or traditional institutions and accepted practices have a presumption in their favor because we have an idea of what to expect from accepting them. Their likely consequences or potential side effects are known better than those of a system or practice that is yet untried. This suggestion tied presumption into practical reasoning under uncertainty in concluding toward a prudent course of action, a conceptual tie-up also later advocated by Clarke (1989, 10). The idea is that some presumptions at least can be justified on a practical basis because our practical knowledge of their expected consequences makes them a safer basis for prudential action.

This pragmatic view of presumption was developed into a fuller analysis of presumptive reasoning by Ullman-Margalit (1983a). According to this analysis, a presumptive inference from one proposition A to another proposition B is based on a rule of the following form: given that A is the case, you (the rule subject) shall proceed as if B were true, unless or until you have sufficient reason to believe that *B* is not the case (147). This rule is not meant by Ullman-Margalit (149) to make any claim on its subject's "cognitive or epistemic systems" which involves a commitment to, or guarantee of the truth-value of the derived presumption *B*. The analysis is meant as a pragmatic explication of presumption in the sense that it entitles one only to hold that *B* is true "for the purpose of concluding one's practical deliberation on the impending issue . . ." (149). In this analysis, presumption is understood as based on a kind of practical inference that sanctions a pragmatic passage from one proposition to another in the context of some overarching practical deliberation or discussion on an issue regarding some contemplated course of action or policy. Ullman-Margalit (1983b) also shows how presumption relates to Grice's maxims (especially the Cooperative Principle), indicating how a presumption can be rebutted when it violates a maxim.

This pragmatic type of analysis suggested by Perelman and Olbrechts-Tyteca, Ullman-Margalit, and Clarke is very promising, but it depends on how we are to understand practical reasoning as a distinctive type of reasoning.

Practical Reasoning

Burden of proof is characteristically linked to the problem of an agent who must decide on a course of action or inaction in a rapidly changing, complex particular situation where certain knowledge, or even probable knowledge, cannot be acquired in time to make the best decision. Very often, in such situations, an agent must act on the basis of plausible presumptions about what can reasonably be expected to happen in the given situation, based on usual expectations, customary routines, and commonsense understanding of institutions, functions, and familiar sequences of actions. This type of decision is based on what is reasonably foreseeable, even if such an outcome is improbable.

Much commonplace reasoning in deliberation is based on the idea that as human agents, we are *in the world,* in a given environment of the moment that is constantly in a state of flux. In this situation, even doing nothing can be a form of action (significant omission or refraining). In this predicament, reasoning starts with a basic horizon, so that the decision-maker is pre-

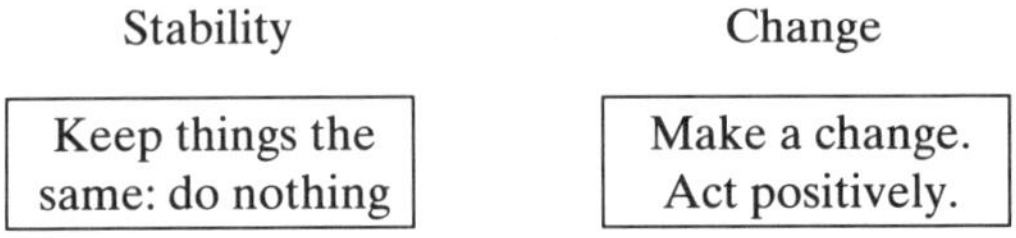

Stability	Change
Keep things the same: do nothing	Make a change. Act positively.

Fig. 7.1

sented with a choice (see Fig. 7.1). This choice is forced upon us where even doing nothing is a significant course of action (omission) that could influence the changing course of events. In such a case, there is no room left to opt out of deciding what to do. Even "doing nothing" may count as doing something, because it could preserve or disrupt the status quo, or have other significant consequences (see case 3.16, for example).

This type of reasoning in deliberation is especially prevalent on important topics of controversy that affect the conduct of one's life, yet where reasoned conviction is the best anyone can aspire to. For example, despite the uncertainties of political controversies, ethical convictions, religious beliefs, and legal evidence, nevertheless a person must decide how to vote, what ethical goals to adopt, whether to join a church, and what verdict to vote for when on a jury. All such living and momentous choices fall within the province of practical reasoning in deciding how to act in the world; to do nothing is, in effect, a kind of action that implies a certain stance on the issue.

The problem with all these kinds of decisions is that acting on the basis of presumptions by setting a burden of proof is inherently risky. One could turn out to be wrong. One conclusion that could be drawn from the observations that presumptive reasoning is essentially subjective and, by its nature, inherently unreliable to some extent, would be that acceptance of presumptions on pragmatic considerations rather than on strictly objective evidence is not rationally justifiable, or is even fallacious. This point of view would counsel that logical reasoning should never be based on presumptive opinion, for that opens the floodgates to mere rhetorical persuasion as a standard of good argument.

This conservative type of view could be based on W. K. Clifford's argument (1877) that belief should never be based on insufficient evidence: "[I]t is wrong always, everywhere, and for anyone, to believe anything upon insufficient evidence." From this viewpoint, any conclusion based on anything less than objective (and sufficient) evidence, cannot be rationally justified.

The difficulty inherent in this conservative viewpoint was well brought out, however, in William James's (1896) reply to Clifford's argument. James argued that such an extremely conservative view must stifle action, because reasonable action must be based on beliefs that are reasonable even if they cannot be confirmed, and must also undermine knowledge by leading to an unwarranted skepticism.

Some of the sting can be taken out of Clifford's repugnance with practical reasoning if it is acknowledged that: (i) objective evidence is to be given priority over presumptive reasoning where the former is available, and (ii) it is to be stressed that efforts to collect objective evidence are to be strongly encouraged when such evidence is available at reasonable cost and effort. Thus it should be clear that practical or presumptive considerations should be no substitute for objective evidence based on observation, experiment, or mathematical calculation.

Practical reasoning has to do with shifts in a reasoner's commitments in reasoned dialogue on issues that are controversial or practical, meaning that despite lack of access to deductive certainty or even probability, some presumptive conclusion must be acted upon. Such reasoning is inherently fragile, and therefore follows the principle of drawing a conclusion on the basis of a balance of considerations. Although you may be committed to a plan of actions, you must also be prepared to retract or change your goals. Therefore, the reasonable person must not stick to a plan too dogmatically in every situation. Hence the reasonable person will adhere to a plan *to some degree*—to a degree commensurate with the given knowledge base of the plan.

The plan can be identified with the arguer's position, or set of commitments in dialogue. A set of propositions can be adopted or accepted by conviction, on a disputable issue, where the real truth of the matter is not known, because to act on reasoned conviction, one must adopt a point of view or stance, as a basis for action or inaction. In the loaded gun example (case 3.14), the person doesn't know whether the gun is loaded or not, but he must act in some manner or other in the situation. Perhaps even if he leaves the gun alone, it could be dangerous. If so, it is better that he presumes it is (may be) loaded, and then carefully checks to see, all the time operating on the presumption that it is loaded.

Practical reasoning is a goal-directed sequence of linked practical inferences that seeks out a prudent line of conduct for an agent in a set of particular circumstances known by the agent. Where a is an agent, A an action, and G a goal, the two basic types of practical inferences are, respectively, the *necessary condition scheme* and the *sufficient condition scheme* (D. Walton, 1990b, 41).

G is a goal for *a*
Doing *A* is necessary for *a* to carry out *G*
Therefore, *a* ought to do *A*

G is a goal for *a*
Doing *A* is sufficient for *a* to carry out *G*
Therefore, *a* ought to do *A*

The second premise, in both types of inferences, is to be understood as relative to what *a* knows or reasonably takes to be the case, as far as he grasps the particular circumstances in the given case. These circumstances can change, and practical reasoning is therefore to be understood as a dynamic kind of reasoning that needs to be corrected or updated as new information comes in.

The concepts of necessary and sufficient conditions incorporated in the second premise need to be understood as typically flexible rather than strict relationships. Both need to be judged in relation to the given knowledge base of the agent, subject to exceptions and overriding circumstances that can come to light in a particular case. These are very special kinds of conditionals that have a special kind of logic in their own right (analyzed below, "Internal and External Burden of Proof").

The conclusion of a practical inference guides an agent to a prudent course of action, subject to the conditions set in the premises. The conclusion is a practical imperative directing the prudentially wise to do something, given the circumstances, as the agent sees them, expressed in the premises. If the agent is committed to the premises, then he ought (prudentially) to be committed to the course of action to which he is directed by the conclusion. Otherwise, his set of commitments is practically inconsistent.

As argumentation, practical reasoning is used in a context of dialogue. Most commonly, practical reasoning is used in deliberations, but it is also often used in advice-solicitation dialogues, and in critical discussions. Four kinds of critical questions function alongside a practical inference as a means of indicating a proper weight of commitment to be assigned to the conclusion in a given context of dialogue.

Q1:   Are there alternative ways (other than *A*) of realizing *G?*
Q2:   Is it possible for *a* to do *A?*
Q3:   Does *a* have goals other than *G* that should be taken into account?
Q4:   Are there other consequences of bringing about *A* that should be
       taken into account?

In weighing these critical questions against a practical inference in a given case, in a context of dialogue, burden of proof plays an important role. If the premises of a practical inference are well supported as reasonable commitments for an agent, a weight of presumption is thrown against a respondent who questions the practical validity of the practical inference in the given situation. To shift the burden back onto the proponent, the respondent must pose one or more of these appropriate critical questions. Thus practical reasoning has a kind of validity that should be judged in relation to the requirements of burden of proof in a given situation.

The kind of analysis of practical reasoning briefly outlined above and further developed and elaborated in D. Walton (1990b) makes room for the pragmatic view of presumption of the sort advocated by Perelman and Olbrechts-Tyteca (1969), Ullman-Margalit (1983a) and Clarke (1989).[1] Presumptions can be justified in reasoning, on a practical basis, on the grounds that it can enable the line of reasoning to go ahead, even in the absence of absolute knowledge of what will happen in a particular situation where some commitment to action or inaction needs to be made. Guidance toward a prudent course of action typically necessitates operating on presumptions that could turn out to be wrong, and drawing conclusions (tentatively) from these presumptions by practical inferences, even if such reasoning is a kind of careful guesswork.

Legal Burden of Proof

The best-known instance of the working of burden of proof in legal argumentation is the familiar requirement that the prosecutor in a criminal case must prove guilt "beyond reasonable doubt" to win its case. Then in such a case, the defense needs only show weakness in the prosecution's argument

---

1. Note the account of presumption in Leibniz in Dascal (1987, chap. 6).

in order to win its side of the case. The purpose of this set imbalance between the two sides of the argument in criminal cases is clear. In criminal cases, the evidence may be unclear or uncertain because it is based on the reconstruction of past events that must be conjectured. Since therefore there is the possibility of error, the goals of dialogue should be set up in such a way to minimize the conviction of innocent persons, even at the cost of letting guilty persons go free. The former is judged the greater injustice, and therefore the legal requirement of evidence is really based on an intent to safeguard against a particularly grave danger of injustice inherent in the system of argumentation.

Generally, the prosecution bears the burden of proof in criminal cases. According to legal scholars, this general requirement is an instance of the principle, "He who asserts must prove." And in civil cases, the plaintiff bears the burden of proof on more issues than the defendant. But there are many exceptions to these general rules (see Degnan, 1973, 914). An example would be contributory negligence, the doctrine that one injured through another's negligence cannot recover if his own negligence contributed to his injury. In some U.S. states, the plaintiff must prove his freedom from contributory negligence, while in England and other U.S. states, this proof is up to the defendant.

Legal rules of evidence are formulated generally for each type of case so that, in principle, both sides to the dispute should know at the outset where the burden of proof lies. There can be a shift in the burden of proof during the course of a trial, depending on the issues being argued. But how burden of proof changes with the advent of a specific issue is also determined by rules of evidence known at the outset of the case. For example, in a criminal case, the prosecution may have to prove guilt beyond reasonable doubt. But if the defendant pleads insanity, then the burden of proof is upon him to prove that he was insane at the time of the act at issue.

The party who bears the burden of proof in the law must produce a strong enough argument to permit a reasonable person to conclude that his contention is established. However, there are three recognized degrees of persuasion: (1) by preponderance of the evidence, (2) by clear and convincing evidence, and (3) beyond reasonable doubt (Degnan, 1973, 914).

Presumptions are legal devices that can be used to alter a burden of proof. A presumption is a rule that allows one proposition to be inferred from another. It is a kind of rule of plausible inference that states what can normally or customarily be deduced from a particular fact in an argument.

For example, if it can be shown as a fact that someone has disappeared without explanation or being heard of for more than seven years, it may be presumed that this person is dead. This presumption holds, however, only so far as it goes uncontradicted by further evidence of the person's being alive (Degnan, 1973, 914).

Presumptions in law usually occur where a proposition at issue would be difficult to prove. A presumption can lighten the burden of proof. Presumptions come into play in a recurring type of situation where normal expectations about an expected type of outcome in this situation can be defined or codified according to a preestablished standard.

The concept of a presumption in law is closely tied to the concept of burden of proof. Both of these factors can be set by the rules of evidence before a specific case is actually tried. Both factors can be important in determining, in a particular case, what is to count as a successful realization of the goal of dialogue by either side of the dispute. But how does burden of proof work in less strictly organized types of argumentation? Is it similar to the way it works in the law? It does seem to be similar in certain important respects because burden of proof is an important requirement in all persuasive reasoned dialogue. Yet many contexts are different. The goal of the criminal law is to determine guilt or innocence (responsibility). Other contexts of dialogue may not share this goal. Even so, certain general patterns stand out as common to all persuasive reasoned dialogue.

The burden of proof gets set, ideally, in reasoned dialogue, at the outset of the round of exchanges between the two participants. Each participant sets out his thesis, which is a proposition. By declaring a proposition as his thesis, a participant thereby incurs a burden or obligation of proof—meaning that he is obliged to offer proof, or at least evidence or backing, for this thesis, if challenged by the other participant in the argument. The ideal point in reasoned dialogue to set the burden of proof for both participants is at the beginning of the dialogue, at the initial stage of discussion.

Van Eemeren and Grootendorst (1984, 85) call this first stage *identifying the dispute,* where one participant advances a point of view, and another participant advances a different point of view, or casts doubt on the first point of view. Then the second stage of dialogue may be an attempt to resolve the dispute posed by the two different points of view, by subsequent discussion.

Rescher (1977, 27) also writes of a probative burden, set at the initiating stage of a dialectical situation, which then remains constant throughout the subsequent dialogue. Rescher (27) calls this type of burden the *initiating* or I-burden, which is characteristically "static, and rests with the inaugurating side constantly and throughout" the dialogue. In Rescher's analysis of reasoned dialogue, the burden of proof, once set for a proposition *A* in an argument, establishes a presumption that not-*A* stands, until the burden of proving *A* has been discharged (32).

Generalizing on these insights from Rescher, van Eemeren and Grootendorst, and legal rules of evidence, some basic principles can be set down.

Internal and External Burden of Proof

In reasoned dialogues generally, there are two ways in which burden of proof can be set. First, burden of proof is set *externally* by the rules of procedure and goals of dialogue set by the participants, or agreed to by them. The first item to be noted in a critical discussion is that each participant is required to have a thesis to be proved, and once this thesis is set, that participant has a burden of proof (obligation). His goal or obligation is simply to prove that thesis. However, particular types of dialogue, once identified, will also serve to sharpen formulation of the burden of proof for both sides. In a dispute, the burden of proof is equally distributed. In a weakly opposed difference of opinion, the burden of proof falls exclusively on one side.

External burden of proof is set at the global level of reasoned dialogue. External conventions affect arguments over the whole course of the dialogue, from beginning to end. From this perspective, the commitment rules of dialogue can be viewed as part of the external burden of proof requirement. For the commitment rules define, over the whole sequence of dialogue, whether an arguer is committed to a specific proposition, and whether, as a consequence, he is obliged to prove it if challenged.

In general, there are four factors that influence how burden of proof is set externally in reasoned dialogue: (1) the theses to be proved by the participants, (2) the rules of dialogue, especially the commitment rules, (3) the initial plausibility of the theses to be proved, and (4) presumptions required by special contexts of dialogue (e.g., safety). The fourth factor refers to special kinds of issues where there may be reason to set the burden of proof higher against one side. For example, a physician, in an emergency situation where the patient's life may be in danger, is expected to "err on the side of life" by acting to presume that there is a danger if the situation is not clear and the costs of acting to preserve life are acceptable. The general principle at work here is that of tutiorism, or taking the safer, known way for the purpose of safety where there is both risk and uncertainty.

Burden of proof is set *internally,* at the local level of dialogue, where requirements of proof or argument are set relative to one specific move, or pair of moves, in a sequence of dialogue. For example, the maxim "He who asserts must prove." may dictate that a participant who actively assents to a specific proposition may be called upon or challenged by another participant to prove or support that proposition. Or an asker of a question may be called upon to give evidence for presuppositions of the question. Of course, these are external commitment rules, but they can apply at the local level of one specific question-reply interchange. When they do, specific burdens of proof are set internally, and can be altered or shifted internally, at specific moves in the sequence of dialogue.

There can be different methods of setting the burden of proof externally in reasoned dialogue, and there is room for controversy on the subject of which is the best general method from a theoretical point of view on dialogue. Generally the goal of persuasive dialogue is to shift the burden of proof so that one's own side of the argument has become predominant. And in a dispute one participant's thesis is proved if, and only if, the other participant's thesis is refuted.

In an evenly matched dispute, the plausibility of each participant's thesis is roughly equal to the other. Hence any plausible argument newly advanced during the course of dialogue will tilt the burden of proof against one side by raising the plausibility of the other. Therefore, it might be proposed that whichever side has the higher plausibility at the end of the dialogue should be declared to have the winning (strongest) argument.

However, in dialogue on some controversial issues, the initial plausibility of the thesis on one side of the issue to be disputed may be much greater than that of the other. Thus the burden of proof is much heavier on one side than the other. Here, a different procedure for evaluating the respective merits of the arguments on both sides needs to be followed.

Several years ago there was a program shown on Canadian television called *The Great Debate.* At the beginning of the program, a controversial issue was stated, and two speakers were introduced, each of whom was slated to argue for one side of the issue. But before any debating began, the audience was asked to vote for whichever side of the issue each person at present accepted. This count was recorded, and then after the debate had taken place, another count was taken of each member of the audience's new position on the issue. Whichever direction the count had gone from the first voting to the second indicated the winner of the debate.

This suggests a different approach. It might be proposed that whichever side has altered the plausibility of his thesis to a higher plausibility at the end of the dialogue, from the level of plausibility set at the beginning of the dialogue, should be declared to have the winning (strongest) argument. Here the external burden of proof, set for the course of the game, is equal, even if the initial, apparent burden of proof set by the plausibility of each thesis at the outset of play, was unequal. The inequality of the relative plausibility of each disputant's thesis is offset by the rule that sets the goal of the dialogue.

In this type of persuasive dialogue, which could be called a *Pierre Berton dispute,* after the host of the program, the disputant wins who has the greatest positive difference between the initial plausibility value (at the first move) and the final plausibility value (at the last move) of the sequence of dialogue.

In a Pierre Berton dispute, each participant has two goals. One is to persuade the audience to accept his thesis as more plausible than they thought it to be at the outset of dialogue. The other is to induce a plausibility increase greater than that effected by the opponent's arguments.

One problem in formulating the requirement for burden of proof in a Pierre Berton dialogue is to deal with the cases where neither participant induces a net increase of plausibility, over the course of the dialogue, for his thesis. This could happen where both arguments are ineffective, and the plausibility value of each thesis remains the same at the final move as it was at the initial move. Or it could happen where one or both arguments are counterproductive and there is a drop in plausibility over the course of the argument.

The best way to deal with these cases is to rule that in each of them, the burden of proof requirement fails to be met. The reason behind this way of proceeding lies in the first goal of dialogue in a Pierre Berton dispute. The first goal is to persuade the audience to accept one's thesis as more plausible. And if this fails, the argument as a whole fails, and the burden of proof requirement should not be regarded as having been met.

Moving on to the cases where there is some increase in plausibility value for a thesis over the course of the dialogue, the burden of proof requirement is met by the disputant who induces the greatest net increase in plausibility. This requirement stems from the second goal of dialogue in a Pierre Berton dispute.

Pierre Berton Dispute

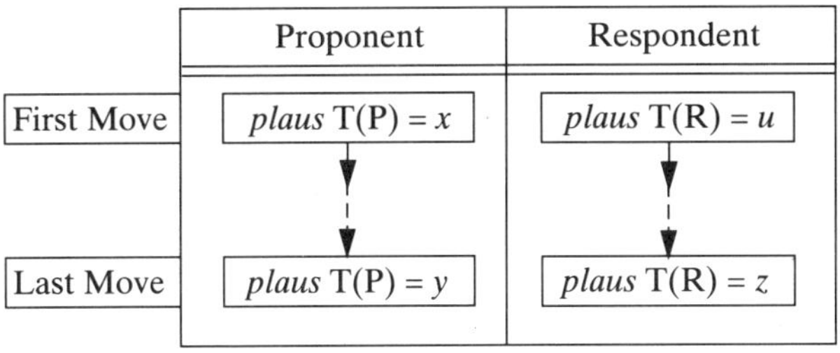

	Proponent	Respondent
First Move	*plaus* T(P) = x	*plaus* T(R) = u
Last Move	*plaus* T(P) = y	*plaus* T(R) = z

Fig. 7.2

Two technical conventions of burden of proof can make these rulings easier to carry out. One is to rule that if a participant either induces a decrease in plausibility for his thesis over the course of the argument, or induces no net increase, then the differential plausibility of his argument is given a value of zero. Then if one arguer is assigned a value of zero, for either of these reasons, any positive gain at all by the other will win the dispute. Here even a very weak argument could swing the burden to one side. A second useful rule is to declare the dispute a *tie* if the two differential plausibility values for each side are equal.

The burden of proof requirements for a Pierre Berton type of dialogue can be represented in relation to Figure 7.2 above, where $T(P)$ is the proponent's thesis, and $T(R)$ is the respondent's thesis. Generally, we are assuming that $x \geq 0$, $y \geq 0$, $u \geq 0$, and $z \geq 0$, to begin with. The arrows and dotted lines represent the sequence of moves during the course of the dialogue; *plaus* stands for "plausibility." Generally, it is a requirement that for any arguer to meet the burden of proof requirement, at least one of them must have a net plausibility increase of greater than zero. Given this is so, then whoever has the greater increase (if one does) wins the dispute. Thus the burden of proof requirement for each participant can be expressed as follows.

Proponent: $(y - x) > (z - u)$
Respondent: $(y - x) < (z - u)$

The direct opposition of these win-requirements makes it clearly evident that a Pierre Berton dialogue is indeed a dispute. For although both conditions can fail in the event of a tie, if either requirement is met the other cannot be.

A dialogue, as defined in Chapter 6, is an orderly sequence of exchanges between two participants where each participant has a goal and the dialogue, as a whole, has a goal. In some main types of dialogues that are especially important as contexts of argumentation the goal of one or both participants is to prove that a proposition is true.

The critical discussion is a dialogue of this type. The goal of a critical discussion (van Eemeren and Grootendorst, 1984) is to resolve a conflict of opinions. In a simple critical discussion, the goal of one participant is to prove that his thesis (point of view) is true (right), and the goal of the other participant is to raise doubts (critical questions). In the type of dialogue we call a dispute above, which van Eemeren and Grootendorst call the *compound critical discussion,* both participants have a thesis to be proved, and the one thesis is the opposite of the other.

Other types of dialogues, outlined in D. Walton (1989a, 10) include the information-seeking dialogue, where the goal is for information to be transmitted from the one participant to the other, and the negotiation dialogue, where the goal is for the parties to "make a deal" by dividing up some goods or interests that are in short supply.

The concept of an obligation applies to all types of dialogue. The obligation is the function the participant has to perform, according to the rules of the dialogue, in order to fulfill his goal in the dialogue. Burden of proof is a subcategory of obligation. In a type of dialogue, called a *probative dialogue,* where the goal of a participant is to prove (or disprove) something, his obligation is matched with a *weight,* a rough rating (heavy, medium, or light) which is an estimate of how difficult or easy it is to prove that particular proposition in the given context of dialogue.

Burden of proof can be thought of as a balance in a compound critical discussion. Where the burden of the one side is relatively light, the burden of the other side will be matchingly heavy (and vice versa), at the beginning (opening stage) of the dialogue (D. Walton, 1988).

A critical discussion (van Eemeren and Grootendorst, 1984, 85–87) has four stages: the opening stage, the confrontation stage, the argumentation stage, and the closing stage. The global (technical) burden of proof is set in the confrontation stage, and fixed for the duration of the discussion, through to the closing stage. However the local burden of proof (burden of proceedings) varies during the course of the discussion, depending on the type of speech act put forward by a participant at a particular move, and

Subarguments (Rounds) in the Argumentation Stage
of a Dialogue

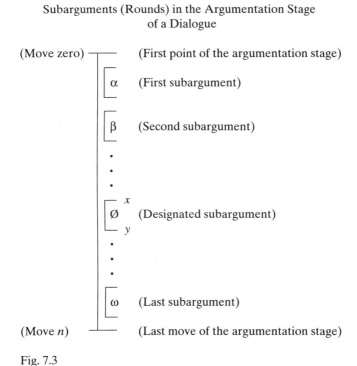

(Move zero) ⊤⎯⎯ (First point of the argumentation stage)

α (First subargument)

β (Second subargument)

.
.
.

x
Ø (Designated subargument)
y

.
.
.

ω (Last subargument)

(Move *n*) ⊥⎯⎯ (Last move of the argumentation stage)

Fig. 7.3

the state of his commitment-set at that move. The commitment-set of a
participant (Hamblin, 1970, 263), varies during the sequence of the dialogue.

The argumentation stage of a dialogue is best thought of as a sequence
of connected subarguments on both sides, as one side is pictured in Figure
7.3 above. The burden of proof is the obligation to prove the initial thesis,
set at the beginning of the dialogue. But this changes as the dialogue proceeds. Burden of proof, at the local level, depends not only on the argumentation scheme (type of argument) that has been put forward at that move,
but also on the sequence of argumentation the proponent has put forward
at prior moves. Depending on the strength of a participant's sequence of
argumentation at a particular point in the sequence of a dialogue, the burden of proof can shift toward the other participant, meaning that he must
reply with a correspondingly strong argument if he is to successfully fulfill
his obligation in the dialogue.

Burden of proof is an especially important and useful idea where conclusive resolution of a disputed issue by appeal to decisive evidence (knowledge) is not practical or possible. The problem, in such a case, is that the argumentation could go on and on, and never reach a resolution (see case 4.11, the *ad ignorantiam* tug-of-war, and its formal structure, profile 5.1). Burden of proof is a practical solution to this problem which works by setting a required weight of strength of argumentation as sufficient to prove (disprove) the contention, and thereby close the dialogue off from further argumentation.

At the global level, burden of proof can be set in various ways—by preponderance of evidence, by convincing evidence, or beyond reasonable doubt, for example—on a scale of increasing heaviness of the burden. At the local level, some ways of apportioning burden of proof are relatively clear; for example, "He who asserts must prove." In the case of speech acts other than assertions (e.g., questions), the apportionment of the burden may depend on many factors (such as the type of question) in judging whether the questioner or respondent is committed to presuppositions of the question.

But the most fundamental problem, for this chapter, is how the speech act of presumption is related to, or determined by the burden of proof. Traditionally these two notions have been thought of as partners, but the exact nature of their relationship has never been clearly defined. Indeed, presumption and burden of proof are often confused, or treated as the same thing. Can we help to clarify this situation?

The way to begin is to observe that presumptive reasoning often plays an important role in argumentation at a local level of a dialogue, represented by subargument φ in Figure 7.3. At this level, for example, there may be a weight of presumption in favor of a particular proposition that is brought forward in a dialogue, even if hard evidence, of the sort normally required to meet a burden of proof in that type of dialogue, is not forthcoming. Presumption at this level functions as a way of absolving or excusing a subargument from the usual demands of burden of proof.

Commitment and Burden Shifting

In refining Hamblin's notion of commitment in dialogue, we have to make two important distinctions between kinds of commitments. First, we need to distinguish between concessions and substantive commitments. A *substantive commitment* is a proposition that a participant in dialogue is obliged to defend, or retract, if challenged by the other party to give reasons to support it. In a word, it has a burden of proof attached to it. This is the type of commitment to a proposition that goes along with having asserted it in a dialogue. A *concession* is a commitment where there is no such obligation to defend, if challenged. Concessions are assumptions agreed to "for the sake of argument." By nature, they are temporary, and do not necessarily represent an arguer's position in a dialogue (Hamblin, 1970; 1971).

Second, we need to distinguish between explicit commitments and implicit commitments. The commitment-set of each participant in a dialogue is divided into two sides: a light side, a set of propositions known, or on view, to all the participants; and a dark side, a set of propositions not known to, or visible to, some or all of the participants. This dark-side set represents the implicit commitments of a participant in a dialogue. These are propositions that he is committed to, but has not explicitly agreed to, or otherwise given a clear indication in the dialogue of his commitment to them.[2] They have to be guessed, or plausibly conjectured from what we know about the nature of his explicit commitments, as they have become apparent in the dialogue.

Case 7.2

> For example, if George has been consistently socialist in a dialogue, so far, and shows plenty of evidence of being a committed socialist, we can make plausible conjectures about his commitments on an issue on which he has, so far in the dialogue, expressed no explicit opinions, e.g. on how to finance the postal service. Although he has not explicitly committed himself to the proposition that the postal service should be funded by the government, and we do not know that he is committed to this proposition on the evidence of the dialogue, still, we can conjecture that he is likely to be committed to it, as a presumption inferred from what we know of his position so far. (Walton and Krabbe, 1995)

2. D. Walton (1984; 1992c) and Walton and Krabbe (1995) give accounts of dark-side commitments.

The games CAVE and CAVE+ in Walton (1989b, 296–311) have this dark-side commitment feature, and the reader who wishes a fuller exposition of how the rules of a dialogue incorporate this notion can find some answers there. Suffice it to note here that many of an arguer's commitments in argumentation are not explicitly stated, or agreed to as such, in a dialogue, and therefore have to be inferred or conjectured, on a provisional or presumptive basis. Otherwise, we could not make sense of ordinary argumentation in everyday conversations based on unexpressed premises and other kinds of important but unstated presumptions.

Given these distinctions then, how can we give a clear and useful account of the distinction between presumption and burden of proof? What is the essential difference between these two concepts?

Presumption is clearly connected to burden of proof in argumentation, but how? To begin with, we should note the difference between (pure) supposition and assertion as kinds of speech acts. Assertion always carries with it a burden of proof, because assertion implies substantive commitment to the proposition asserted. Supposition (or assumption) however, requires only the agreement of the respondent, and carries with it no burden of proof on either side. Presumption, as a speech act, is halfway between (mere) supposition and assertion. Presumption essentially means that the proponent of the proposition in question does not have a burden of proof, only a burden to disprove contrary evidence, should it arise in the future sequence of dialogue. The burden here has three important characteristics: it is a future, conditional, and negative burden of proof. It could perhaps be called a burden to rebut, in appropriate circumstances.

Presumption is functionally opposed to burden of proof, meaning that presumption removes or absolves one side from the burden, and shifts the burden to the other side. In this respect, presumption functions as a speech act in dialogue as a switching of roles of the two participants. Fallacies can arise, however, because this shifting back and forth can be tricky.

One fallacy that can be explained in relation to this shifting of the burden of proof from one party to the other in a dialogue is *petitio principii,* the fallacy of circular reasoning or begging the question. If the proponent of a thesis *A* in a critical discussion has the burden of proving *A,* but then puts *A* forward as a presumption in the discussion, his argument is circular. He is "begging the question" in the sense that he is begging the respondent to accept, as a presumption (i.e., without proof), a proposition that he is obliged to prove. This type of move is dialectically incoherent, in the sense that the arguer asks to be granted, without having to prove it, a proposition he is supposed to be proving.

The fallacy of begging the question is actually much more complicated than this simple sketch of it indicates, when it comes to the interpretation and evaluation of particular cases. But even this bare conceptual sketch of the basis of the fallacy shows that burden of proof is different from presumption. The existence of the fallacy of begging the question as a fallacy proves that there is a difference, in general, between burden of proof and presumption. The fallacy is precisely the fusing (or confusing) of the difference between these two things.

Whately (1846; 1963, 113), as noted above, saw astutely how failure to be attuned to shifts in a burden of proof in argumentation can be disastrous in allowing one party unfairly to get the best of another in an exchange. Ignorance of such matters can be a major tactical failure in argumentation. Whately, in case 2.8, compared it to the case of troops in a fort who are strong enough to defend it against all attacks, but foolishly sally forth to engage the enemy in the field, and are defeated. Whately (case 2.8), asked us to imagine a case where a person who, confronted with an unsupported accusation, tries to prove his own innocence by collecting all the facts he can muster, instead of defying his accuser to prove the charge. Such a reply would be ineffective, and even rouse a strong suspicion of guilt by appearing too defensive. The attacked person has overlooked his strongest weapon of defense—the burden of proof. The problem is that the attacker falsely appears to have the weight of presumption on his side, to the extent that the underlying shift in the burden of proof has gone unnoticed.

It is this kind of tricky, unperceived, and unlicensed shift in a burden of proof in a speech act of presumption in dialogue that underlies the working mechanism behind other fallacies as well, like the *ad ignorantiam* and the fallacy of many questions, as we have seen. In the next section, a set of speech act conditions defining the movement and sequencing in the functioning of presumption in dialogue are given. This set of conditions shows how the back-and-forth shifting of presumption should work as a speech act in any sequence of argumentative dialogue generally. In conjunction with the requirements for a particular type of dialogue in a given case, this set of conditions can be used as a general framework for evaluating presumptive reasoning.

Speech Act Conditions Defining Presumption

In the speech act analysis of presumption given by the twelve conditions below, presumption is understood as a kind of speech act that is halfway between assertion and (mere) assumption. An assertion normally carries with itself in argumentation a burden of proof: "He who asserts must prove!" By contrast, if a participant in argumentation puts forward a (mere) assumption, she (or anyone in the dialogue) is free to retract it at any subsequent point in the dialogue without having to give evidence or reasons that would refute it. Assumptions are freely undertaken and can freely be rejected in a dialogue.

Presumptions are between these other two types of speech acts somewhere. A presumption is a proposition put in place as a commitment tentatively in argumentation to facilitate the goals of a dialogue. Presumptions are often put forward for practical reasons, to enable the dialogue or an action to go ahead, even if there is a lack of hard evidence that would confirm or refute the proposition in question definitively, one way or the other.

The key thing about the speech act of presumption in argumentation, according to the analysis given below, is that it reverses the burden of proof in a dialogue. More generally speaking, presumption reverses the roles of the two participants in argumentation. Normally, the burden to prove is on the one who asserts a proposition A in argumentation, as something he is committed to in the dialogue. However, when a presumption is brought forward by a proponent, the burden is on the respondent to refute it, or otherwise it goes into place as a commitment.

The basic idea is that a dialogue is an extended (global) sequence of exchanges of speech acts that has a goal-directed overall structure. But within this global structure there are "rounds" or subarguments that are woven together into the larger fabric of the dialogue. For example, a dialogue could be a critical discussion of whether the practice of tipping is generally a good thing or not, and a subargument within the larger dialogue could be a discussion of whether or not tipping creates some problems for fairly assessing income tax.

The idea is that a presumption stays in place for a certain number of moves in a dialogue, but is not a permanent or nonretractable commitment for either party that must stay in place for the whole duration of the dialogue. Typically, a presumption stays in place long enough for the participants to finish the round of argumentation in which they are currently engaged. In order to be useful, presumptions must have a certain amount of "sticking power," but by their nature, they are tentative and subject to later retraction.

In the analysis below, a summary of the fuller account given in D. Walton (1992c), I shall speak of the subargument as a "round," a sequence of argumentation that can be isolated as having a structure (premises, conclusions, inferences) of its own. This round provides a useful place, a localized setting, where a presumption can be set in place, during the opening moves of the round. We will call the actual point at which a presumption is brought forward for consideration "move x." The round also has a duration, lasting to a move or point y, where the presumption can be given up or cancelled.

I. Preparatory Conditions
    1. There is a context of dialogue that involves two participants, a proponent and a respondent.
    2. The dialogue provides a context within which a sequence of reasoning could go forward with a proposition A as a useful assumption in the sequence.

II. Placement Conditions
    1. At some point x in the sequence of dialogue, A is brought forward by the proponent, either as a proposition he explicitly asks the respondent to accept for the sake of argument, or as a nonexplicit assumption that is part of the proponent's sequence of reasoning.
    2. The respondent has an opportunity at x to reject A.
    3. If the respondent fails to reject A at x, then A becomes a commitment of both parties during the subsequent sequence of dialogue.

III. Retraction Conditions
    1. If, at some subsequent point y in the dialogue $(x < y)$, any party wants to rebut A as a presumption, then that party can do so, provided she can give a good reason for doing so. Giving a good reason means showing that the circumstances of the particular case are exceptional, or that new evidence has come in that falsifies the presumption.
    2. Once having accepted A at x, however, the respondent is obliged to let the presumption A stay in place during the dialogue for a sufficient time to allow the proponent to use it for his purposes of

argumentation (unless a good reason for rebuttal under clause III.1 above can be given).

IV. Burden Conditions

1. Generally, at point x, the burden of showing that A has some practical value as a useful presumption in a sequence of argumentation is on the proponent who proposes to use A as a presumption in his argument.

2. Past point x in the dialogue, once A is in place as a working presumption (either explicitly or implicitly) the burden is on the respondent to rebut the presumption by giving a good reason for rejecting it.

These essential conditions for the speech act of presumption in dialogue make it clear that the key idea is the shifting of the burden of rebuttal. At a particular point in the dialogue, the participants switch roles. The burden was first on the proponent, but then at this particular point, the burden of providing a good reason shifts to the respondent.

The basic way that a presumption operates in a dialogue is to give the argument some provisional basis for going ahead, even in the absence of firm premises known to be true. Once the presumption is lodged into place, the respondent is temporarily obliged to leave it in place for a while, giving the proponent a fair chance to draw conclusions using it as a premise. How firm a weight of commitment is put into place in such a lodging depends on the type of dialogue, and other global factors, such as the burden of proof, as well as local requirements defined by the type of argumentation scheme used at the local level. But quite generally, in any of the contexts of dialogue suitable as frameworks for argumentation as considered above, this set of speech act conditions for presumption shows how the shifting back and forth of presumptive argumentation should work. Thus it provides a general normative framework for the use of presumptive reasoning in dialogue that can help in the determination of certain kinds of argumentation as fallacious or nonfallacious.

Presumptions and Presuppositions

Presumption is a notion that is fundamental to philosophy as a subject, but has generally been ignored as a concept for serious investigation. In contrast, presupposition is a concept that has been studied in great intensity by both philosophers and linguists, resulting in a prolific variety of different theories, summarized by Levinson (1983). Both concepts can be put to use for varying purposes, and there is some flexibility in how they can be interpreted. Consequently, it is not easy to tell the two apart, or to firmly fix their key differences. It seems that, in many cases, they refer to roughly the same thing. Given the existing literature, it is especially hard to say what presupposition is, briefly, with much confidence.

However, in what follows, a brief sketch is given of what is taken to be the key differences between the concept of presumption that is the target of analysis for this chapter, and the broad notion of presupposition that seems—if not very clearly—to have emerged as a technical term in linguistics and the philosophy of language.

Presupposition relates to a specific type of speech act and the appropriate type of response when that type of speech act is used in a dialogue. It is not so much a question of burden of proof, or of bringing forward evidence, but of what happens to the respondent's commitments when he gives the normal or appropriate type of response in a dialogue.

Case 7.3

> For example, the concept of a presupposition of a question can be defined pragmatically as follows. A presupposition of a question asked by a proponent in dialogue with a respondent is any proposition the respondent becomes committed to in giving any direct answer to the question. For example, a presupposition of "Have you stopped cheating on your income tax?" is the proposition "You (the respondent) have cheated on your income tax." It is a presupposition because no matter which direct answer the respondent gives, the preferred answer (yes), or the nonpreferred answer (no), he becomes committed to that proposition (Walton, 1989a, chap. 1).

The proposition that the respondent has cheated on his income tax could also be described as a presumption of the proponent's question, meaning that once the respondent commits himself to it by giving a direct answer, a burden is put on him to then disprove it, if he decides that he no longer accepts it.[3] And in general, presuppositions can often be described or explained

3. Recall the analysis of case 3.18 given by Reiter (1987).

as presumptions. But there is a key difference. When you describe a proposition as a presupposition, the essential thing is not the burden of proof, or the shifting of it from one party to the other, as it is in a presumption.

Presupposition has to do with the order in which propositions put forward by a proponent in a dialogue are taken on as commitments by a respondent. With the income tax question above, the problem is that asking it in a dialogue, in such a way that a direct answer can be given, presumes (prior to this, in the logical sequence of dialogue) that the respondent has already committed himself to the proposition that he has cheated on his income tax. But this may or may not be the case. If it is the case, there may be no problem. But if it is not the case in the real context of dialogue in a given, particular instance of the asking of this question, there could be a serious problem. The fallacy of many questions (complex question) could have been committed.

Of course, the respondent can always reply: "Your question has a false presupposition; I have never cheated on my income tax!" In other words, he could refuse to give a direct answer by questioning, or objecting to the question. In most ordinary contexts of conversation, fortunately, this option is available.

But if there is textual evidence from the context of dialogue that the proponent is adopting a tactic of trying to seal off this option, or badger the respondent into not taking advantage of it, this is precisely the type of context where the charge that he is committing the fallacy of many questions is appropriate.

Case 7.4

> In a familiar type of case of everyday conversation (for example, in asking directions), the speaker is operating on the presumption that the proposition advanced by the respondent is right or reliable. But he is not thereby (necessarily) presupposing that the answer will be right. Nor is it a presupposition of his question "Which way to room C300?" that the answer given by the respondent is right. The proponent waits until he gets the answer, and then if it seems reasonable, and there is no reason to question it, or think it is wrong, he goes ahead and presumes that it is (plausibly) right.

This shows a difference between presumption and presupposition, because the questioner is not presupposing that the answer is right, in asking his question.

The question has presuppositions, it is true. For example, the question presupposes that room C300 exists, that there is a way to get there, and so forth. These can also be described as presumptions inherent in the asking of the question. But although the questioner presumes that the answer given is correct or reliable, it is not (necessarily) the case that he, or his question, presupposes that the answer given is correct or reliable. That would only be the case if the proponent (questioner) had some reason, to which he was committed previously, to believe that this particular respondent was a particularly reliable source, who could be trusted to give a correct answer (conclusively defeat) the conditional generalization. This property does not work for the default (defeasible) conditional, or at least we cannot assume that it applies in all cases. It only works in the case where the individual is typical of some reliable type of source. But one has to be open-minded (not rigid) here, because there is the open possibility, which we may discover in the future, that the individual is not typical in some significant way.

Default conditionals are inherently pragmatic because they must be evaluated in relation to a given type of dialogue, and the goals for that type of dialogue, which impose practical requirements on commitments in argumentation, including prior requirements of global burden of proof. As Rescher (1977, 6) put it, the kind of conditional involved here is "provisoed" to how things go "normally" or "naturally," subject to dialectical countermoves that could possibly defeat it in the future course of a disputation. Rescher concludes (19) that the logic of this defeasible type of conditional has to be evaluated in relation to a sequencing of moves and countermoves in an organized argumentative exchange of disputation.

The kind of exceptive argumentation or defeasible reasoning involved in the *secundum quid,* modeled using the default conditional as a major premise, it seems, can be reasonable in some cases, fallacious in others. A common problem with presumptive reasoning is that it is pressed ahead too aggressively or dogmatically by an arguer who appears to forget its provisional nonmonotonic nature, and dogmatically fails to retract it, even when evidence to rebut it has come into the dialogue.

Implications for Argumentation and Fallacies

Much more remains to be learned about presumptive reasoning, but what we have learned in this chapter about its leading characteristics has fundamental implications for the project of analyzing informal fallacies as types of errors of reasoning, and for the project of the normative evaluation of argumentation generally. In the past, presumptive reasoning has been too often and severely condemned and neglected as inherently untrustworthy, erroneous, or even fallacious. Surprisingly, it has often been cast aside as being of little or no importance to philosophy.

Presumptive reasoning should be understood as inherently nonmonotonic, in the sense that it is always subject to revision or correction on the basis of new information that may come in at some future point. This means that nonmonotonic reasoning is often circular, in the sense that the new information introduced by the particular circumstances of a given case at issue often provides feedback, subjecting a conclusion based on presumptive inference to correction or enrichment. This circularity of reasoning is not necessarily a fallacious circularity, however (D. Walton, 1991a). In fact, it is characteristic of the self-correcting aspect of presumptive reasoning generally. Here, we have to overcome the prejudice against circular reasoning as being inherently fallacious.

In some cases of default reasoning, a list of kinds of exceptions can be well-defined. For example, in the Tweety case (case 3.7), we may have a list of the nonflying birds, including penguins, ostriches, and so forth. But in other cases, new information could come in that could not have been anticipated on any list of standard exceptions. Tweety may be a canary, normally a flying type of bird, but in fact, it could be that Tweety has an injured wing. Thus the presumptive conditional must generally be regarded as an open-ended generalization that is subject to unanticipated objections in a given case. Hence the job of evaluating presumptive reasoning is inherently pragmatic, in that it depends on the particular circumstances of a given case, as far as these are known, to a given point. This context-sensitivity and openness to revision is also characteristic of practical reasoning generally—a kind of reasoning that takes as its object an inherently variable situation unfolding in time.

As we have seen, there are many different kinds of basis for making presumptions, and it is also true that the evidence for judging a presumptive inference as successful (correct, justified, acceptable) or not are inherently pragmatic, fitting a context of dialogue. First, it depends on the type of dialogue involved (e.g., a critical discussion). Second, it depends on the speech act. Presumption is a type of speech act, but presumptions are also put forward in questions, arguments, and other kinds of speech acts. Third, it depends on the stage of the dialogue the speech act occurs in; here we have been concentrating on the argumentation stage primarily. Fourth, it depends on the burden of proof, on the conditions for the speech act of presumption in the given context of dialogue, and generally on the obligations of the proponent and respondent of the presumption. Fifth, it depends on the information given in the text of discourse of a dialogue explicitly, or on information that can be inferred by conventions of politeness and implicature from the given discourse. Thus judging presumptive reasoning often depends on expectations and contentions of politeness that are not explicitly stated in discourse.

Generally, presumptive reasoning can be seen as a forward-moving sequence in a dialogue; Figure 7.4 outlines the sequence. At the choice point, the inference goes forward or not, subject to default. And then, even when the inference succeeds and the conclusion is drawn, that conclusion remains subject to possible future defeat by new circumstances that may arise. As portrayed here, presumptive reasoning is neither deductive nor inductive in nature, but represents a third distinct type of reasoning of the kind classified by Rescher (1976) as *plausible reasoning,* an inherently tentative kind of reasoning subject to defeat by the special circumstances (not defined inductively or statistically) of a particular case. Rescher also sees this kind of reasoning as inherently dialectical in nature, meaning that it needs to be judged in a context of dialogue. The recognition of this third type of reasoning has important and fundamental implications for the analysis of informal fallacies. Cases 7.3 and 7.4 show how the *argumentum ad ignorantiam* can be a reasonable argument based on presumptive reasoning from data that is not known explicitly or given explicitly, in positive form, as part of a given knowledge base. The fact that a particular proposition is *not* in a knowledge base can sometimes license a presumptive inference to a negative conclusion. We can presume that a particular proposition is false, on the grounds that it is not known to be true. As an instance of presumptive, nonmonotonic reasoning, such an inference can be reasonable. Hence, we cannot take it for granted that the *argumentum ad ignorantiam* is a fallacy.

The fallacy of many questions turns on the order in which a sequence of questions should reasonably be asked and answered in a dialogue. It is a question of the order in which a logically connected sequence of commitments should be taken on or rebutted by a respondent. The problem type of case, like "Have you stopped cheating on your income tax?" concerns a complex question that combines several commitments in the one question. The problem arises when a question is posed aggressively, in a manner that incorporates a tactic of preempting an affirmative response to taking on a commitment that the respondent should have an opportunity to reject. The

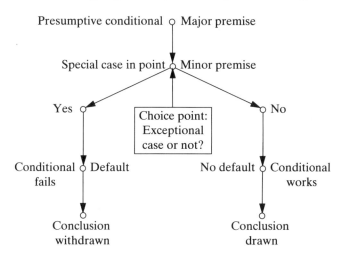

Fig. 7.4

problem revealed here is that presumptions need to be put forward in an open-ended way that allows for defeasibility in the future sequence of dialogue. Closed ways of putting them forward can go against their nonmonotonic nature, which demands certain requirements on how they should be used correctly and reasonably in a context of dialogue. As case 3.18 showed, these requirements are tied to communicative conventions of dialogue that license presumptive inferences.

Cases 7.1, 7.2, 7.3, and 7.4 show how common presumptive reasoning is in everyday conversations, persuasive arguments, and practical reasoning. Seen as an instance of presumptive inference to a defeasible conclusion, often as a provisional basis for prudent action in the absence of hard knowledge, the *argumentum ad verecundiam,* that traditional fallacy, can now be revealed as a type of argumentation that is, in many cases, quite reasonable and nonfallacious. Although drawing conclusions based on testimony of a reliable source has not been given its due as a type of reasoning in traditional logic, viewed as a species of presumptive reasoning, it can be seen in a new light. From this new point of view, there is less of a tendency to condemn it reflexively as fallacious, without carefully examining the given circumstances of a particular case.

Finally, the *secundum quid* fallacy is the major fallacy that highlights the need to see presumptive reasoning as a distinctive type of reasoning in its own right, with its own distinctively pragmatic standards and requirements. Making sense of the fallacy of *secundum quid* requires coming to grips with case-based reasoning which is dependent on argumentation that weighs the similarity of one case to another (argument from analogy), and that takes into account shifts in the weight of presumption derived from the special features of a particular case.

Hedging, as defined by Fogelin (1978, 42) is a tactic for protecting arguments from attack by weakening one's commitment, say, from "all" to "most" to "typically," or from "certainly" to "probably" to "presumably." In principle, hedging is legitimate in argumentation. It is not inherently fallacious. But as a critic, you have to look at each individual case carefully. In some cases, the overly defensive, evasive instances of hedging can be the opposite type of error from the fallacy of *secundum quid.* It is the opposite failure from dogmatic rigidity.

In case 7.1, the physician would be committing the *secundum quid* fallacy if he were to persist in arguing that Bob must take medication *M,* because it is the prescribed treatment for patients in Bob's condition, even after it was told to him that Bob's (apparent) father had condition *X.* But the physician did not commit this fallacy, because he reasoned appropriately, once this information came in. And then again, showing an appropriate flexibility, he changed the course of his presumptive reasoning, once Alice brought forward new information again about Bob's paternity. Now the operative presumption in the case is that Bob's father, whoever he is, presumably does not have condition *X,* as far as anyone privy to the discussion knows. In this case, the physician kept changing the conclusion, and the presumptive reasoning leading to it, but this was not inappropriate or fallacious hedging. Nor was it reasoning that committed the *secundum quid* fallacy. It represented a "middle way" of reasoning appropriately in line with the known or presumed circumstances of the given case.

There is still much to learn about case-based reasoning, but it is clear that this type of reasoning is typically presumptive and practical in nature, its major faults and failures inherently dialectical in nature.

The Maieutic Function of Dialogue

The question of how far we should admit presumptive reasoning into logic, as being a kind of reasoning that can be legitimate and correct, in at least some instances, is bound to remain controversial. Positivists, or those inclined toward a positivistic viewpoint, feel that the only kind of really good reasoning, that should be recognized or supported by logicians as respectable, is reasoning based on hard evidence, of the kind recognized in scientific methodology. Those who are inclined to evaluate reasoning from this point of view remain very suspicious about presumptive opinion-based reasoning, no matter how carefully it is pointed out that presumptions do have a genuine relationship to hard evidence—admittedly a negative, conditional relation via the *argumentum ad ignorantiam* to future evidence, should it arise in an argument. Positivists are still inclined to reject, or to be suspicious about presumptive reasoning, because the real basis of its justification is more practical than cognitive in nature.

Those of us in the field of informal logic and argumentation study, however, are increasingly inclined toward accepting presumptive reasoning, as, in principle, a legitimate kind of reasoning, even though we recognize its potential for error and abuse in fallacies, in some cases. The basic reason we are so inclined is that we can see that so much of the practical reasoning used in everyday conversations is inherently presumptive in nature. To turn our backs on this kind of reasoning is simply to perpetuate our ignorance of how practical reasoning is used in everyday conversations of all sorts, including political debates, ethical disputes, legal argumentation, and even philosophical argumentation. Most important, the recognition and analysis of presumptive reasoning has been shown here to be a required step toward the reasoned evaluation of the kinds of arguments traditionally classified as informal fallacies.

Proper evaluation of presumptive reasoning requires a flexible tolerance, a readiness to acknowledge and correct errors and biases, and finally, an appreciation of the finer shades of meaning and shifts of presumption in argumentation. The positivist point of view is more absolutistic and "black and white," tending to see presumptive reasoning as inherently sloppy, vague, or subjective, and trying to eliminate such hedging wherever possible. Unfortunately, too heavy a leaning toward the positivistic view in affairs of everyday life tends toward the kind of rigidity, prejudice, and dogmatism that does not deal very well with the exceptions and irregularities commonly encountered in practical reasoning in the real world of changing circumstances in a particular case. But this rigidity is typically the very sort of dogmatic attitude in dialogue that is associated with committing fallacies of the kind we have examined. It is hard to live with presumptive reasoning, but harder still to live without it.

One of the most trenchant and fundamental criticisms of presumptive reasoning as a method of arriving at a conclusion is that argument on a controversial issue can go on and on, back and forth, without a decisive conclusion ever being determined by the argument. The only defense against this criticism lies in the use of the concept of the burden of proof within reasoned dialogue. Once a burden of proof is set externally, then it can be determined, after a finite number of moves in the dialogue, whether the burden has been met or not. Only by this device can we forestall an argument from going on indefinitely, and thereby arrive at a definite conclusion for or against the thesis at issue.

Admittedly this way of arriving at a conclusion could be viewed as a form of *argumentum ad ignorantiam,* but of course it does not follow that all argumentation of this type is fallacious or erroneous. It does show that such argumentation is very often, and typically, a species of practical reasoning.

Argument in a critical discussion has to do with shifts in the burden of proof according to the rules of dialogue. These rules may include specific rules for deductive argument, inductive argument, presumptive argument, and other procedural rules of asking questions and replying to them. There are many special contexts of dialogue, but we still need to ask, Is there some deeper, fundamental purpose of reasonable persuasion dialogue? And if so, What is its principal benefit? Why evaluate practical reasoning as correct in many cases if it is so notoriously subject to fallacies, errors, and subtle shifts that can easily lead us astray?

It is a natural presumption that the most significant benefit of critical discussion—where the goal of dialogue is for the one participant to convince or persuade the other by reasonable argument—is the insight, or information increment, produced by the dialogue in the one to whom the argument is directed. Thus if I become convinced of some proposition I was not previously committed to, by your argument, then the value or benefit of the dialogue has been my increased understanding, awareness, or insight with regard to my own position in the argument. Good dialogue has altered my position, and thereby deepened, refined, or articulated that position in some positive way.

However, it may be less often recognized that there may be an important benefit of argumentative dialogue for the one who has advanced the reasoned argument, as well as the benefit gained by the recipient. For by constructing and successfully mounting the reasoned argument, the arguer may have also succeeded in refining and articulating his own position. Sometimes at the outset of argument, an arguer's position may be clear in some respects, but murky and shapeless in others, and through the process of having to defend his position against an opponent's queries and criticisms, that position may be more clearly and broadly defined. This clarifying, called the *maieutic function* of dialogue, can give the arguer significant insight into his own position.

This description of reasoned dialogue as a process of deepened insight into one's own position on a controversial issue is consistent with the Socratic view of dialogue as a means to attain self-knowledge. For Socrates, the process of learning was an ascent from the depths of the cave toward the clearer light of self-knowledge through the process of reasoned, and primarily verbal, dialogue with another discussant, on controversial issues. What Socrates emphasized as the most important benefit or gain of dialogue was self-knowledge. It was somehow through the process of articulation and testing of one's best arguments against an able opponent in dialogue that real knowledge was to be gained.

This Socratic point of view draws our attention to the more hidden and subtle benefit of critical discussion. Not only does it enable one to persuade an opponent or coparticipant rationally in discussion; it is also the vehicle that enables one to come to understand better one's own position on important issues, one's own reasoned basis behind one's deeply held convictions. It is the concept of burden of proof that makes such shifts of rational persuasion possible, and thereby enables dialogue to, as Locke put it, prepare the way for knowledge. We recall from Chapter 2, Locke's contention that the *argumentum ad ignorantiam* could "dispose . . . for the reception of truth," even though it does not actually establish knowledge directly. One way to explain how this "disposing" works is through the maieutic function of arguing in a critical discussion with an able opponent in an adversarial testing of arguments to see which party has the stronger weight of presumption on his side.

8

Identification and Analysis of the Argument

In this chapter, we take the first steps of identifying the *ad ignorantiam* as a distinctive type of argument that has an identifiable form or structure we call an argument scheme. Having done this, we go on to analyze how the argument is used correctly or reasonably, to make a contribution to the different types of dialogue, or normative models of argument identified in Chapter 6.

Characteristics of the Argument from Ignorance

What is most characteristic generally of the *argumentum ad ignorantiam* as a distinctive type of argument is its negative logic: it goes from a premise that *A* is not known to be true (false), to an opposite conclusion that *A* is false (true). But this negative logic breaks down into several subparts. First, every argument from ignorance starts from a lack-of-knowledge (lack of proof, lack of evidence, failure to establish) premise that is inherently negative. It is inherently negative in the sense that the negation operator goes before (and governs) the knowledge claim.

Krabbe (1994, 4) calls this characteristic "reasoning from a premise of ignorance." In his notation, where E is some "positive" epistemic (knowledge-related) operator, a premise of ignorance of the form $\neg EA$ or $\neg E \neg A$ is characteristic of the general form of the argument from ignorance. As we saw in Chapter 5, we must be careful not to confuse this form with $E \neg A$, which is not the same as reasoning from a premise of ignorance. Despite the presence of the negation symbol, this form of premise is actually a species of reasoning from a premise of knowledge (knowledge that something is not the case).

Perhaps this characteristic is the reason why the expression *argumentum ad ignorantiam* (*ad* meaning "to") is sometimes called the argument *from* ignorance, and sometimes the appeal *to* ignorance. It is the premise of ignorance that the argument begins *from* or appeals *to* that defines it. But contrary to what you might expect, the Latin *argumentum ad ignorantiam* literally means "argument *to* ignorance." Would it be perhaps more accurate or consistent to start calling it the *argumentum ab ignorantia,* as does Rescher (1980, 66)? This translation can be a source of confusion, because, in the presumptive use, arguments from ignorance are also arguments to (or toward) ignorance in the sense that the conclusion is only inferred tentatively, subject to default (in the absence of knowledge).

At any rate, the second characteristic of the *argumentum ad ignorantiam* (or *ab,* if you prefer) is the presence of the conditional or search premise, of the form "If A were true (false), it would be known to be true (false)." These two types of premise, the premise of ignorance and the search premise, are the two basic components of the *argumentum ad ignorantiam.*

But then it is how the two are put together to generate a conclusion that fully defines the argument from ignorance as a distinctive species of argumentation. The presence of some knowledge (usually incomplete), is combined with the absence of other knowledge (i.e., ignorance) to draw a conclusion about the significance of this lack of knowledge or missing knowledge. This inference takes a *modus tollens* form, as we saw in Chapter 3: if A were true (false), A would be known to be true (false) but A is not known to be true, therefore A is false (true). These three components, the ignorance premise, the search premise, and the *modus tollens* inference, characterize the *argumentum ad ignorantiam* as a distinctive species of argument.

As we saw in Chapter 3, the problem of identifying the *argumentum ad ignorantiam* is nontrivial. Students first learning about this fallacy tend to start finding it everywhere, and sometimes think they spot a fallacy of *argu-*

mentum ad ignorantiam where the argument in the given case is not really of this type. One further case will illustrate this subtlety of identification.

In this case, Karen and Doug were riding their bikes past a house in an adjoining neighborhood that had been up for sale for quite a long time.

Case 8.1

Karen: I wonder if that place ever sold.
Doug: Well, the sign is no longer up there.

This is perhaps an instance of an argument from negative evidence, because the premise is based on the observation of no sign being there. Formerly, a sign had (positively) been there for a long time. But it is not really an *argument from ignorance,* as defined above, because the premise is of the form $E \neg A$, i.e. Doug made the positive observation of something not being the case (the sign not being there). It's not a case where it is appropriate to say that we don't know the sign is there.

It might be fair enough, however, to identify this case as an instance of the argument to ignorance, on the grounds that it is a presumptive inference that is inconclusive. It could be that the sign was removed because the owner decided not to keep the house on the market, even though it did not sell. Perhaps he couldn't get the price he wanted, and so decided to keep the house himself. So the argument could be wrong. But still, the fact that the sign is no longer there is some (admittedly weak and inconclusive) indication that the house sold.

Of course, in this case, we aren't explicitly told that this is the conclusion Doug drew, or is indicating that Karen should draw. As we saw in Chapter 3, often conclusions have to be extrapolated by implicature, on a basis of interpreting the discourse in a context of dialogue. In this case, we can infer by presumption from the context of dialogue, given the existing profile of dialogue, that Doug is drawing such a conclusion by virtue of his giving a definite reply to Karen's question. So here Doug is putting forward an argument. But it is just not an argument from ignorance.

On the other hand, you could argue that the *argumentum ad ignorantiam* is involved in this case, on the following grounds. Part of Doug's argument could be that he looked, and did not find a sign on the property, and that since normally such signs are placed in a visible spot, he would have seen it, if one were there. By *argumentum ad ignorantiam* then, Doug concludes that there is no sign there.

Admittedly, this is an *argumentum ad ignorantiam,* but it is surely not the whole argument, or the main argument in case 8.1. The main argument in this case uses the premise that no sign is there to conclude that the house has sold.

This again shows the nontrivial nature of the job of identifying instances of the *argumentum ad ignorantiam.* As we saw in Chapter 5, it is sometimes a judgment of whether the glass of water is perceived as half empty or half full.[1] For in some cases, it could be possible to describe the case either in positive or negative terms. Case 8.1 is not really one of these cases, however, as far as the main line of argument is concerned.

This first task in giving an account of any fallacy is the identification of the type of argument used when the fallacy is committed. But the *ad ignorantiam* is a type of argument that is, in many instances, reasonable, not fallacious. Hence another task is that of separating the nonfallacious cases from the fallacious ones. This is the task of evaluation. This is the task of judging whether the argument is correct or erroneous, which I reserve for Chapter 9.

Defining Key Terms

Our thesis is that the *argumentum ad ignorantiam* has been too often presumed to be a fallacy because an important but implicit part of its form as a characteristic type of argument was too often overlooked. In many of the textbook accounts, it was presumed that the argument from ignorance has the form: *A* has not been proved true (false), therefore *A* is false (true). This portrayal of its form does appear to make the *argumentum ad ignorantiam* an unjustifiable leap from ignorance to positive knowledge.

However, what was overlooked is that many arguments from ignorance, and this type of argument generally as a reasonable kind of argument scheme, have an implicit conditional premise that links knowledge to ignorance, in the sequence of argument in a given case. This conditional premise is to effect: If *A* were true (false), *A* would be known to be true (false).

---

1. In other words, even though we defined the terms "knowledge" and "ignorance," as they should be understood for our purposes, in Chapter 5, there will still be room, in a particular case for judging whether the case (as known or interpreted from the given discourse) fits the requirements of the definitions.

Hence you could say that according to our reconstruction of the form (scheme) of the argument from ignorance, this type of argument is also, partly, an argument from knowledge. Hence, at least in the nonfallacious cases, it is not *purely* an argument from ignorance. It is a type of argument that combines knowledge and ignorance together, to generate a presumptive conclusion that shows the way to the direction of increasing knowledge, in a given case.

Some of the standard accounts of the *argumentum ad ignorantiam* as a fallacy, however, as noted in Chapter 3, would reject this definition of it as a type of argument. They would say that once you have added in the conditional premise, it is no longer an argument from ignorance. Instead, it is now a species of argument from (positive) knowledge. No wonder then, that such an argument is no longer fallacious.

Kahane (1992, 64) defines the fallacy of *appeal to ignorance* as "to take the absence of evidence for a claim as proof that the claim is false." Like most of the textbooks, Kahane recognizes the possibility of cases where arguments that appear to fit this description are not fallacious. He deals with such cases by claiming that they are not really appeals to ignorance.

> However, there are cases in which the failure of a search does count as evidence against a claim. These are the cases in which the thing searched for would very likely have been found if it were really there. Thus, if someone were to claim that a planet exists between Earth and Mars, the absence of favorable evidence would count against the existence of such a planet, given all the sky watching that has gone on in the last 10,000 years. Similarly, when a careful test fails to find blood in a urine specimen, a doctor is justified in concluding that no blood is there. These are not cases of reasoning from ignorance, but rather of reasoning from the *knowledge* that we've appropriately looked for but failed to find the thing in question.

As we saw in Chapter 5, Copi (1982, 95) uses this same definitory move to explain away the apparently nonfallacious instances of the *argumentum ad ignorantiam.*

This definitory move allows one to continue to condemn the argument from ignorance as always being a fallacious argument. It removes the need to distinguish between the fallacious and nonfallacious uses, in different cases. Like all definitory moves in argument, it is hard to dismiss this one categorically. For there are open possibilities of defining the argument from ignorance in different ways, and the disagreements on this matter evident in the textbook treatments show that the issue is still open.

However, we do not see this definitory move—to insist that all genuine arguments from ignorance must be *purely* arguments from ignorance—as a good one. For the real strength of the argument from ignorance is precisely that it does combine partial ignorance with partial knowledge in order to direct a discussion or inquiry along the path to increased knowledge by showing the way toward the truth of a matter. Its function is pragmatic. It applies at one particular stage of a dialogue or inquiry, based on the knowledge or commitments accrued to that point, and then uses lack of knowledge or presumption to guide the dialogue forward, contributing to the goal of the dialogue: to resolve a conflict of opinions, or to prove a proposition based on a pool of relevant evidence that expresses both knowledge and lack of knowledge. To overlook this function, or to define this important and very commonly used type of argument away as an unpersuasive move or fallacy, is to take a one-sided view of it.

This tendency to categorize presumptively all arguments from ignorance as fallacious is perhaps encouraged too much by the negative-sounding connotation of the label "argument from ignorance." Ignorance sounds bad, encouraging the approach that any such argument can be routinely condemned as fallacious. If it would help, this type of argument could be relabeled as *argument from negative evidence,* or *lack-of-knowledge reasoning.* There are precedents for both of these terms of classification in the literature (see Chapter 3). The term *argument from negative evidence* is in common use in the natural sciences, and the term *lack-of-knowledge inference* is in common use in the social science and computer science literature (see Chapter 3).

Two Different Types of Arguments from Ignorance

Knowing that you don't know something, or "Socratic wisdom" is different as a kind of reasoning from the type of argument from ignorance mainly concentrated on by the logic textbooks as the *argumentum ad ignorantiam.* Knowing that you don't know, as a basis for drawing inferences, is associated with a different fallacy.

The advantage of knowing that you don't know about something, or awareness of limitations, is an asset in critical reasoning, because it warns you that you may be about to commit an error, or to look at a problem too simplistically, or that your best next move may be to seek out new knowledge. The flip side of this attitude is that of being *dogmatic* in argument: of thinking you have knowledge of a situation, and so being unwilling to look at the situation more carefully, and recognize that there may be important exceptions to the rule you are at present following.

Dogmatism is associated with the *secundum quid* fallacy: the fallacy of neglecting or ignoring qualifications to a general rule as it applies to a particular case (D. Walton, 1990a). The opposite of the dogmatic attitude is the open-minded and flexible attitude of being able to recognize exceptions to a rule as a situation changes. This attitude requires an openness to new knowledge or information that may come in to a situation. Hence it is based on a premise of awareness that one does not know something, even though one may have previously thought that one did know all about it.

The kind of argument scheme that might be appropriate in this kind of situation is: I now find out that I don't know that *A* is true (false), therefore, before acting on *A*, I had better look to see if it may need to be qualified in this situation, or subjected to further study. I have described this principle as *tutioristic;* that is, being on the safe side epistemically, where there is a likely or possible risk of falsehood or error in a situation where caution might be less costly than error.

This type of argument from ignorance is different from the type typically associated with the *argumentum ad ignorantiam,* where lack of knowledge or evidence that a particular proposition is true (false) is a basis for concluding that this proposition is false (true). The two are similar, because both proceed from a premise of ignorance, and both point the way or path toward searching for more knowledge or information. But the one starts from an iterated premise concerning knowledge about knowledge, while the other generally does not. And the one just calls for open-mindedness, whereas the other concludes to a specific proposition being true or false.

Although both these forms of argument are arguments from ignorance, it would be confusing to give them both the label of *argumentum ad ignorantiam,* especially in the logic textbooks, where pedagogy of the fallacies is the purpose. It is better to call the Socratic argument the *argument from awareness of ignorance* or *argument from limitations of knowledge* to distinguish it from the other type. This Socratic form of argument is based on an iterated knowledge premise of the form $K\neg KA$, and would be analyzed in artificial intelligence research as a species of autoepistemic reasoning (see Chapter 3, "Autoepistemic Reasoning").

I now turn to the main problem of determining the argument scheme or form of the argument from ignorance.

The Argument Scheme

We now put forward a new analysis of the structure of *ad ignorantiam* arguments. On this analysis, the basic structure of the argument has two premises, a base premise and a conditional premise. The base premise is a finding of negative evidence. Roughly it says that an investigator looked or searched for such-and-such a thing in a certain place, and did not find it there. The conditional premise is a counterfactual which says that if that thing you were looking for was in that place you were looking for it, then you would have found it there. These two premises link together to generate the conclusion, which says that the thing you were looking for is not there.

The form of this basic type of *ad ignorantiam* argument has the structure of a *modus tollens* argument:

If it were there, I would find it.

But I didn't find it.

Therefore, it is not there.

Put very simply, this is the basic argument structure of all three types of *ad ignorantiam* arguments initially identified by Woods and Walton (1978b). The reason it was not discovered in Woods and Walton (1978b) is clearly evident: the conditional premise was overlooked.

A very simple example exemplifying this form of argument very clearly is case 2.5, given by Machina (1982, 43), called (C), repeated below.

> (C) I've looked all though the drawer for my pen, and I found no sign of it.
>
> The pen is not in the drawer.

According to the account given by Machina (43) this argument is a nonfallacious argument from ignorance because there exists a "background condition." According to our analysis of the basic structure of the argument from ignorance, this background condition amounts, in effect, to the conditional premise: If the pen were in the drawer, I would see it there (if I looked all through the drawer carefully).

The same analysis applies to case 2.4, the case cited by Michalos (1970, 52) of the elephant in the room. The reason that the *ad ignorantiam* argument is reasonable in this case relates to the satisfiability of the conditional premise. What this amounts to, in this case, is the assumption that if the person were to look for an elephant in his room, and if it were there, then he could "hardly fail to find evidence for the fact." Hence the argument from ignorance is reasonable; the failure to find any elephant there allows us to infer that there is no elephant there.

This basic structure of the argument from ignorance, as having two premises—a base premise and a conditional premise—can now be applied to all three variants of the *argumentum ad ignorantiam* identified in Woods and Walton (1978b). Once the conditional premise is added into the forms identified there, a clear account of the structure of the argument from ignorance can be given.

Basically, the *argumentum ad ignorantiam* has to do with searching around for something, whether it is searching for something around the house, or in a database, or searching for evidence to support a hypothesis. How it functions as a useful argument is to rule out or eliminate dead ends, so you can narrow down the search, and proceed down a new avenue, or seek out a different alternative. It is not a conclusive argument, in the sense that the end of the search has been reached, and all need for continued searching is now at an end. Instead, it only shows you the way for continuing to search.

It should be noted, however, that my definition of the *argumentum ad ignorantiam* as a type of argument is controversial. Not everybody in the textbook accounts agrees with it—notably Kahane and Copi—and some would feel that it is too liberal. Many of the cases I have classified as being instances of the argument from ignorance would not be so classified by others who view this type of argument differently. This remark would especially apply to cases 2.8, 3.8, 3.9, 3.14, 3.15, 4.1, 4.15, 5.1, 5.3, and 5.11, but potentially to many of the other cases we have studied as well.

Some thinkers would say that my analysis of the argument scheme of the argument from ignorance in the *modus tollens* form above is not argument from ignorance, because it also includes an appeal to (positive) knowledge (in the conditional premise). However, I see the matter differently. I do not see the argument from ignorance as operating in the vacuum of pure ignorance, but see its strength as its clever combination of knowledge and ignorance, in a given case, to draw a conclusion.

The Role of the Conditional Premise in Closure

In both the knowledge-based and the scientific reasoning types of *ad ignorantiam* arguments, the role of the conditional premise is fairly clear in most cases. In the knowledge-based cases, the conditional premise is a depth-of-search premise. For example in Copi's case of Mr. X the suspected spy, the worth of the argument from ignorance depends on how thorough a search has been conducted by the FBI. In the scientific cases, the conditional premise has to do with the verifiability or observability of the evidence. Most of the problem cases in this area have to do with the use of hypotheses on the fringes of science—ghosts, the paranormal, ESP, etc.—where, if there is relevant evidence at all, it is hard to identify or confirm it, in a given case.

The problem in determining the role of the conditional premise is in the shifting of burden of proof–type cases (the Lockean type of *ad ignorantiam*). The question is, What is the conditional premise in this type of argument from ignorance? The reason that the answer is not so evident as in the two other types of arguments from ignorance is that the conditional premise is expressed differently in two distinctively different types of cases where the *ad ignorantiam* argument can be a fallacy in the shifting of burden of proof cases.

The second type of case has to do with the shifting of presumptions during the argumentation stage of a dialogue. We return to this type of case below. The first type of case, which we now turn to analyzing, is that where the conditional premise works at the closing stage of a persuasion dialogue. In a persuasion dialogue, there are two opposed theses formulated at the confrontation stage, and the idea is that during the argumentation stage, both sides will put forward the strongest possible case for their thesis, using all the relevant evidence that was available. Hence for a thesis, a proposition *A,* the conditional premise makes the following claim:

(CP)   If *A* were true (false), *A* would be proved to be true (false) by the closing stage of the argument.

Here the (CP) functions as a closure principle that states an article of faith about the value and effectiveness of persuasion dialogue as a way of finding the truth of a matter. It licenses us to conclude by an *argumentum ad ignorantiam,* that if A was not proved true (false) by its proponent's arguments by the closing stage of the dialogue, then we can conclude (by presumption) that A is false (true). The conclusion states that relative to the discussion that preceded, A may be asserted as false (true), as shown by the outcome of the discussion. Here then, the conditional premise functions as a closure principle for the persuasion dialogue as a type of framework of argument.

But the *ad ignorantiam* fallacy can occur here as a type of fallacy that van Eemeren and Grootendorst (1987, 292) call *absolutizing the failure of a defense.*[2] The problem is that someone may infer that just because A has been shown to be true (false) by the persuasion dialogue in which both sides mounted their strongest possible arguments, we must conclude that A is absolutely true (false), as though this outcome were the result of an inquiry, and therefore absolutely final, even if new relevant evidence should come to be known. The fallacy here is a species of misuse of *argument from commitment,* a scheme of argument in which one party proves a proposition A by inferring it by logical types of argument accepted by both sides in a persuasion dialogue, from premises that are commitments of the other side. Traditionally this type of argument has been called the *ex concessis* type of argument. Many have identified it with the *ad hominem* argument—most notably Locke—but I now feel that this is a mistaken classification. The *ad hominem* argument is a subspecies of the argument from commitment where the one party uses personal attack against the other—either (primarily) by attacking the character of the other, or by alleging a pragmatic inconsistency said to exist in the commitment set of the other.

When Is Closure of a Dialogue Appropriate?

Whether it is in the knowledge-base variant or the Lockean variant, the basic *ad ignorantiam* fallacy is the same kind of tactic: the attempt to close off a whole dialogue or search of a knowledge base, or a subargument in a sequence of dialogue, by trying to induce closure at a stage where closure is not appropriate.

2. Krabbe (1994) has also observed this connection.

Generally however, strong closure of dialogue is not a reasonable assumption for most contexts of persuasion and inquiry appropriate for most of the examples studied in this book. Indeed, the characteristic form of tactic that is open to severe criticism as an *ad ignorantiam* fallacy in argumentation is the attempt to shift presumption to close off dialogue and shut down any further argument by an opponent.

The tactic of shifting a presumption in order to make a dialogue appear to be strongly closed is often a highly objectionable subterfuge for trying to force premature foreclosure of acceptance of a proposition by stifling further critical questioning. Thus basically, the fallacy of argument from ignorance ties in to the problem of closure in reasonable dialogue: When can discussion of an issue be reasonably terminated, and the assumption be made that no further evidence will be relevant? This question is the key problem in assessing many contexts of dialogue, where an *ad ignorantiam* failure is suspected.

In a legal trial, the judge determines when closure obtains; that is, when enough evidence is in to determine the issue to be decided. In a university committee meeting, the chairman of the committee decides when discussion is to be ended and a vote taken. In a case like 2.7, Copi's case of "a serious F.B.I. investigation" that fails to find evidence that Mr. X is a Communist, a competent, professional investigating agency itself will presumably have standards of when a professionally adequate investigation has been carried out. However, such a standard of closure may well be disputed in some cases by the subject of the investigation himself. And in law, an appeal may be made, and the case reopened, if it is found that significant, new evidence has come in. In such a case, a new trial may be ordered. Thus the problem of closure is nontrivial in reasoned dialogue, as a practical problem. In a case like the Watergate scandal, various parties having a stake in the issue may argue vehemently whether or when the debate should be terminated. Hence the reasonableness of an argument from ignorance in a particular case turns on pragmatic aspects of the context of dialogue.

The most general problem of the critical discussion as a method of resolving controversies, where conclusive knowledge of the truth of the matter is typically lacking, is the danger that the dialogue could go on and on interminably with no real conclusion becoming decisively established. The danger is that dialogue can (notoriously) be subjective and inconclusive, a waste of everyone's time that yields no gain in definite, verifiable, reproducible knowledge. Dialogue can become "idle chatter" and yield no proof or disproof, as in the tug-of-war type of case (case 4.11).

The problem is one of closure. The process of dialogue must terminate after a reasonable duration (often for practical reasons), and the sequence of argumentation leading to this termination point must then be susceptible to evaluation as having "proved something" or not. If not, that finding should be significant as well, in relation to proving or disproving something.

As we have seen, the main device for solving this closure problem is the mechanism of burden of proof, which sets a reasonable target, a weight of evidence required to prove a particular proposition that is at issue in the controversy. If the target is reasonably achievable in relation to what is known—the evidence available to the participants in the dialogue—then either reaching the target (proving) or not reaching the target (failure to prove) are significant outcomes of interactive reasoning.

In effect, this framework sanctions the *argumentum ad ignorantiam* as a valid principle of interactive reasoning, at least in those instances where the right conditions of dialogue exchange are met. A failure to disprove a proposition by one side of a dispute, by the agreed time of termination of the dialogue, can rightly be taken as a conclusion that the proposition has been proved, at least to be provisionally confirmed or acceptable by the dialogue. The proposition has survived the test of contestive, reasoned, dialogue. And this means that if the dialogue was good (met criteria for being a reasoned dialogue), its conclusion is provisionally acceptable to a degree determined by the burden of proof that has been met. Similarly, a failure to prove the proposition that was the subject of the dispute enables us to draw the inference (*argumentum ad ignorantiam*) that the proposition is disproved. It follows that, in this context of argument, the proposition in question may be regarded as refuted, and it may be rejected.

In general then, the validity of the *argumentum ad ignorantiam,* and with it the validity of persuasion dialogue as a useful way of arriving at conclusions by proving contended propositions, presupposes the existence and practicality of some mechanism for bringing dialogue to a point of closure. Rules for the concluding stage of an argumentative discussion have already been given by van Eemeren and Grootendorst (1984, 173f.), as noted in Chapter 6. They require a participant to retract his doubts about a proposition if the other participant sufficiently defended it. This brings the discussion to an end, and resolves it in favor of one side. Thus the *argumentum ad ignorantiam* can be seen as a kind of methodological principle of the conduct of a reasoned discussion that pertains to the method of closure of the discussion. It is, therefore, a technique of argumentation that can be used well or badly to contribute to the goal of a dialogue. Used well, it is an important basic technique of argumentation.

On the other hand, the *argumentum ad ignorantiam* can become a fallacy—meaning, in this instance an inappropriate deployment or misuse of the method of closure proper for a dialogue—where one participant attempts to force premature closure by prevailing on the other party to give up too soon (where the burden of proof has not really been discharged by the first participant). The problem here involves a kind of confusion between the closing stage of a dialogue and the earlier stages, where the one participant tries to "leap ahead" from one of the earlier stages to the closing stage without making the required intervening moves in the dialogue. The illicit move is a kind of argument tactic designed to short-circuit the proper mechanism for closure of a dialogue.

However, it is characteristic of arguments used as sophistical tactics that there are variations on a basic theme. Where the basic tactic does not seem to be working very well to deceive an opponent, arguers will devise subtle variants to overcome resistance. To see how a fallacy works, or is really used as an effective tactic of deception in realistic cases, one must study how it is used as a technique of persuasion, or for other purposes in argumentation in a dialogue.

The Role of the Conditional Premise in Shifting Presumptions

We now turn to the analysis of the second kind of function that the conditional premise has in the use of arguments from ignorance in persuasion dialogue. This second function relates not to the closure stage of the dialogue, but to the prior argumentation stage, where the argument on neither side is conclusive, and the burden of proof can typically shift back and forth in relation to a contested claim.[3]

The second type of case is that where the conditional premise is part of an argument from ignorance where there is a presumption against a proposition A in a persuasion dialogue. This is different from the previous type of case, because it typically occurs during the argumentation stage of a persuasion dialogue, as opposed to the closing stage.

In this type of case, the conditional premise takes the following form:

---

3. Krabbe (1994) has distinguished between two types of *ad ignorantiam* fallacy in this same way.

(CP)   If *A* were true, then there would not be a presumption against *A*.

The problem for evaluating the argument from ignorance in this kind of case has already been indicated by profile 5.1, reprinted below.

Profile 5.1

Speaker: Why *A*?
Respondent: Why ¬*A*?

The problem is to determine when an instance of this profile of dialogue is a reasonable type of *ad ignorantiam* argument and when it is a fallacious one. The answer is that it depends on the previous sequence of argumentation in the persuasion dialogue up to that point, and in particular, whether the weight of presumption at this point is for *A* or for ¬*A*. It depends, in short, on the burden of proof, at that point in the dialogue.

To show the profile characteristic of a reasonable use of argument from ignorance in a case like this, we reconstruct the profile of dialogue 5.1, adding an intermediate move by the respondent.

Profile 8.1

Speaker: Why *A*?
Respondent: There is a presumption against *A*. Hence your question is illegitimate. We are presuming that *A* is false. Hence I can ask you, in return, a supplementary question.
Respondent: Why ¬*A*?

In this type of case, the *ad ignorantiam* argument can be reconstructed as a reasonable (nonfallacious) sequence of argument, using the version of the conditional premise (CP) above as part of the argument.

Here the argument takes the characteristic *modus tollens* form:

Base Premise: There is a presumption against *A*; i.e., the presumption is that ¬*A* is true.
Conditional Premise: If *A* were true, then there would not be a presumption against *A*.
Conclusion: *A* is not true.

Hence by Hamblin's rule *S3* (see Chapter 5, "Three Types of Argument from Ignorance"), it is inappropriate for the speaker to have asked the question "Why *A?*" at this particular point in the argumentation stage of the persuasion dialogue. By Hamblin's rule, it would therefore be appropriate for the respondent to pose a supplementary question of the form "Why ¬*A?*" at the next move. This represents a reconstruction of the profile of dialogue appropriate for a nonfallacious use of the argument from ignorance in a persuasion dialogue.

However, if the presumption were to be on the other side, the burden of proof is turned around. Suppose the presumption were in favor of *A* at that point in the dialogue. Then the question "Why *A?*" would be legitimate, and the use of the forking technique, by replying "Why *A?*" at the next move, would be inappropriate. In Hamblin's framework, it would violate the rule *S3* for the asking of why-questions (see Chapter 6, "Argument Interpretation").

The failure or fallacy, in such a case, is the inappropriate shifting of burden of proof in lieu of giving a proper answer that would meet the obligation to furnish proof or justification for a proposition one is committed to defending.

Status of the Conditional Premise

The conditional premise is part of a *modus tollens* type of inference that is characteristic of the *argumentum ad ignorantiam,* but that does not imply that this type of argument, as used in dialogue, is generally or always deductively valid. It is deductively valid, as we saw in some of the cases of knowledge-based reasoning, where the knowledge base is assumed or known to be closed. But in the majority of cases of reasonable uses of the *argumentum ad ignorantiam,* this assumption was not applicable. Instead, the argument took a presumptive and defeasible form.

It is generally the case with reasonable *ad ignorantiam* arguments that the conditional premise should be judged on a presumptive basis as being more or less plausible, or not, in a given case. For example, in the cases of knowledge-based reasoning, the argument from ignorance is strong or credible to the extent that the search premise is justified and credible, in the given case. For example, in the case of Mr. X the suspected Communist spy, the conditional premise becomes more and more credible—better and better justified—to the extent that a search into Mr. X's activities have been undertaken by a reputable and competent authority like the FBI. The more the search premise is supported by the known facts of the case, the stronger is the *ad ignorantiam* inference to the conclusion that Mr. X is not a Communist spy.

However, the argument in this case would not be deductively valid because, as we saw in the Alger Hiss case, proof and disproof on matters of spying is rarely, if ever, absolutely conclusive. It is a matter of presumptive weight of evidence, depending on the depth of the search that has been undertaken.

In the *ad ignorantiam* arguments of this kind, the evaluation of the conclusion should be a function of (a) the structural correctness or validity of the argument form (scheme) and (b) the plausibility value of the premises. Generally, the rule is (D. Walton, 1992d) that the plausibility value of the conclusion should be no greater than that of the least plausible of the premises.

What tends to happen in many weak and insufficiently supported instances of the *argumentum ad ignorantiam* is that the conditional premise, which is often not explicitly stated in the given text of discourse, is insufficiently supported, in the given case. Thus the attempt to make the whole argument from ignorance hang on the lack-of-knowledge base premise alone produces an argument that is, at best, weak and questionable.

However, frequently there is a tendency to try to cover up for this failure to fulfill reasonable requirements of burden of proof of justifying the premises by trying to shift the burden to the other side to disprove them. Basically then, in such cases, the *ad ignorantiam* fallacy is the use of a deceptive technique of shifting to avoid one's primary obligation in a persuasion dialogue, to justify a proposition one is committed to, or claims as a premise, if challenged to do so by the other party.

This willingness to fulfill reasonable requirements of burden of proof if challenged is a mark of the persuasion dialogue as a type of argument exchange that displays a commitment to rationality in the form of paying attention to matters of evidential support for claims made. The sophistical attempt to evade this burden by shifting it inappropriately to the other party is a symptom of what Aristotle called "peevishness" or nonseriousness in a persuasion dialogue (or in a dialectical argument), to use Aristotle's somewhat comparable notion (*Topica* 161a.17–27). As Aristotle observed, sometimes a party who is questioned takes this criticism personally, and the dialogue shifts from a critical discussion to a quarrel.

Sources of Contextual Evidence

Now that we have an argument scheme for the argument from ignorance, the job of seeing whether it is present and has been used correctly in a given case depends on how it was used in a given case, in a context of dialogue. A correct argument from ignorance is one that contributes to the goal of dialogue the arguers are supposed to be engaged in.

Evidence for the correctness or incorrectness of an *argumentum ad ignorantiam* in a particular case comes from two main sources of information in the context of dialogue. First, in a critical discussion, each participant has an obligation to prove his thesis from concessions of the other party, in order to realize the goal of the dialogue, successful persuasion. This requirement means that each party to the argument has a (global) burden of proof: each party has a particular proposition to be proved, and the rules of the game define the acceptable mechanisms of proof. At the global level, in a critical discussion, each party has a distinct proposition to be proved. In a dispute, the one thesis (proposition to be proved) of the one party is the negation (opposite) of the thesis of the other party. Hence it may be tempting for one participant to cite his opponent's failure to disprove his (the opponent's) thesis as a kind of proof that fulfills the first participant's burden of proof. Indeed, this tactic of the *argumentum ad ignorantiam* may be a reasonable strategy of proof, in some cases. But it can also be illicit, in other cases, depending on where the burden of proof really lies.

The second source of textual evidence, from a context of dialogue, which can be used to evaluate the correctness or fallaciousness of an *argumentum ad ignorantiam* comes from the local level of dialogue. The commitment rules of the particular dialogue define the allocation of burden of proof at each move. For example, normally in a critical discussion, if a participant makes an assertion move of the form "I assert A," then he becomes committed to the proposition A, and if challenged, he is obliged to prove A. The function of the why-question in persuasion dialogue is to enable one participant to challenge another with respect to the other's commitment to a specific proposition by requesting that the second participant provide reasons or grounds to back up his commitment to this proposition (see Hamblin, 1970, 271).

Questions also function as devices to allocate burden of proof at the local level. For example, if a participant does not indicate that he is not committed to a proposition A, at the next move after he is asked the question

"Why *A?*" then he will become committed to *A*. And therefore, at each subsequent move, unless he retracts his commitment to *A*, he will have incurred a burden of proof with respect to *A*. At any rate, this is an example of how responding to a question can affect allocation of burden of proof in dialogue at the local level. For a more detailed description of the function of why-questions in distributing burden of proof in dialogue, the reader could consult Walton (1987, 297–302). Generally, each context of dialogue in a particular case must be looked at on its own merits in determining proper allocation of burden of proof between two parties.

In contrast to the dialectical type of *argumentum ad ignorantiam* fallacy, it is useful to distinguish an epistemic type of *argumentum ad ignorantiam* fallacy which can occur where the context of dialogue is that of an inquiry. This distinction was elaborated in "Three Types of Arguments from Ignorance" below.

The inquiry is different from the persuasion dialogue in that persuasion dialogue is adversarial (contestive) whereas the inquiry is a more cooperative type of dialogue that has as its goal an accumulation of proof (knowledge) that will satisfy all parties concerned that the truth (or knowledge) has been established by a complete body of evidence. In persuasion dialogue, the fallacy of *argumentum ad ignorantiam* arises through the use of the overaggressive tactic of shifting the burden of proof or disproof (illicitly) onto the other party. In the inquiry, the fallacy of the *argumentum ad ignorantiam* arises from the unwarranted leaping ahead from a presumption that is not yet well established to a claim that it is known (proved) to be true. Both variants of the fallacy are types of tactics to try to induce premature closure of an argument. Both errors are faults of putting too much weight on a presumption in argument.

In both the critical discussion and the inquiry, there is a pragmatic sequence from the opening stage to the closing stage of the argumentation. An inquiry opens with a given depth of knowledge on the subject of the inquiry, and the goal is to increase that depth of knowledge to the point where some particular proposition (representing the problem or question) can be proved or disproved. As the inquiry progresses, if all goes well, the depth of knowledge is increased. Therefore, an *argumentum ad ignorantiam* that was weak at the beginning of the inquiry, may become a very strong argument at a later stage. At the closure of a successful inquiry, the *argumentum ad ignorantiam* may be a very strong and well-established argument.

The strength or weakness of an *ad ignorantiam* argument, in a particular case, depends on how far along the process of inquiry has gone in that case. In Copi's case 4.5 of the foreign agent suspect (Copi, 1982, 102), the "serious" security investigation had checked Mr. X's record. But how seriously or thoroughly did they check? The more carefully and completely their investigation was carried out, the stronger is the *ad ignorantiam* conclusion that Mr. X is not a foreign agent.

Theoretically, the *ad ignorantiam* could even be a deductively valid argument in some cases, but only on the (often idealistic) closed world assumption that the information yielded by the inquiry is complete, and not subject to appeal, correction, or addition. In effect, the closed world assumption made here is that any proposition not included in the finding of the inquiry can be declared *false,* for the purpose of the inquiry. This means that the inquiry is declared *strongly closed,* meaning that the findings to date represent all the relevant facts from which conclusions may be drawn.

The problem here seems to be that since the time of Descartes in modern European history, scientific inquiry has been seen only as the increment of positive knowledge; the ignorance aspect of scientific research has been ignored, or even suppressed. As Ravetz (1993, 18) put it, the formulation of science as "the art of the soluble" implies that what is not soluble is simply not part of science.

> This restricted view of science as "the art of the soluble" may well have enhanced its power in the past, to the point where it now presents perils for the future. It also has other, even deeper effects on our vision of knowledge and the world. For it entails a total exclusion of ignorance from our view. Uncertainty exists only so far as it can be managed interestingly, in the form of the soluble research problems at the margin of our scientific knowledge. Ignorance is not soluble by means of ordinary research; therefore it does not exist. In the classic image of science, purveyed by philosophers and publicists, and imbibed by generations of teachers and their pupils, science is about certainty. Uncertainty is there to be banished, and ignorance is to be rolled back beyond the horizon.

This "simplistic vision of the triumphal advance of science" (Ravetz, 1993, 18) exclusively emphasizes the positive aspect of scientific inquiry as a build-up of knowledge, and dismisses arguments from ignorance as simply being not a part of science (or "hard" science; see also Ravetz, 1987). But surely a more realistic view of scientific inquiry should see it as a progression from relative ignorance to relative knowledge.

In many cases, the *argumentum ad ignorantiam* is used (or abused) in policy discussions that are practical deliberations on what prudent course of action to take where some dilemma has arisen. Ice (1987) cites the decision to launch the ill-fated Challenger space mission in 1986, where there was a determination in place to launch, and the burden of proof was put on the engineers to disprove flight readiness. When engineers from Morton Thiokol, the company that manufactured the O-rings, questioned conditions for the launch, they were told to reexamine their data (Ice, 1987, 632).

> Thus when the members of the Thiokol group were sent into caucus, they felt they needed to come back to the main teleconference with "conclusive" data which demonstrated that they should not certify flight readiness.
>
> Indeed the members at Thiokol believed that they had to prove that the flight was not ready. As Robert Lund put it: " . . . we [the engineers at Thiokol] were trying to find some way to prove to them it wouldn't work and we were unable to do that. We couldn't prove absolutely that the motor wouldn't work." (*Report of the Presidential Commission on the Space Shuttle Challenger Accident,* Washington, D.C.: GPO, 1986, 4:632)

According to one of these engineers (148), "There was a meeting where the determination was to launch, and it was up to us to prove beyond a shadow of a doubt that it was not safe to do so." This reversal of polarity of the normal burden of proof turned out, in retrospect, to be a very questionable *argumentum ad ignorantiam.*

Dunn (1992, 46) contrasts usable ignorance with inadvertent ignorance (error) and deliberate ignorance (fraud); and supporting Ravetz (1987), Dunn claims that usable ignorance is a very important part of successful policy discussions that led to a good decision. Part of this process, according to Dunn (51–52) is the discovery or recognition of ignorance, and the use of that ignorance.

- Policy analysts should be rewarded for conducting research and practice syntheses, as well as standard meta-analyses, which expose significant sources of error and bias in the conclusions and recommendations of other policy analysts. These syntheses and meta-analyses promote mutual criticism and self-criticism with a framework of commonly accepted standards, fostering the discovery of usable ignorance.

- Policy analysts should be rewarded for replicating, crossvalidating, and evaluating promising synthesis, development, and dissemination strategies attempted elsewhere. Replication, crossvalidation, and evaluation facilitate the search for usable ignorance.

- The unit of evaluation and object of incentives (rewards and discipline) should be the synthesis, development, and dissemination strategy, not the policy analysis unit or its staff. The evaluation of strategies depersonalizes rewards and discipline, minimizes deviance from accepted professional standards for reasons of self-preservation, and enhances awareness that failures are not personal but stem from the organized complexity of the knowledge system.

This strongly suggests that not every argument from ignorance should be condemned as "fallacious." Policy analysis is seen by Dunn as an applied social science that can achieve results having what he calls a "pragmatic validity" (51). He sees it as a type of dialogue that uses mutual criticism, self-criticism, and argument from ignorance to develop progressively an improved policy analysis useful for making practical decisions on how to apply specialized scientific knowledge.

This same kind of progression is evident in the critical discussion, although the nature of it is different as a kind of argumentation. At the opening stage, a burden of proof is allocated for the proposition that is to be evaluated by the discussion. At this beginning stage, if the proposition in question is not yet proved, that does not mean it is disproved. Here, the *argumentum ad ignorantiam* is a very weak argument at best. As the dialogue progresses successfully, however, by examining the strongest arguments for and against this proposition, the *argumentum ad verecundiam* becomes much stronger as a way of dealing with this proposition. And then, at the closure stage, the *argumentum ad ignorantiam* can become a very strong argument indeed. Once the critical discussion has been successfully concluded, and the issue decided, the proponent's failure to prove this proposition allows us to conclude that this proposition has been refuted, that it may be rejected as a conclusion.

Generally then, the evidence for evaluating an *ad ignorantiam* argument in a particular case has to come from what can be surmised about the context of dialogue in that case. It is not a matter of taking the logical form of the argument and evaluating it by means of a noncontextual calculus, as we are familiar with doing in deductive formal logic. Instead, the context of use in a conversational setting is the source of the evidence used to evaluate the form or scheme of the argument.

Different Stages of the Inquiry

One of the problems of evaluating arguments from ignorance in the context of scientific reasoning is that people tend to confuse or fail to distinguish two stages of the inquiry as a framework of this kind of reasoning. During the discovery phase, hypotheses are put forward on a tentative or best-guess basis. At this stage presumptive reasoning associated with the *argumentum ad ignorantiam* is highly appropriate and useful.

Black (1946, 247–49) and Beardsley (1950, 517–47) have given accounts of the structure of the inquiry that emphasizes the kind of conjectural reasoning in constructing a plausible hypothesis characteristic of this initial, discovery phase. For example, in a case given by Black (1946, 248–49), a student tries to figure out where he lost a textbook; he might have left it in a restaurant, but can't remember the name of it. To collect information to verify or falsify various plausible conjectures, he starts phoning likely looking restaurants listed in the Yellow Pages, eliminating many of them by their locations. When he hits one that reports having found his book, he has verified one of his plausible conjectures. Then the proposition that his book was lost at such-and-such a restaurant becomes a verified hypothesis—an item of knowledge—as opposed to being simply a plausible conjecture that might turn out to be wrong.

This particular example is one of a commonsense type of inquiry—a kind of empirical verification of a hypothesis that we often use in everyday argument and deliberation in solving the practical problems confronted in daily life. However, another type of inquiry is the scientific investigation of a hypothesis by empirical or experimental methods in a scientific discipline like chemistry or demography. In such cases, the methodology and arguments used must be judged in relation to the specialized standards and accepted methods that have been adopted at any particular time by the specialists in the field. The participants in the argument are experts in a particular discipline, and this must be taken into account in any evaluation of the argument.

Here too, however, the *ad ignorantiam* as an argument does have a legitimate place if used during the initial, discovery stage of the dialogue. At this stage, it has the function of guiding the construction of potentially fruitful hypotheses by narrowing down the less plausible hypotheses and the less likely to be fruitful lines of inquiry. It is a form of reasoning from negative evidence so it is a less worthy or plausible type of argument than that of reasoning from positively established evidence by successful verification of a hypothesis on empirical or mathematical evidence. But it has a negative, guiding, or heuristic function that gives it some positive value as an argument, at the discovery stage.

Once we move forward from the collection of evidence and verification of hypothesis stages to the closing stage of the inquiry, however, where the practitioners of a science present the results of their findings to their colleagues and to outsiders, the *ad ignorantiam* argument is evaluated differently. At this stage, the argument from ignorance can still be used legitimately, but it is regarded as a much weaker form of argument, and in certain respects unsatisfactory—indicating that the inquiry was, to some extent at least, unsuccessful. The intent of the inquiry is always to decisively prove or disprove a particular proposition by amassing all the relevant evidence and, in effect, closing the knowledge base. However, in some instances, a careful inquiry will be forced to the conclusion that despite all efforts to collect such evidence, the base of knowledge gathered was insufficient to definitely prove or disprove the proposition in question. In one respect, this is a successful outcome, because it has shown that the proposition in question cannot be proved—incompleteness results in mathematics like those of Gödel would be a case in point here.

Yet in another respect, such an outcome is a disappointment, because the aim of inquiry is always definitive proof or disproof, if this is possible, and it is generally hoped that it is possible. Hence to have an argument from ignorance as the outcome—say, in the form of an incompleteness proof—is somewhat disappointing. On the other hand, in some instances, an argument from ignorance can be decisive—as in the case of Gödel's incompleteness proofs in logic. They showed that certain propositions simply cannot be demonstrated, at least using the existing methods of logic, because the only way to prove them leads to a contradiction.

Whatever the ultimate lessons of these aspects of the inquiry, they show that foundationalism seems most plausible and persuasive as an account of scientific reasoning when it focuses on the presentation of the results or closing stage of the inquiry. Here the use of a presumptive type of argument from ignorance seems unfavorable or perhaps inappropriate or fallacious. When you shift attention to the discovery phase, however, the evaluation of the use of the argument from ignorance is quite different. Here, negative evidence can be justified as a type of argument that, while less desirable than a collection of positive experimental results, still has a guidance function.

9
Evaluating the Fallacious Cases

In Chapter 7, we saw how the basic dialectical sequence of putting forward a presumption in a dialogue actually has the same structure as the *argumentum ad ignorantiam*. A presumption is always granted provisionally in the absence of evidence to the contrary (or strong enough evidence to refute it). If this is correct, and *ad ignorantiam* arguments are often reasonable, if tentative and defeasible arguments, how can they be fallacious? And if they are fallacious in some cases—as Chapter 4 strongly indicates—what criteria can we use to determine whether an argument from ignorance is fallacious or not, in a particular case? These are the questions addressed in this chapter.

A prior problem is what is meant by the term "fallacy." According to van Eemeren and Grootendorst (1984; 1987; 1992), a fallacy is a violation of a rule of a critical discussion. Although the pragmatic and dialectical framework of this definition is very favorable, I use a broader definition here (D. Walton, 1984; 1989a; 1992b; 1992c; 1992e) according to which, a fallacy is a sequence of argumentation used in a context of dialogue (of which there can be many types) as a tactic of deception to trick a speech partner in an exchange, or as an underlying, systematic, and serious type of error of reasoning. Note that a fallacy, according to this conception, is not just any error, weak argument, or violation of a rule of dialogue, but a particularly serious and systematic type of error or sophistical tactic of an identifiable kind, used in argumentation to obstruct a goal of dialogue, or interfere with its realization.

According to this viewpoint, there is no one-to-one correspondence between a fallacy and a violation of a rule of rational discussion. To identify, analyze, and evaluate a fallacy, one first of all has to distinguish it as a distinctive type of argumentation—represented by an argumentation scheme or form of argument. Then one has to study how this distinctive type of argument is used in different types of dialogue, correctly, to make a contribution to the goal of the dialogue exchange of arguments. This can be done using profiles of dialogue. Then one has to construct another profile of dialogue, and then separately, show how this type of argumentation has been used incorrectly, when the profiles are compared, as a serious instrument of deception (D. Walton, 1995).

Weak Arguments, Sophistical Tactics, and Fallacies

How can one tell, in a particular case, whether an *ad ignorantiam* argument is correct or erroneous? As we saw in so many cases, one has to look for evidence in the context of dialogue. But we have also found that *ad ignorantiam* arguments occur in different contexts of dialogue: they can occur in an inquiry, in a critical discussion, or in the context of advice-giving dialogue; for example, in cases of computer reasoning in expert systems. In any of these contexts the *argumentum ad ignorantiam* can be stronger or weaker, depending on factors in the context of dialogue.

In advice-seeking dialogue, the *argumentum ad ignorantiam* is stronger or weaker, depending on the depth of knowledge at the particular stage of the dialogue where the argument occurs. The greater the consulted expert's depth of knowledge in the domain of proposition *A,* put to him as a query, the greater is the plausibility that *A* is false, if the expert cannot find *A* in her knowledge base.

In a critical discussion, the important factor is the burden of proof, and in particular, how close that burden is to being fulfilled at the particular stage of dialogue where the *ad ignorantiam* occurs. In effect, the *argumentum ad ignorantiam* is absolutely plausible once the burden of proof has been fulfilled. If *A* has not been proved true by the point of closure of a dialogue, then *A* must be presumed to be true, according to the requirements of burden of proof set at the opening stage of the dialogue.

In an inquiry, the *argumentum ad ignorantiam* for a particular proposition becomes stronger and stronger as the knowledge cumulated by the inquiry becomes more and more firmly established. However, even at the beginning stages of an inquiry, where very little is known about a subject or hypothesis, the *argumentum ad ignorantiam* can still be a correct, even if weak, kind of argument. It can be a speculative argument that only yields a small degree of plausibility for its conclusion. Even so, in such a case, it can be a correct, as opposed to an erroneous argument.

However, in a case where there is no evidence at all, it is a fallacy to suppose that pure ignorance can change a burden of proof, as in case 2.28, the McCarthy case. But most of the cases examined in this book have been arguments from partial ignorance, not arguments from total ignorance on how to prove something. They have been arguments based on knowledge that a particular procedure did not lead to a particular sort of knowledge. Should we call these "arguments from ignorance?" Yes, because the basic problem is how to proceed further with them, given the situation of incomplete knowledge. The problem is one of burden of proof. Who has it, and who has enough knowledge, evidence, or basis for presumption so that the burden should properly be shifted to the other side?

When a charge is made, there needs to be at least enough evidence to make the charge go forward for further investigation. In case 4.11, the charge that the treaty was being violated rested on a recent television report that quoted American officials (unnamed) as conceding that Canadian uranium was being used in U.S. nuclear weapons. Unless these allegations are brought forward with specific details, they cannot be investigated further, assuming the government has no other evidence of violations of the treaty. When making a serious charge, there should be a burden, not to prove it conclusively, but at least to give enough evidence to show that the charge should be further investigated.

The requirements for burden of proof depend very much on the context of dialogue. A high burden of proof may be appropriate for a scientific inquiry, but inappropriate in practical deliberation on how to act when human safety is a practical consideration. In case 4.8, Bristol-Myers Squibb used the argument from ignorance, saying: "We have no scientific evidence. We are ignorant!" It may have been true that a scientific inquiry into the safety of polyurethane breast implants had not yet been carried out. But if Bristol-Myers Squibb had anecdotal evidence, based on reports of health problems by women who had complained about the bad effects of their implants, these practical considerations should have been acknowledged as a basis for deliberations, and warnings to other women who might have been considering using these implants. The problem in this case is a dialectical shift from a deliberation concerning human safety to an inquiry based on scientific standards of research and investigation.

The *argumentum ad ignorantiam* can be incorrect, or even fallacious where there has been a dialectical shift, of an unannounced or illicit sort, between one context of dialogue and another. For example, to cite Copi's classic case of the ghosts (Chapter 2, "The Standard Treatment as a Fallacy"), it may be a reasonable presumption to draw in a persuasion dialogue on the subject of ghosts that, given the absence of good evidence in favor of their existence, we can provisionally conclude that their existence should be subject to doubt. In effect, this *argumentum ad ignorantiam* places a burden of proof on the would-be prover of the existence of ghosts.

Now, it could be argued whether this way of placing the burden of proof is appropriate for the particular context of dialogue. But the argument is not inherently bad or fallacious per se. However, in the text of this case, Copi used the term "established" in the conclusion, suggesting both that the context of dialogue is that of an inquiry, and that the existence of ghosts (a proposition most of us take to be highly implausible) has been established by some inquiry. But of course, the premise that nobody has ever proved the nonexistence of ghosts is highly problematic as a premise for such a strong conclusion, given the verifiability problems with entities such as ghosts, ESP, and so forth. The shift to the inquiry, the implausible conclusion, and the problematic premise, all combine to make for such a hopelessly implausible argument that Copi can safely label it a "fallacy." This is an example of the "tarring and feathering" of presumptive argumentation schemes like the *ad ignorantiam* in the logic texts, by picking examples that appear so implausible, or even silly, that they can be clearly and easily classified as a fallacy. We have already seen, however, that the *argumentum ad ignorantiam* is not generally that bad. It can be a reasonable argument in some cases, and in still others it is a blunder, an error, or a weak argument, but not such a bad case that we can justifiably call it a "fallacy."

The *argumentum ad ignorantiam* can be, in some cases, simply a weak or inconclusive argument that fails to meet its burden of proof or search standard in setting a depth of knowledge required for an inquiry. But in some cases it is also a fallacy, a sequence of argumentation that exploits an argument tactic that can apparently be used in the same way in different contexts of dialogue. But generally, it is a sequence of argumentation modeled by the use of an argument scheme in a profile of dialogue, that can be used correctly or sophistically in different contexts of dialogue.

What makes the *argumentum ad ignorantiam* a fallacy, when it is a bad argument, is not simply its occurrence in one of these contexts of dialogue. It is its misemployment as a tactic to make an argument seem (unjustifiably) stronger than it really is. Wreen (1989, 302) supports the idea that a much more "complete context" has to be supplied in order to determine whether a fallacy has been committed, or how strong the argument is, in judging the standard textbook cases of the *argumentum ad ignorantiam*.

Locke's characterization of the *argumentum ad ignorantiam* as an assent-producing tactic in dialogue that can be used either well or badly (see Chapter 2, "The Lockean Origin"), has turned out to be one that is not only supported by our casework, but can be modeled normatively. His suggestion on what can go wrong with the *argumentum ad ignorantiam,* when it is wrong, has also turned out to be fruitful. It goes wrong when the proponent adopts the forking tactic of trying to drive the respondent harder than the procedures of the dialogue reasonably permit, in order to force him to submit to her (the proponent's) opinion in the argument.

What makes the *argumentum ad ignorantiam* a fallacy, as opposed to being simply a blunder or a weak but not totally worthless argument, is its manner of use in a context of dialogue as an overaggressive tactic of argumentation. Locke's insight brought out this tactical element very well when he wrote (Hamblin, 1970, 60) that men use the *argumentum ad ignorantiam* to "drive" others and "force" them to "submit" in debate. There is nothing wrong with vigorous advocacy of your point of view in a critical discussion, or with basing your arguments on presumptions, in cases of partial ignorance. The fallacy comes in when there is the use of a tactic of forcing or pushing ahead too strongly to be commensurate with the knowledge or ignorance appropriate for the stage of dialogue that one has arrived at in reasoning together with others.

To judge when a "forcing" or "pushing ahead too strongly" has occurred in a particular case, one must compare the actual sequence of dialogue in that case with the type of profile appropriate for the normative model of the dialogue.

The Basic Fallacy

According to the account of the structure of the *argumentum ad ignorantiam* given in Chapter 5, there are two different subtypes, one a knowledge-based conception modeled by (KBS) and (PPS), the other a dialectical conception modeled by the Lockean profile of dialogue. It may appear that these are two completely different types of argument, with nothing in common. But they both share the same negative logic, as reasonable arguments. And the basic *ad ignorantiam* fallacy has the same structure as a fallacy in both subtypes.

In (KBS) and (PPS), the underlying structure is that of a knowledge base and a search process through that knowledge base that is at some stage of completion. In the Lockean profile, the underlying structure is that of a dialogue in which two parties are reasoning together, and the argument in question is at some stage in the sequence of that dialogue. The basic fallacy in the knowledge-base type of *argumentum ad ignorantiam* is that the search process is not far enough along to justify the claim made in the argument. Or to put it another way, there is not enough evidence to fulfill the burden of proof appropriate for the conditional premise of the argument.

But that is not enough in itself to determine an *ad ignorantiam* as being fallacious (a strong charge), as opposed to simply being weak or insufficient, in the sense of being not strong enough, or not containing enough evidence, to prove the conclusion. The fallacious cases are the more extreme cases where some dubious tactic is used to imply or suggest that the argument is strong, or conclusive, or able to shift the burden of proof, when really it is not. For example, in case 2.28, McCarthy's argument implies, by an innuendo, that there must be already strong evidence against the person accused of being a Communist, so that there being nothing in his file to disprove his Communist connections is a powerful indictment. Here the reversal of polarity in the tribunal itself is the contextual factor that makes it seem reasonable (in the circumstances of this era) to presume guilt instead of the opposite.

Van Eemeren and Grootendorst (1987, 291–92) classify the *argumentum ad ignorantiam* as a violation of their Rule IX of a critical discussion,[1] which

---

1. Rule IX (van Eemeren and Grootendorst, 1987, 291) says: "A failed defence must result in the protagonist withdrawing his standpoint and a successful defence must result in the antagonist withdrawing his doubt about the standpoint."

pertains to the concluding stage of the discussion, where both parties agree on whether the original question of the dispute was resolved, and then adjust their attitudes according to this agreement. So conceived, the *ad ignorantiam* fallacy is a species of the fallacy van Eemeren and Grootendorst call (1987, 291) *absolutizing the failure of a defense,* the argument that just because a proposition *A* has not been given a successful defense, it follows that *A* is false.

This account of the *ad ignorantiam* fallacy does capture the kind of case analyzed in Chapter 8, where the fallacy occurs at the closure stage of a dialogue. And, from the viewpoint of our analysis, the expression "absolutizing the failure of a defense" is a good one to describe what goes wrong when the Lockean profile can be judged to be an instance of the closure type of *ad ignorantiam* fallacy in a particular case.

However, in one respect, this account of the fallacy is too limited, because the Lockean profile can become fallacious not only at the closing stage of a dialogue, but anywhere along the way. In many cases, it is during the earlier or middle phases of the argumentation stage that one party in a discussion tries to shut off proper critical questioning by trying to get the other party to concede a proposition as proven, just because he (the other party) has so far failed to disprove it. But the fallacy here is that the other party should be given more room for argument to eventually come up with such a disproof, precisely because the dialogue is not even near the closing stages yet.

Yet it is true that the *ad ignorantiam* fallacy often has to do with premature closure. In the knowledge-base subtype, in reality it is not often that the closed world assumption applies. As Dohnal (1992, 1157) put it, in connection with reliability reasoning in microelectronics: "For large knowledge bases a complete set of uncertain information is very often not (in real life actually never) available." In most cases, (PPS) and not (KBS) is the more applicable model of the argumentation in a realistic description of an actual case. Thus the *ad ignorantiam* fallacy often trades on the appearance that (KBS) is the model of reasoning (i.e., that the closed world assumption is appropriate), when in reality, it is not.

At the most general level, however, what is characteristic of the argument from ignorance as a fallacy is the attempt to evade appropriate critical questioning, in the form of a reasonable request to fill the appropriate burden of proof to justify a proposition one is committed to in a dialogue, by trying to shift the burden to the other side unfairly. The move generically takes the form of the reply: "If you can't disprove this proposition, then you had better accept it!" Exactly when and why this type of shifting (forking) move is inappropriate is indicated by the profiles of dialogue constructed in Chapter 5. Basically, it is a tactic to try to force commitment in a profile of dialogue where suspension of commitment would be the appropriate stance.

How the *ad ignorantiam* argument works is by itself shifting a weight of presumption from one party to the other in a dialogue. This type of argument takes the following form:

If A were true, it would be known (proved, presumed) to be true.

A is not known (proved, presumed) to be true.

Therefore, A is (presumably) false.

When put forward as an argument in a dialogue, this form of argument gives rise to several appropriate critical questions.

1. If A were true, would it be known (proved, presumed) to be true?
2. Is it the case that A is not known (proved, presumed) to be true?

These are legitimate and appropriate questions for a respondent to ask when confronted (at the prior move) by the argument from ignorance in a dialogue. The fallacy is the use of the forking tactic, in its various guises, to evade or suppress these critical questions, by pushing aggressively ahead.

Three Main Subtypes of the Fallacy

In coming to understand the *ad ignorantiam* fallacy, it is important to begin with the realization that the argument from ignorance is basically a reasonable type of argument that has a distinctive argumentation scheme. Thus we cannot just assume it is a fallacy. We have to explain what is wrong with it, when it goes wrong, or is used as a fallacy.

While the basic fallacy involves the same type of argument, the *ad ignorantiam* particularly occurs as a common fallacy that is effective in deceiving arguers in three different forms or guises. The first form is the kind of shifting of burden of proof that typically occurs in a persuasion dialogue. This fallacy is well described by the Lockean forking tactic: instead of proving a proposition she is supposed to prove, an arguer replied, "You disprove it! Otherwise it stands!" What is fallacious here is revealed by the profile of dialogue. This type of shifting or forking tactic is not always a fallacious argument. In some cases, it is legitimate. But in other cases, it represents a profile of dialogue characteristic of fallacious use.

The second common form of the *ad ignorantiam* fallacy is the knowledge-based or epistemic variant. The fallacy here is characterized by a shift in the scope of the negation sign over an epistemic operator, formally speaking. But in some cases, a shift of this sort in an argument is justified. What especially makes it unjustified, in cases most typically associated with the *ad ignorantiam* fallacy, is the failure to justify the conditional search-premise. Normally, some sort of searching in a relatively deep or complete database has been undertaken in an argument from ignorance. At least, such a search is a premise of the *argumentum ad ignorantiam,* properly used. But if the shift of negation operation from the base premise to the conclusion is pressed forward with a degree of confidence (plausibility) not justified by the evidence supporting the conditional premise, then we have the typical kind of case associated with the committing of an *ad ignorantiam* fallacy.

Now, as we have seen, in some cases, the argument from ignorance is actually a deductive form of argument, where the knowledge base is said to be closed, or complete. But in real life, this situation is rarely the case. Normally, the argument from ignorance in the knowledge-base guise, is a presumptive type of argument, like the first guise, above. Normally, a knowledge base in an investigation is open to the future of the investigation, where new knowledge might come in to reverse or defeat the current weight of presumption in support of (or against) a proposition. So in this type of guise as well, the strength of the argument rests on the search premise: the failure of this premise to be justified in a case is the most common sort of failure identified with the fallacious use of the argument from ignorance.

The third subtype of *ad ignorantiam* fallacy most common as a deceptive tactic of argument is the use of negative evidence in the context of verification or falsification of a scientific hypothesis. In scientific reasoning in a research inquiry, as we saw in Chapter 1, negative evidence has been somewhat grudgingly admitted by scientists in recent times, as an admissible way of reporting research results for publication. But it is regarded as a weaker form of argument than reporting of positive findings that tend to confirm a hypothesis. The justification for allowing it at all in scientific reasoning is that it reveals blind alleys or pathways that do not appear promising, thereby cutting down waste of scientific research effort and expenses by narrowing the possible pathways for future research efforts. Even so, it is regarded as a plausible or presumptive (heuristic) type of argumentation that is no real substitute for finding positive results that build on (positive) knowledge in an inquiry.

What creates the fallacy here, then, is that the *ad ignorantiam* argument is put forward or taken as some sort of stronger or more conclusive argument than it really is. Instead, we should always see such arguments from ignorance, based on negative evidence only, as mere heuristic guides or indicators of direction for future research, and not as positive scientific findings or established results of inquiry in their own right. They are presumptive in the sense that they are temporary indicators or direction signs that are inherently open to correction or refutation by future investigations.

This third type of *ad ignorantiam* fallacy becomes most worrisome and deceptive when it occurs in conjunction with arguments where it is inherently difficult to get access to data, especially where there is a strong suspicion that a hypothesis may not even be verifiable at all (e.g., the cases of ESP, ghosts, the paranormal, etc.).

Innuendo as Another Basis of the Fallacy

Innuendo is not itself a fallacy, but it is certainly at the basis of many of the informal fallacies—most notably the *ad hominem* fallacy, which is often put forward by innuendo or suggestion. And it was shown by Weddle (1978), in case 4.15, how the *ad ignorantiam* can be used to create doubt and raise suspicions. Damer (1980, 19) cites the fallacy of *argument by innuendo* as the use of suggestions, as opposed to assertions, to create an impression that a veiled claim is true, even though no relevant evidence is presented to support the claim. We would not go so far here as to claim that argumentation using innuendo is inherently fallacious. But the dangers implicit in this type of argumentation have already been indicated in Chapter 4.

Innuendo leads to the raising of doubts or suspicions and to the creation or shifting of presumptions. Argumentation using innuendo typically performs these functions by means of using tacit conversational postulates or conventions of dialogue that are not explicitly stated along with the argument itself. How this kind of inference or "conversational implicature" works has been well illustrated by a case given by Grice (1975, 71).

Case 9.1

> *A* is writing a testimonial about a pupil who is a candidate for a philosophy job, and the letter reads as follows: "Dear Sir, Mr. X's command of English is excellent, and his attendance at tutorials has been regular, Yours, etc." (Gloss: *A* cannot be opting out, since if he wished to be uncooperative, why write at all? He cannot be unable, through ignorance, to say more, since the man is his pupil; moreover, he knows that more information is wanted. He must, therefore, be wishing to impart information he is reluctant to write down. This supposition is only tenable on the assumption that he thinks that Mr. X is no good at philosophy. This, then, is what he is implicating.)

This case contains a concealed or subtle *argumentum ad ignorantiam,* because what *A* leaves unsaid, the information he fails to give, naturally leads the reader of the letter (in context) to conclude that *A* is saying Mr. X is no good at philosophy. Since *A* fails to mention the good skills or quality that the reader is looking for, and expects to be mentioned, the reader concludes that Mr. X does not have them (at least in *A*'s opinion).

The argument conveyed in this case is not fallacious, however, at least as far as we can tell from the information given. But one can see that it is a device used by the writer of the letter to suggest a particular conclusion without actually coming out and explicitly saying it or drawing it. Since this device is being used, in effect to shield the writer off from the burden of proof—say, having to prove in court that Mr. X is no good at philosophy, after Mr. X brings suit—one can easily see, however, that it is a technique that could easily be used to help commit fallacies of various kinds.

Because of its inherently presumptive nature, innuendo is especially dangerous, because the burden of proof can even be avoided altogether. An accuser can say, "Well, of course this is just a rumor I heard from someone else, and I don't believe it. In fact, I would even deny it, but that is just the rumor I heard the other day. Shocking, isn't it?" Here, burden of proof is avoided altogether by denial, but still the suggestion is still there that the rumor may be true, because, "Where there's smoke, there's fire." The suggestion is that the proposition conveyed in the rumor may be true, because it has not been proved false or true.

What is important in the passing on of rumors and gossip of this sort is the naming of the original source of testimony who supposedly made the allegation in the first place. This is where the burden of proof lies, and the using of unnamed and unidentified sources enables another party to use the tactic of "plausible deniability" indicated above. The fallacy implicit in this kind of argumentation is the creating of suspicions and doubts, particularly in attacking someone's character or personal integrity, while escaping any real responsibility or obligation to fulfill requirements of burden of proof appropriate for a claim, even if it is a presumptive inference.

Another kind of situation where innuendo is really dangerous as a basis of the fallacious *argumentum ad ignorantiam* is the case where, for various reasons, some particular type of claim or accusation is extraordinarily powerful. In this type of case, you have to look at the broader context of dialogue to see that the whole procedure for judging and evaluating evidence is somehow stacked to one side. Typically this occurs because of a social climate of acceptance for some particular belief or point of view that builds up such a heavy burden of proof on one side. During the cold war period of the McCarthy era, for example, a kind of polarization of public opinion in North America was part of a climate of fear in which the claim that someone was a Communist became a powerful accusation. In the atmosphere of the Red Menace, the innuendo that so-and-so was a "Communist sympathizer" became an extraordinarily powerful weapon of political attack.

Reversal of Polarity

The Salem witchcraft trials, the McCarthy tribunal, and the Alger Hiss case shared many properties as contexts of dialogue. They all occurred during a time of rapid social change where there was a shift in values. During this time of change, there seemed to be a period where feelings ran very high, almost a hysteria, so that a certain type of accusation became very powerful, even devastating. To allege that someone was a witch, during the one period, or a Communist in the other, carried such a social stigma that the person accused could not defend herself against the charge. In this atmosphere, a reversal of polarity, characteristic of the *argumentum ad ignorantiam*, occurred. Instead of there being a presumption of innocence, once the victim was "fingered," a presumption of guilt was set into place.

The problem in these cases was that the accused person could not prove she was not guilty, partly because of the inherent difficulty of either verifying or refuting the charge. Proving you did not have "Communist affiliations," as shown so well in the Hiss case, was practically impossible. And because of the nature of "spectral evidence" and other peculiar procedures of the witchcraft trials, there was really no realistic possibility of proving yourself not guilty, once the accusation was brought to trial.

In these cases, the fallacy is not to be sought just in the local use of the *argumentum ad ignorantiam,* in its argumentation scheme, or just in the local profile of dialogue even, just by itself. It is whole or global burden of proof that has shifted, or been reversed. Normally, by the principle of "he who asserts must prove," the accuser has the burden of proof. But in these cases, there is a reversal of polarity; for all practical purposes, the accused bears the burden of proving herself innocent (and a very heavy burden at that, given the public hysteria surrounding this particular type of accusation).

The thing to remember here, however, is that reversal of polarity is not, in itself, fallacious. We saw in the loaded gun cases (3.14 and 3.15), that the burden of proof can go to one side in one context, quite properly, and the opposite side in another context. In other cases, it can be questionable, and subject to controversy, whether a reversal of polarity is justifiable or not. In August 1993, prior to a coming election, Prime Minister Kim Campbell expelled three members of the Conservative Party on the basis of legal charges of corruption that could later be thrown out of court.

Case 9.2

The Prime Minister said in Montreal on Monday that she would not allow three Quebec MPs to run again as Tories in the next federal election because the party has to set the highest possible standards of trust and public confidence.

Carole Jacques, Gilles Bernier, and Gabriel Fontaine face corruption charges related to activities while in Parliament. Although police investigations or charges were public knowledge at the time, the party allowed the three MPs to be renominated in their ridings last spring.

But that was during Brian Mulroney's leadership. The expulsion move on Monday presented an opportunity for the new leader, Ms. Campbell, to define new standards for the party, which suffered a string of charges or convictions against MPs under Mr. Mulroney.

In declaring that political parties can have standards that exceed those of the courtroom presumption of being innocent until proved guilty, Ms. Campbell took her party a step beyond tradition. (Ross Howard, "Tories Have Tradition of Refusing Candidacy," *Globe and Mail,* August 4, 1993, A3.)

Traditionally, presumption of innocence would have applied in such cases, and charged offenders would not be expelled until the charge was proven in court. However, the previous leader, Mr. Mulroney, had expelled a minister, André Bissonnette, in 1987 for being under police investigation for corruption, although Bissonnette later was found not guilty, in connection with a multimillion-dollar land sale (A3).

Is reversing the innocent until proven guilty principle legitimate, in such a case, or not? It appears controversial and hard to say, definitively, one way or the other. Whatever the answer should be, the tradition is changing, and reversing the original polarity of burden of proof.

The answer to whether there is an *ad ignorantiam* fallacy in such a case, however, is not to be sought in tradition, or in what the actual practice is. It is a normative question of where the burden of proof should lie in the context of dialogue the participants were originally supposed to be engaged in. In case 9.2, the dialogue is political, and not legal, at least in the sense of being part of a trial. Political debate is a mixed type of dialogue, as we saw in Chapter 6, that has some aspects of a critical discussion (presumably) involved in it. But it is a very different type of dialogue from that of a legal trial. So the reversal of polarity in the shift from one context of dialogue to the other could, in case 9.2, be quite legitimate. At any rate, it is not, by itself, an indication that an *ad ignorantiam* fallacy has occurred in this case.

If we go back to the Salem case, the McCarthy case, or the Hiss case, the situation is quite different. Here the participants were supposed to be engaged in a legal trial, or some tribunal where innocence was presumed until guilt was proven, and that was appropriate.

In a case reported on *20/20* (ABC News, 1994), a young woman was diagnosed with an eating disorder (bulimia), and treated by a therapist, who convinced her on the basis of repressed memories that her father had sexually abused her when she was a child. Without any further evidence, her

father was arrested and tried. Financially ruined, he faced life imprison-
ment, depending on the testimony of his daughter. During the trial, she was
heavily drugged by therapists, having been in treatment for nineteen
months, and claimed to have sixty-five personalities, as discovered by the
therapists. The trial ended in a hung jury. Later, the daughter, having recovered from her "treatment," declared that the abuse never happened. A
commentator, Dr. Paul McHugh (ABC News, 3) said "everything about this
case is very similar to the witch trials of Salem." Although it did end in a
hung jury, the presumption of the therapists, who testified as expert witnesses, was that the father was guilty.

The analysis of the *ad ignorantiam* fallacy in this type of case, then, is to
be sought in the context. There is a dialectical shift from a more balanced
type of dialogue like the critical discussion, the inquiry, or the legal trial to
a kind of partisan or eristic dialogue where a vested interest pushes ahead
for advocacy of its "cause," and extreme views are carried forward on the
crest of a wave of some temporary public enthusiasm. There is a shift from
a more open and balanced type of dialogue to an eristic type of dialogue
that pushes ahead so strongly for one side that no real room is left for
rebuttal or critical questioning by the other side.

This reversal of polarity is a common phenomenon in wartime, when the
enemy are routinely described in negative terms as "terrorists," "brutal,"
etc., and one's own side is perceived in enthusiastic positive terms. Anyone
who tried to say that there might be good people on the other side would—
at least during this time of public emergency and fear—be socially ostra-
cized or otherwise not listened to as having a legitimate point of view. These
periods of social upheaval are accompanied by fear: both fear of the enemy
(or the devil or the Communists) and fear that one may be accused of
somehow being associated with the enemy, or their cause.

The problem is that in the context of a "good cause" that we fervently
support, an *ad ignorantiam* argument may look very good (or bad), but
then later, in hindsight, or in a different historical context, the polarity may
be reversed. In many cases it is one thing to judge an *ad ignorantiam* in the
context of the climate of opinion and what is known at a particular time,
and quite another thing to judge it later, when new, relevant information
may have come in, and the context may be quite different. As a sequel to
case 4.2 for example, it could be noted that the Israeli Supreme Court found
John Demjanjuk not guilty, on July 29, 1993, of being Ivan the Terrible. The
Supreme Court reversed Mr. Demjanjuk's earlier conviction in an Israeli
district court, because evidence from Nazi war crimes compiled by the So-

viet KGB indicated that the real Ivan the Terrible was a Ukrainian named Ivan Marchanko (a different man).[2]

This brings out the nonmonotonic nature of many arguments from ignorance, and their relativity to the known information in a given case at a particular stage of the dialogue. In Chapter 4, we judged the *ad ignorantiam* argument in case 4.2 as fallacious. However, as part of a larger picture, once later developments were included, the argument actually came out as being on the right track.

For this reason, it is best to be clear that any evaluation of an *argumentum ad ignorantiam* as fallacious or not in a given instance, should be seen as a conditional judgment relative to what is known about that case at a given stage. In historical hindsight, when an issue is no longer so controversial, and many of the facts are in, a relatively conclusive determination may be possible. But in the midst of an upheaval of social values, where there is tremendous pressure to make and enthusiastically prosecute a particular type of accusation that is powerfully stigmatic, it may be extremely difficult or even impossible to make such a judgment (especially one that goes against the popular opinion of the time) without being dismissed as partisan.

The reality of many *ad ignorantiam* arguments is that they are presumptive, and are best seen as tilting a burden of proof where there are strong arguments on both sides of an issue.

Evidence on Balance of Considerations

The key to evaluating the *argumentum ad ignorantiam* is to begin with the realization that typically this type of argumentation is most useful in a case that must be decided on a basis of balance of considerations. In this type of case, the given knowledge is insufficient to decide the outcome, or, for various reasons, it is impractical to collect this knowledge so that the decision between the competing hypotheses or claims could be made on what Locke called an *ad judicium* basis. Burden of proof steps in as the tie-breaker.

2. Associated Press and Staff, July 30, 1993, Demjanjuk acquitted, has nowhere to go, *Globe and Mail,* A1 and A5; Associated Press, July 30, 1993, Another Nazi gas-chamber operator fingered as real Ivan, *Globe and Mail,* A5.

The initial situation in such a dialogue is modeled by profile 5. 1. The defender of each of the conflicting claims tries to occupy the high ground by posing the issue as though the other party must prove his claim, or he (the first party) wins the exchange. This is precisely the kind of situation exemplified by case 4.11, the *ad ignorantiam* tug-of-war. Each side tries to shift the burden to the other side. What can be done to break such a deadlock?

The problem in such a case is that the Lockean forking–tactic form of the *argumentum ad ignorantiam* can be deployed indefinitely by both sides. The result, as indicated in case 4.11 and profile 5.1, is that this pattern of pro and contra *ad ignorantiam* argumentation can cycle on endlessly, coming to no conclusion of the argument, and no resolution of the issue.

It is presumably just this problem of endless protraction of a dispute that the legal use of burden of proof, as a principle of argumentation underlying a trial, is designed to deal with. But can this concept be extended to cases outside the legal framework of rules of evidence, which is very much a highly artificial and conventionalized, codified set of rules? The same could be said of a forensic debate, where explicit rules governing procedure, burden of proof, methods of proof, and so forth, are all laid down and agreed to in advance of the argumentation stage. Is this kind of model applicable to everyday reasoning?

The answer, as we saw in Chapter 6, is that it is not, exactly. In common cases of argumentation in everyday conversation, typically there is a context of dialogue, and rules of implicature that can, in many cases, be identified and made explicit. But they are generally presumptions that are not explicitly stated, or codified in any explicitly written down set of rules that can be appealed to as "the letter of the law." Instead, they are implicit maxims of polite conversation that tend to be in the background, in a context of dialogue of one of the types identified in Chapter 6.

What needs to be identified in a given case, in order to evaluate an *argumentum ad ignorantiam* used in that case, are several factors already indicated generally in Chapter 5: the type of dialogue supposedly engaged in by the participants; the stage of that dialogue reached in the argument; and, in particular, the type of proof and level (burden) of proof required for the argument to be successful, on either side.

These factors, insofar as they can be extracted from the context of a case, function as the "evidence" to evaluate an *argumentum ad ignorantiam* used in that case. But as Locke pointed out, this is not *ad judicium* evidence, or empirical evidence collected by observing nature in the orderly way characteristic of scientific verification of hypotheses. It is presumptive evidence, based on assumptions about what is normally expected in a certain type of conversation, according to implicit expectations of politeness. Some would deny this is even "evidence" at all, or at least good evidence that meets scientific or empirical standards of accuracy and verifiability.

It is just this kind of problem about "evidence" that was at the bottom of cases 4.8, 4.9, and 4.10, on the silicone breast implant controversy. There was plenty of so-called anecdotal evidence, but physicians interviewed denied that this was good enough to be called "scientific evidence." For example in case 4.9, Dr. Glassman used the *argumentum ad ignorantiam,* claiming a lack of "hard scientific evidence linking these implants to these serious diseases." By standards appropriate for medical research, there was "no evidence" of harmfulness. But by ordinary standards of safety and caution from a point of view of the women who had had these implants, or the women who were considering having them, there was plenty of evidence strongly suggesting they are unsafe.

This seems to be a contradiction, because the implants are either unsafe or not. But what it indicates once again is that an *ad ignorantiam* argument of this type is best evaluated as acceptable or not within the context of dialogue in which it is being used to make a point. The women contemplating this type of surgery had to make a decision to go ahead or not. And the women who already had these implants had to decide whether or not to have them removed. In one sense there was "no evidence," because the proper medical studies had not been done. But in another sense, based on presumptive argumentation, there was plenty of "evidence" accumulating, suggesting that these implants were unsafe.

Things like "anecdotal evidence" or a "gut feeling" based on experience may not be so-called hard evidence, of the kind that would qualify as evidence in a scientific inquiry. Yet for practical purposes, in a deliberation on what to do in a particular situation in the everyday affairs of life, it may be unwise to ignore this fallible, presumptive type of evidence. It is worthwhile stressing then, that in our view of "evidence" and "argument," the argument from ignorance has too often wrongly and prejudicially been dismissed as fallacious.

The Function of Burden of Proof

In a critical discussion, the goal is to prove (or disprove) something. The burden of proof is a useful device that allocates a weight of evidence which is required to fulfill this goal, and distributes it between the participants in the discussion (see Chapter 7). The function of burden of proof is to shorten the discussion. This function is especially important in dialogues where there is a lack of hard knowledge about the issue being discussed. The tug-of-war problem in such cases is that the dialogue could go on and on, never terminating in a decisive outcome, one way or the other, in time for practical purposes. The burden of proof is a practical device used to close the discussion, once one side has made a strong enough case to fulfill the practical purpose of the discussion. Thus any argument evaluated as successful in meeting the requirements of a burden of proof is only "correct" or "sound" in a relative sense: it is good enough for practical purposes in a context of dialogue, yet not absolutely correct or sound in the sense of being beyond default in the future, or not subject to refutation in a different context.

This relativity of arguments from ignorance has led, as we saw in Chapter 2, to a general mistrust and even condemnation of them. Gaskins (1992) reflects this negative point of view by describing the argument "I win my argument unless you can prove that I'm wrong," as a gambit used by the skillful advocate in polemical battles and public debates to shift a burden of proof. Gaskins (xvi) sees the argument from ignorance as thriving in a cultural climate that casts profound suspicion on all forms of authority other than the judicial power of the courts.

This point of view casts a pall over the argument from ignorance, suggesting it is a usurper of objective, scientific evidence, and that basing arguments on burden of proof is responsible for the crumbling of respect for scientific rationality in the postmodern period. What this neglects to appreciate, however, is how much we generally rely on arguments from ignorance to make practical, wise decisions in everyday deliberation and reasoned conversation. To understand fully the strengths and weaknesses of burden of arguments based on burden of proof, we must see practical reasoning as reasonable and useful on its own terms, and not as a defective type of scientific or theoretical reasoning.

Burden of proof is a technical or artificial device based on conventions or rules of a discussion, or on prior agreements at an early stage of a discussion. Such rules can be highly institutionalized in some cases. For example, in a criminal trial, the burden of proof is on the prosecuting side to prove guilt "beyond a reasonable doubt." In other cases, burden of proof is a natural notion based on common knowledge, experience, or expectations. If your audience is strongly inclined to presume something as true, you will need sufficiently strong arguments in order to convince them that the opposite really should be accepted as a new commitment. If they are inclined to presume the opposite proposition in the first place, you may not need to argue for it at all. Burden of proof as a working concept is applicable to much everyday argumentation, especially in goal-directed deliberations on how to act in particular situations, and in critical discussions on controversial issues of public policy, as Gaskins (1992) shows. The reason is that we often have to take action in these cases personally, even though knowledge of the facts is far from decisive and one's real goals may not be clearly articulated. In these situations, admittedly, even a weak presumption may be enough to tilt the argument to one side, serving as only a provisional guide on how to proceed on the best reasonable basis available at the time. Granted, such arguments can not only be weak, in some cases, but even fallacious. But that should not cast a pall over them as being somehow a symptom of postmodern degeneracy.

Presumption as a Practical Device

Practical considerations can be very important in setting up an appropriate burden of proof in realistic cases of deliberation, and in judging the worth of an argument. To make a presumption is to "take something for granted." But granted by whom? A presumption is to be granted by the other participant(s) in the argument. Hence the concept of presumption requires a concept of argument as an interactive dialogue with two participants, a proponent and a respondent, as we saw in Chapter 7. Thus an inference drawn by presumption is, in a sense, subjective: it is an artifact of dialogue. The proponent makes, or creates, a presumption. And the respondent grants, or allows, that presumption.

   If the respondent does not reject a presumption, then it stands provisionally, according to the analysis put forward in Chapter 7. Therefore, the basic principle of reasoning behind presumptions is the *ad ignorantiam* (as noted at the beginning of Chapter 7). Once a presumption is advanced, if there are no grounds for rejecting it, the presumption stands, provisionally in the dialogue, until at some future point in the dialogue, it may be discharged or refuted. Commitment to presumptions in dialogue is inherently based on ignorance because presumptions are useful and appropriate precisely when it is not known whether or not the proposition at issue is true. Even in the absence of knowledge, an inquiry must often proceed, on the basis of soft (defeasible) evidence, and in the face of (relative) ignorance. Instead of hard knowledge, presumptions in practical reasoning often rest on general experience, policy, convenience, safety, or plausibility.

A presumption is a kind of assumption or concession made in an argument. But it is not just any assumption: it is an assumption that carries a certain amount of weight during at least part of the subsequent argumentation in which it is made. For this reason, the word "presumption" has a prefix that rightly indicates its function in argumentation. Once made at any particular point in a sequence of argumentation, the presumption holds for the succeeding sequence of points; that is, until the presumption is dropped or rebutted, or until the argumentation is concluded.

As well as being linked essentially to the posterior context of argumentation, a presumption is also linked to the prior context. The weight of the presumption is determined by the type of argumentative discussion that it occurs in, and in particular by the burden of proof that is appropriate for arguments in that type of discussion. Thus presumptive arguments are fragile, and are dialogue-relative. But to see their virtue, you have to realize their practical use.

The practical operation of presumption is related to knowledge in the situation. It is not a substitute for knowledge, but it is a way of proceeding to do something in the absence of relevant knowledge (of a high-enough grade). Note also that the presumption must be given up or cancelled, should knowledge or sufficient evidence become available, in the course of the discussion, to rebut the presumption (see Ullman-Margalit, 1983a, 147). Presumptions are defeasible, and subject to cancellation.

Presumption comes into play where there is an issue or question that is open in the sense that the relevant, available evidence does not decide the issue one way or the other with sufficient weight to close discussion of the issue. In order to proceed tentatively—until such evidence may become available—it may be useful to act on a presumption, one way or the other. Thus a presumption is a kind of provisional concession or acceptance of a hypothesis that is reasonable to act on for the present, but may have to be given up in the future.

In a scientific investigation where the researchers want to "establish the facts" conclusively as a basis for building up a solid body of evidence, it may be thought desirable to avoid presumptions if at all possible. For presumptions may have to be withdrawn as further evidence builds up in the inquiry, thus necessitating revisions which could complicate a well-established theory that has been carefully constructed and drawn out. However, in practical reasoning, this luxury of all but the most secure presumptions is very often not available. Much practical reasoning has to proceed on a trial-and-error basis that depends on presumptions that may later be found to be false or inadequate.

In effect, this means that practical reasoning often has to be based on guesswork—but it should be intelligent guesswork that is corrected and improved as actions are carried out and feedback knowledge of the consequences of those actions come into the knowledge base of the practical reasoner. Practical reasoning is therefore characteristically circular in nature whereas discursive reasoning in an inquiry has a tree-like structure where the goal is to "move ahead" from a well-established base of prior premises. In certain ways, then, it is inferior to discursive reasoning, but it is important not to condemn it categorically as though it were a species of defective discursive reasoning.

Presumption is basically a practical idea. Its use is to enable action to go ahead in a practical manner, instead of being stifled by lengthy investigations and inquiries that would delay any action past the point where action could be useful. This is not to say that inquiry is bad, but only that action often needs to be prompt in order to be effective.

Although presumption is primarily practical in nature, it also has a proper place in cognitive contexts. A critical discussion, where the goal is not action but rather to test which side of an argument has the best reasons for its thesis (point of view) may need to use presumptions in order to allow the argument to go ahead. The use of a presumption here is to facilitate discussion—more a cognitive than an action-oriented goal.

Presumptions are also used in scientific investigations and inquiries, but scientific methodology tends to be unfriendly to presumptions if they can be avoided or dispensed with by gathering evidence to confirm or disconfirm the hypothesis, one way or the other. Presumptions are often necessary in scientific investigations, but science is a quest for evidence, and therefore scientists tend to be uncomfortable with presumptions and try if possible to turn them into hypotheses where some hard evidence can be found either to confirm or disconfirm them. Presumptions exist in science, but the goal of scientific inquiry is to eliminate them (as presumptions) if possible.

To evaluate any argument based on presumption as reasonable or not, we must look at the context of dialogue in which the presumption has supposedly been made, and we must understand the purpose of making the presumption in that context. A common problem is that the context of dialogue may not be clearly specified or apparent. Another common problem is that there can be a dialectical shift from one context of dialogue to another. It is in these kinds of cases where fallacies can be traced to abuses of presumptions or misunderstandings about presumptions.

A case in point is the fallacy of *petitio principii,* where a proponent tries to get a respondent to accept a particular proposition as a presumption when in fact this proposition is supposed to be proved by the proponent (as his obligation in the discussion). This kind of attempted violation of conventions of reasoned dialogue is a species of failure to fulfill burden of proof, or trying to make something appear to be a fulfillment of burden of proof when it is really not (D. Walton, 1991a).

Presumptions can be used correctly in a discussion to facilitate the goals of the discussion. But they can also be used fallaciously or sophistically to try to get the best of an adversary in discussion through unfair tactics. In such cases, presumptions can be abused, and these illicit moves can hinder the goals of a discussion. Presumptions are valuable because of their use as a provisional way of steering ahead in a particular case where knowledge to form the basis of a conclusive inference is lacking.

To sum up, the best way to analyze and justify presumptive reasoning based on burden of proof is to see it as useful in practical reasoning in particular "real-life" situations where a prudent course of action must be arrived at on a tentative basis of intelligent guesswork, because "hard" knowledge is lacking. Ravetz (1987) and Dunn (1992) advocate usable ignorance as a basis for useful argumentation in policy discussions where the scientific evidence is too complex, abstract, or inconclusive to be brought directly to bear on applied policy decisions. But those who are suspicious about burden of proof and the argument from ignorance, like Gaskins (1992), tend to see it as a challenge to scientific authority, a kind of illicit substitute of legal bargaining for making a decision based on scientific evidence.

This controversy about the *argumentum ad ignorantiam* is likely to continue, but what I have tried to show is that practical reasoning should be evaluated in a context of its use in a given case. And each case needs to be judged on its merits.

Classification of Subtypes of the Fallacy

From our case studies of the fallacious instances of the argument from ignorance, it is evident that this type of fallacy has three main subtypes. The presumptive type is the use of the shifting of burden of proof to unfairly evade the obligation to prove or justify a claim by shifting the burden to the other party in a dialogue. The knowledge-based type of *ad ignorantiam* fallacy has to do with lack-of-knowledge inferences in a knowledge base, where the conditional or search premise has not been justified adequately, but where the arguer tries to slip the negative evidence claim through anyway. The scientific reasoning type of instance of the *ad ignorantiam* fallacy has to do with cases where there is a problem of verifiability of the alleged evidence, and generally concerns cases of fringe science, such as ESP, ghosts, UFOs, the paranormal, recovered memory, and so forth. Here the use of an argument from ignorance where the conditional premise is not supported by evidence (or perhaps never could be, because of the unverifiable nature of the claim or prediction), and this uncertainty about how to verify or falsify, by evidence for the conditional premise, is what makes the fallacy dangerous and confusing. In such cases, the *ad ignorantiam* seems reasonable, when really it is not, because of the uncertainty of knowing what would count as evidence either to support or refute the conditional premise. These three main subtypes of the *ad ignorantiam* fallacy, along with various other subtypes identified in our case studies, are illustrated in Figure 9.1.

As indicated in Chapter 1, probably the witch-hunt cases are the most dangerous, and also the most complex cases of the *ad ignorantiam* fallacy. They combine a number of features. First, they are based on the shifting burden of proof move characteristic of the presumptive type of *ad ignorantiam* argument. Second, as we saw in the Salem case, they also involve a strong aspect of nonverifiability of the "evidence" characteristic of the scientific reasoning cases. In the Salem case, a key problem was the unverifiable aspect of the "spectral evidence" used to convict those accused of witchcraft. Also, in those cases, reversal of polarity was present globally. There was a powerful factor of hysteria in the prevailing public opinion and fear, at the time, making the allegation of being a witch so powerful and damaging as a charge that a general presumption was set in place against anyone so accused. In this atmosphere of hysteria, conditions were set in place in the court procedures for hearing the evidence that made it difficult

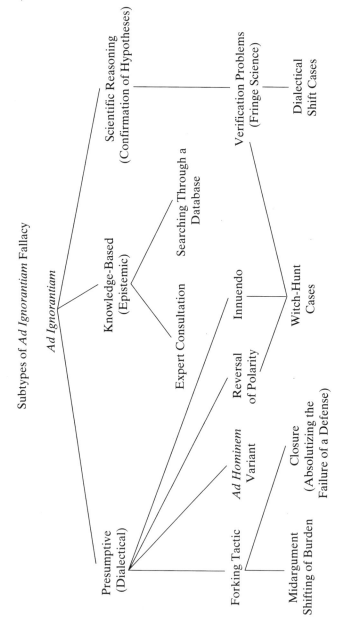

Subtypes of *Ad Ignorantiam* Fallacy

Fig. 9.1

for those accused to give evidence of their innocence. At the same time, a kind of "zero tolerance" framework shifted the burden of disproof onto the accused to prove that she was innocent. Otherwise the *ad ignorantiam* argument was set in place to infer the conclusion that in the absence of such disproof, the conclusion that she was guilty followed. This kind of *ad ignorantiam* argument seems to be supported solely by innuendo, and there is a waiving of the need for any corroborating, objective evidence, other than the allegation itself.

It is these types of cases where the *ad ignorantiam* argument is the most dangerous, because reputations can be damaged; also, the court costs, and costs in personal grief can be enormous. Too often, the accusers in such cases are not punished for the damage they have caused, perhaps on the grounds that they were well-intentioned people who may have been deluded or unhappy, but were acting in support of a "good cause" supported by public fervor at the time.

Criteria for Identification, Analysis, and Evaluation

There are three stages in judging a particular case ostensibly containing an *argumentum ad ignorantiam:* identification, analysis, and evaluation. The beginning point is to identify the specific propositions that are supposedly the premises and the conclusion of the *argumentum ad ignorantiam.* This is a nontrivial job, in many cases, as we have seen, because some of the premises and/or the conclusion may not be explicitly stated. One can use the argumentation schemes (KBS) and (PPS), and the Lockean profile, to aid in this task, but as we saw in Chapter 5, evidence from the context of dialogue may have to be used as well.

Thus here we come to the task of argument analysis. We may be able to identify a proposition being claimed that has the form "We haven't proved that *A* is true." But this may be just a claim. Is it meant to be an *ad ignorantiam* argument? Is the conclusion, "Therefore *A* is false." meant to be inferred from the claim? As we have so often seen, such inferences are often presumptive in nature, and are implicated by tacit conventions of dialogue. So the job of analysis in such cases may involve careful interpretation of the discourse in that particular case.

Another task of analysis is that of identifying the context of dialogue in which the argument was supposedly put forward. Was it in inquiry or a critical discussion, etc.? In some cases, not much information may be given, but in other cases, the title of the book or source of the quotation may give good evidence of the broader context, the type of dialogue in which the argument was used.

In evaluating any particular case, one needs to begin with identification and analysis, before proceeding to the evaluation of the *argumentum ad ignorantiam*. The following sequence of questions indicates the process it is necessary to go through in judging a case.

1. What are the local conclusion and premises?
2. How does the argument fit one of the argumentation schemes or the Lockean profile of dialogue?
3. Are the premises supported by any evidence given?
4. Is the conclusion an assertion or merely a presumption?
5. How does the local argument fit into a larger framework of argumentation?
6. What type of dialogue is the larger framework?
7. What type of evidence is appropriate for this type of dialogue? For example, is it medical evidence, scientific evidence, legal evidence, or some special domain that is involved?
8. What is the amount of evidence (burden of proof) required for both sides?
9. What stage of dialogue are we in?
10. How much evidence (if any) has been collected at this stage?
11. Given the global burden of proof in context, is the balance of presumption for or against the local *argumentum ad ignorantiam* (identified above)?
12. Is the *argumentum ad ignorantiam* reasonable or not?
13. If it is reasonable, is it a strong or weak argument?
14. If it is not reasonable, is it just a blunder or lapse that can be remedied easily, or is the argument fallacious?

Where an *ad ignorantiam* is evaluated as being fallacious in a given case, this means that there is a serious underlying, systematic error, or that the argument is being used as a sophistical tactic to try to get unfairly the best of a speech partner in dialogue. The different subtypes of *ad ignorantiam* fallacy are indicated below.

1. *The Basic Lockean Fallacy.* This is the forking tactic of claiming the respondent's side is defeated if he doesn't give a better argument against one's own claim. Whether a fallacy has occurred depends on the burden of proof at that stage (as revealed by the context of dialogue) and on whether the claim is put forward as an assertion or a presumption.

2. *The Lack-of-Knowledge Base Fallacy.* These are the cases where no real search has been made for evidence to support the conditional premise, "If *A* were true (false), we would know it." The presumption implied is that the burden of proof has been fulfilled by the evidence uncovered by the search, and therefore that the conclusion follows that *A* is true (false).

3. *Verifiability.* These are the UFO cases, and include problems like "spectral evidence." The accused has no way of rebutting the accusation because the vagueness of the claim makes it impossible to falsify.

4. *Reversal of Polarity.* These are the cases where "urgency" or popular hysteria forces a reversal of the appropriate and normal burden of proof (e.g., the Salem and McCarthy cases).

5. *Contextual Ambiguity of Evidence.* These are arguments like the breast implant cases where there is a shift in the meaning of "evidence" from one context of dialogue to another. The basis of the fallacy is a dialectical shift. In this type of case, the standards of evidence appropriate for one type of dialogue may be used where, in reality, the context of the argument is a different type of dialogue. There may be a shift from an inquiry to a critical discussion, for example, or from a critical discussion to a quarrel.

6. *Innuendo.* This is a type of presumptive *ad ignorantiam* argument that has gone too far in suggesting an implicit conclusion by implicature.

7. *Combination with Ad Hominem.* As in case 4.14, the respondent is attacked by an *ad hominem* argument as a way of supposedly closing the knowledge base.

8. *Combination with Ad Verecundiam.* Here the knowledge base appealed to is that of a third party said to be an "expert" in a domain, but such a claim may fail in various ways.

The *ad ignorantiam* fallacies, 1, 2, and 3, are fundamentally the same kind of fallacy in structure. All three are attempts to shift a burden of proof based on a negative premise, used at a particular stage of a dialogue or search where closure is only a matter of appearance, not of reality. One difference is that the Lockean fallacy is dialectical, and the set of propositions that matters is the commitment-set, whereas the lack-of-knowledge-base fallacy is epistemic, and the set of propositions that matters is the knowledge base. One is a fallacy of commitment and presumption, the other a fallacy of knowledge and presumption.

The remaining *ad ignorantiam* fallacies (4 through 8) are variations on this central theme. They represent different tactics used to make the basic fallacies appear plausible in different cases. There is no end to variations on these tactics, in principle. But in practice, we have seen that the techniques noted here tended to recur in the cases we studied, and are the means used to make the *ad ignorantiam* such a powerful tactic of deception in the practices of everyday argumentation.

Thus, very broadly speaking, the *ad ignorantiam* fallacy is a fallacy of relevance, if we mean dialectical relevance in the sense of Chapter 6. It is so, because the fallacy has to do with the situation of a local argument in a wider context of dialogue, especially in relation to who has the obligation to prove what in the global dialogue. But failure of relevance is not the specific failure more precisely characteristic of the *ad ignorantiam* as a distinctive type of deceptive tactic of argumentation.

What is really at the heart of the *ad ignorantiam* fallacy is the idea that participants in argumentation in a dialogue have specific rights and obligations at local sequences or particular stages of the evolution of the dialogue, at junctures where they make particular types of moves, like making assertions, putting forward presumptions, or asking critical questions. A participant is obliged to take on commitment to a proposition urged by the other party only where appropriate conditions at that stage have been met.

The other party, for example, must have allowed the participant sufficient room to ask critical questions, must have fulfilled an appropriate burden of proof by supplying arguments, and so forth. The *ad ignorantiam* fallacy is a characteristic sequence of moves that goes across these obligations and rights, interfering with the proper progress that a dialogue would presumably make were it not for the mischief of the fallacy.

— Selected Bibliography

ABC News. January 3, 1992. Are silicone breast implants safe? *Nightline,* no. 2770. Transcript from Journal Graphics.
———. June 3, 1993. Desperate for help. Transcript 300. Transcript from Journal Graphics.
———. July 22, 1994. My family, forgive me. Transcript 1429. Transcript from Journal Graphics.
Aida, Hitoshi, Hidehiko Tanaka, and Tohru Moto-Oka, 1983. A prolog extension for handling negative knowledge. *New Generation Computing,* 1:87–91.
Arnauld, Antoine. 1964. *The art of thinking.* Trans. James Dickoff, Patricia James and Charles Hendel. Indianapolis, Bobbs-Merrill. (Originally published 1662)
Aristotle. 1939. *Topica.* Trans. E. S. Forster. Loeb Classical Library 391. Cambridge: Harvard University Press.
Barth, E. M., and E. C. W. Krabbe, 1982. *From axiom to dialogue.* New York, De Gruyter.
Bass, Ellen, and Laura Davis. 1988. *Courage to heal,* New York: Harper and Row.
Beardsley, Monroe C. 1950. *Practical Logic.* New York: Prentice-Hall.
Benoit, William. 1990. Isocrates and Aristotle on rhetoric. *Rhetoric Society Quarterly,* 20:251–60.
Berg, Jonathan. 1991. The relevant relevance. *Journal of Pragmatics* 16:411–25.
Black, Max. 1946. *Critical thinking: An introduction to logic and scientific method.* New York: Prentice-Hall.
Blair, J. Anthony. 1988. What is bias? In *Selected issues in logic and communication,* ed. Trudy Govier, 93–103. Belmont, Calif.: Wadsworth.
Blumberg, Albert E. 1976. *Logic: A first course.* New York: Knopf.
Bonevac, Daniel. 1990. *The art and science of logic.* Mountain View, Calif.: Mayfield.
Boyer, Paul, and Stephen Nissenbaum, eds. 1977. *The Salem witchcraft papers: Verbatim transcripts of the legal documents of the Salem witchcraft outbreak of 1692.* Vol. 1. New York: DaCapo.
Boylan, Michael. 1988. *The process of argument.* Englewood Cliffs, N.J.: Prentice-Hall.
Capaldi, Nicholas. 1971. *The art of deception.* Buffalo: Prometheus Books.
Carney, James D., and Richard K. Scheer, 1974. *Fundamentals of Logic.* 2d ed. New York: Macmillan.
Carter, K. Codell. 1977. *A contemporary introduction to logic.* Beverly Hills, Calif.: Glencoe.
Castell, Alburey. 1935. *A college logic.* New York: Macmillan.

Chase, Stuart. 1956. *Guides to straight thinking.* New York: Harper and Row.

Clark, Romane, and Paul Welsh. 1962. *Introduction to logic.* Princeton, N.J.: D. van Nostrand.

Clarke, D. S., Jr., 1989. *Rational acceptance and purpose.* Totowa, N.J.: Rowman and Littlefield.

Clifford, W. K. 1877. The will to believe. *Contemporary Review,* 30:42–54.

Clinton, Henry Lauren. 1897. *Celebrated trials.* New York: Harper and Bros.

Collins, Allan, Eleanor H. Warnock, Nelleke Aiello, and Mark L. Miller. 1975. Reasoning from incomplete knowledge. In *Representation and understanding: Studies in cognitive science,* ed. Daniel G. Bobrow and Allan Collins, 383–415. New York: Academic Press.

Cook, Fred J. 1958. *The unfinished story of Alger Hiss.* New York: William Morrow.

Copi, Irving M. 1953. *Introduction to logic.* New York: Macmillan.

———. 1982. *Introduction to logic.* 6th ed. New York: Macmillan.

Copi, Irving M., and Carl Cohen. 1990. *Introduction to logic.* 8th ed. New York: Macmillan.

Coren,, Michael. April 27, 1994. Fifth column. *Globe and Mail,* A22.

Creighton, James Edwin. 1929. *An introductory logic.* New York: Macmillan.

Damer, Edward T., 1980. *Attacking Faulty Reasoning.* Belmont: Wadsworth.

Dascal, Marcelo. 1987. *Leibniz, language, signs and thought.* Amsterdam, John Benjamins.

Dauer, Francis W. 1989. *Critical thinking.* New York: Oxford University Press.

Davis, Wayne A. 1986. *An introduction to logic.* Englewood Cliffs, N.J.: Prentice-Hall.

De Cornulier, Benoît. 1988. Knowing whether, knowing who, and epistemic closure. In *Questions and questioning,* ed. Michel Meyer, 182–92. Berlin: Walter de Gruyter.

Degnan, Ronan E. Evidence. 1973. *Encyclopedia Britannica.* 15th ed.

DeMorgan, Augustus. 1847. *Formal logic.* London: Taylor and Walton. Reprint, ed. A. E. Taylor; London: Open Court, 1926.

Dohnal, M. 1992. Ignorance and uncertainty in reliability reasoning. *Microelectronics and Reliability* 32:1157–70.

Donohue, William A. 1978. An empirical framework for examining negotiation processes and outcomes. *Communication Monographs* 45:247–57.

———. 1981. Development of a model of rule use in negotiation interaction. *Communication Monograph* 48:106–20.

Dunn, William N. 1992. Assessing the impact of policy analysis: The functions of usable ignorance. *Knowledge and Policy: The International Journal of Knowledge Transfer and Utilization* 4:36–55.

Engel, S. Morris. 1982. *With good reason.* New York: St. Martin's Press. (Originally published 1976)

Fearnside, W. Ward. 1980. *About thinking.* Englewood Cliffs, N.J.: Prentice-Hall.

Fischer, David Hackett. 1970. *Historians' fallacies.* New York: Harper and Row.

Flowers, Margot, Rod McGuire, and Lawrence Birnbaum. 1982. Adversary arguments and the logic of personal attacks. In *Strategies for natural language processing,* ed. Wendy G. Lehnert and Martin H. Ringle, 275–94. Hillsdale, N.J.: Lawrence Erlbaum.

Fogelin, Robert J. 1978. *Understanding arguments.* New York: Harcourt Brace Jovanovich.

Frye, Albert M., and Albert W. Levi, 1969. *Rational belief.* New York: Greenwood.

Gardner, Martin. 1993. Notes of a fringe-watcher. *Skeptical Inquirer* 17:370–75.

Garry, Maryanne, and Elizabeth Loftus. January 1994. Repressed memories of a childhood trauma. *USA Today,* 82–84.

Gaskins, Richard H. 1992. *Burdens of proof in modern discourse.* New Haven: Yale University Press.

Gibson, W. Boyce. 1908. *The problem of logic.* London: Adam and Charles Black.

Govier, Trudy. 1992. *A practical study of argument.* 3d ed. Belmont, Calif.: Wadsworth.

Grice, H. Paul. 1975. Logic and conversation. In *The logic of grammar,* ed. Donald Davidson and Gilbert Harman, 64–75. Encino, Calif.: Dickenson.

Halverson, William H. 1984. *A concise logic.* New York: Random House.

Hamblin, Charles L. 1970. *Fallacies.* London: Methuen. Reprint, Newport News, Va.: Vale Press, 1986.

———. 1971. Mathematical models of dialogue. *Theoria* 37:130–55.

Harrah, David. 1971. Formal message theory. In *Pragmatics of natural languages,* ed. Yehoshua Bar-Hillel, 69–83. Dordrecht: Reidel.

———. 1976. Formal message theory and non-formal discourse. In *Pragmatics of Language and Literature,* ed. Teun A. van Dijk, 59–76. Amsterdam: North-Holland.

Harrison, Frank R., III. 1992. *Logic and rational thought.* St. Paul, Minn.: West.

Heidorn, G. E. 1986. Automatic programming through natural language dialogue: A survey. In *Readings in artificial intelligence and software engineering,* ed. Charles Ritch and Richard C. Waters, 203–14. Los Altos, Calif.: Morgan Kaufmann.

Hibben, John Grier. 1906. *Logic: Deductive and Inductive.* New York: Scribner.

Hintikka, Jaakko. 1962. *Knowledge and Belief.* Ithaca: Cornell University Press.

———. 1981. The logic of information-seeking dialogues: A model. In *Konzepte der Dialektik,* ed. Werner Becker and Wilhelm K. Essler, 212–31. Frankfurt am Main: Klostermann.

Hintikka, Jaakko, and Esa Saarinen. 1979. Information-seeking dialogues: Some of their logical properties. *Studia Logica,* 38:355–63.

Holderness, Mike. June 25, 1993. Information technology: Adventures with form and format. *Times Higher Education Supplement,* 23.

Hopkins, Jasper. 1981. *Nicholas of Cusa on learned ignorance.* Minneapolis, Minn.: Arthur J. Banning.

Huber, Peter. 1991. *Galileo's revenge: Junk science in the courtroom.* New York: Basic Books.

Hughes, William. 1992. *Critical thinking.* Peterborough, Ontario: Broadview.

Hurley, Patrick J. 1991. *A concise introduction to logic.* 4th ed. Belmont, Calif.: Wadsworth.

Hyslop, James H. 1899. *Logic and argument.* New York: Scribner.

Ice, Richard. 1987. Presumption as problematic in group decision-making: The case of the space shuttle. In *Argument and critical practices: Proceedings of the Fifth SCA/AFA Conference on argumentation,* ed. Joseph W. Wenzel, 411–17. Annandale, Va.: Speech Communication Association.

Ilbert, Sir Courtenay. 1960. Evidence. *Encyclopedia Britannica.* 11th ed., 11–21.

Implant danger confirmed. September 25, 1993. *Winnipeg Free Press,* A5.

Jacobs, Scott. 1989. Speech acts and arguments. *Argumentation* 3:345–66.

Jacobs, Scott, and Sally Jackson. 1983a. Speech act structure in conversation. In *Conversational coherence: Form, structure and strategy,* ed. Robert T. Craig and Karen Tracy, 47–66. Beverly Hills, Calif.: Sage.

———. 1983b. Strategy and structure in conversational influence attempts. *Communication Monographs* 50:285–304.

———. 1989. Building a model of conversational argument. In *Paradigm dialogues in communication,* vol. 2, *Exemplars,* ed. B. Dervin, L. Grossberg, B. O'Keefe, and E. Wartella, 153–71. Beverly Hills, Calif.: Sage.

James, William. 1896. *The will to believe and other essays in popular philosophy.* London: Longmans Green.

Jevons, W. Stanley. 1883. *The elements of logic.* New York: Sheldon and Co.

Johnson, Robert M. 1992. *A logic book.* 2d ed. Belmont, Calif.: Wadsworth.

Jose, Paul E. 1988. Sequentiality of speech acts in conversational structure. *Journal of Psycholinguistic Research* 17:65–88.

Kahane, Howard. 1969. *Logic and philosophy.* Belmont, Calif.: Wadsworth.

———. 1992. *Logic and contemporary rhetoric.* Belmont, Calif.: Wadsworth.

Kelley, David. 1994. *The art of reasoning.* 2d ed. New York: Norton.

Kilgore, William J. 1979. *An introductory logic.* 2d ed. New York: Holt, Rinehart and Winston.

Klein, Naomi. January 6, 1994. Why universities feel harassed by zero tolerance. *Globe and Mail,* A7.

Konolige, Kurt. On the relation between default and autoepistemic logic. *Artificial Intelligence* 35:343–82.

Kozy, John, Jr. 1974. *Understanding natural deduction.* Encino, Calif.: Dickenson.

Krabbe, Erik C. W. 1990. Inconsistent commitments and commitments to inconsistencies. *Informal Logic* 12:33–42.

———. 1992. So what? Profiles of relevance criticism in persuasion dialogues. *Argumentation* 6:271–83.

———. 1995. Appeal to ignorance. In *Fallacy theory,* ed. Robert Pinto and Hans Hansen. University Park: The Pennsylvania State University.

Kripke, Saul. 1962. Semantic analysis of institutionistic logic I. In *Formal systems and recursive functions,* ed. J. N. Crossley and M. Dummett, 92–130. Amsterdam: North Holland.

Latta, Robert, and Alexander MacBeath. 1956. *The elements of logic.* London: Macmillan.

Levinson, Charles C. 1983. *Pragmatics.* Cambridge: Cambridge University Press.

Lewis, Charlton T. and Charles Short. 1969. *A Latin Dictionary.* Oxford: Clarendon Press.

Little, J. Frederick, Leo A. Groarke, and Christopher W. Tindale. 1989. *Good reasoning matters.* Toronto: McClelland and Stewart.

Little, Winston W., W. Harold Wilson, and W. Edgar Moore. 1955. *Applied logic.* Boston: Houghton Mifflin.

Locke, John. 1961. *An essay concerning human understanding.* 2 vols. Ed. John W. Yolton. London: Dent. (Originally published 1690)

Machina, Kenton F. 1982. *Basic applied logic.* Glenview, Ill.: Scott, Foresman.

Mackenzie, J. D. 1981. The dialectics of logic. *Logique et Analyse* 94:159–77.

———. 1989. Reasoning and logic. *Synthèse* 79:88–117.

Makau, Josina M. 1990. *Reasoning and communication.* Belmont, Calif.: Wadsworth.

Makin, Kirk. July 3, 1993. Memories of abuse: Real or imagined? *The Globe and Mail,* A1-A5.

Manicas, Peter T., and Arthur N. Kruger, 1976. *Logic: The essentials.* New York: McGraw-Hill.

Marbach, William D., and Michael D. Cantor. July 13, 1987. The search for Planet X. *Newsweek,* 55.

Maté, Gabor. July 25, 1994. Fifth Column. *Globe and Mail,* A18.

Matusow, Allan J. 1970. *Joseph R. McCarthy.* Englewood Cliffs, N.J.: Prentice-Hall.

Maxfield, Valerie A. 1981. *The military decorations of the Roman army.* Berkeley and Los Angeles: University of California Press.

McCaffery, Dan. 1988. *Billy Bishop: Canadian Hero.* Toronto: James Lorimer.

Mellone, Sydney Herbert. 1913. *An introductory text-book of logic.* 6th ed. Edinburgh: William Blackwood and Sons.

Mendelsohn, Richard L., and Lewis M. Schwartz. 1987. *Basic logic.* Englewood Cliffs, N.J.: Prentice-Hall.

Michalos, Alex C. 1969. *Principles of logic.* Englewood Cliffs, N.J.: Prentice-Hall.

————. 1970. *Improving your reasoning.* Englewood Cliffs, N.J.: Prentice-Hall.

Moore, Christopher W. 1986. *The mediation process.* San Francisco, Jossey-Bass.

Moore, James A., James A. Levin, and William C. Mann. 1977. A goal-oriented model of human dialogue. *American Journal of Computational Linguistics* 67:1–54.

Moore, Robert C. 1985. Semantical considerations on nonmonotonic logic. *Artificial Intelligence* 25:75–94.

Moore, W. Edgar. 1967. *Creative and critical thinking.* New York: Houghton Mifflin.

Moore, W. Edgar, Hugh McCann, and Janet McCann. 1985. *Creative and critical thinking.* Boston: Houghton Mifflin.

Mourant, John A. 1963. *Formal logic.* New York: Macmillan.

Munson, Ronald. 1976. *The way of words.* Atlanta: Houghton Mifflin.

Nolt, John Eric. 1984. *Informal logic.* New York: McGraw-Hill.

Owen, William Foster. 1987. Mutual interaction of discourse structures and relational pragmatics in conversational influence attempts. *Southern Speech Communication Journal* 52:103–27.

Pascal, Blaise. 1941. *The provincial letters.* Trans. Thomas M'Crie. New York: Modern Library. (Originally published 1656)

Perelman, Chaim, and L. Olbrechts-Tyteca. 1969. *The new rhetoric.* Notre Dame: University of Notre Dame Press.

Pirie, Madsen. 1985. *The book of the fallacy.* London: Routledge and Kegan Paul.

Pollock, John L. 1991. A theory of defeasible reasoning. *International Journal of Intelligent Systems* 6:33–54.

Post, Tom, Patrick Rogers, and Melinda Lin. November 9, 1992, He was never a Soviet spy. *Newsweek,* 31.

Purtill, Richard L. 1972. *Logical thinking.* New York: Harper and Row.

Radner, Daisie, and Michael Radner. 1982. *Science and unreason.* Belmont, Calif.: Wadsworth.

Ravetz, Jerry R. 1987. Usable knowledge, usable ignorance: Incomplete science with policy implications. *Knowledge: Creation, Diffusion, Utilization.* 9:87–116.

————. May 28, 1993. A leap into the unknown. *Times Higher Education Supplement,* 18.

Reinard, John C. 1991. *Foundations of argument.* Dubuque, Iowa: Wm. C. Brown.

Reiter, Raymond. 1981. On closed world data bases. In *Readings in artificial intelligence,* ed. Bonnie Lynn Webber and Nils J. Nilsson, 119–40. Palo Alto, Calif.: Tioga.

———. 1987. Nonmonotonic reasoning. *Annual review of computer science.* 2:147–86.

Rescher, Nicholas. 1964. *Introduction to logic.* New York: St. Martin's Press.

———. 1976. *Plausible reasoning.* Assen-Amsterdam: Van Gorcum.

———. 1977. *Dialectics.* Albany: State University of New York Press.

———. 1980. *Induction.* Pittsburgh: University of Pittsburgh Press.

Richards, Thomas J. 1977. *The language of reason.* Oxford: Pergamon.

Robinson, Daniel Sommer. 1947. *The principles of reasoning.* New York: D. Appleton-Century.

Robinson, Richard. 1971. Arguing from ignorance. *Philosophical Quarterly.* 21:97–108.

Rovere, Richard H. 1959. *Senator Joe McCarthy.* New York: Harcourt Brace.

Ruby, Lionel. 1950. *Logic: An Introduction.* Chicago: J. B. Lipincott.

Runkle, Gerald. 1978. *Good thinking.* New York: Holt, Rinehart and Winston.

Sacks, H., E. A. Schlegloff, and G. Jefferson. 1974. A simplest systematics for the organization of turn taking for conversation. *Language* 50:696–735.

Schedler, George. 1980. The argument from ignorance. *International Logic Review* 11:66–71.

Schiffrin, Deborah. 1990. Conversation analysis. *Annual Review of Applied Linguistics* 11:3–16.

Schlegloff, Emmanuel A. 1988. Presequences and indirection. *Journal of Pragmatics* 12:55–62.

Searle, John. 1979. *Expression and meaning.* London: Cambridge University Press.

Seech, Zachary. 1987. *Logic in everyday life.* Belmont, Calif.: Wadsworth.

Seligman, Jean, Emily Joffe, and Mary Hager. April 29, 1991. The hazards of silicone. *Newsweek,* 56.

Sextus Empiricus. 1933. *Outlines of Pyrrhonism.* Trans. R. G. Bury. Loeb Classical Library 273. Cambridge: Harvard University Press.

Shapiro, Laura. August 31, 1992. The lesson of Salem. *Newsweek,* 64–66.

Sidgwick, Alfred. 1884. *Fallacies.* New York: D. Appleton.

Smets, Phillipe. 1991. Varieties of ignorance and the need for well-founded theories. *Information Sciences* 57–58:135–44.

Stcherbatsky, F. Th. 1962. *Buddhist Logic.* Vol. 1. New York: Dover.

Sterling, Leon, and Ehud Shapiro. 1986. *The art of prolog.* Cambridge: MIT Press.

Thomas, Stephen M. 1977. *Practical reasoning in natural language.* Englewood Cliffs, N.J.: Prentice-Hall.

Toulmin, Stephen, Richard Rieke, and Allan Janik. 1979. *An introduction to reasoning.* New York: Macmillan.

Ullman-Margalit, Edna. 1983a. On presumption. *Journal of Philosophy* 80:143–63.

———. 1983b. Some presumptions. In *How many questions? Essays in honor of Sidney Morgenbesser,* ed. Leigh S. Cauman et al., 451–73. Indianapolis, Ind.: Hackett.

Vanderveken, Daniel. 1990. *Meaning and speech acts.* Cambridge: Cambridge University Press.

van Eemeren, Frans H. 1986. Dialectical analysis as a normative reconstruction of argumentative discourse. *Text* 6:1–16.

van Eemeren, Frans H., and Rob Grootendorst. 1984. *Speech acts in argumentative discussions.* Dordrecht and Cinnaminson: Foris.

———. 1987. Fallacies in Pragma-dialectical perspective. *Argumentation,* 1:283–301.

———. 1992. *Argumentation, communication, and fallacies.* Hillsdale, N.J.: Lawrence Erlbaum.

Veitch, John. 1885. *Institutes of logic.* Edinburgh: William Blackwood and Sons.

Vernon, Thomas S., and Lowell A. Nissen. 1968. *Reflective thinking.* Belmont, Calif.: Wadsworth.

Vokes, Chris, with John P. Maclean. 1985. *Vokes: My story.* Ottawa: Gallery Books.

Waller, Bruce N. 1988. *Critical thinking.* Englewood Cliffs, N.J.: Prentice-Hall.

Walton, Douglas N. 1984. *Logical dialogue-games and fallacies.* Lanham, Md.: University Press of America.

———. 1985. *Arguer's position.* Westport, Conn.: Greenwood.

———. 1987. *Informal fallacies.* Amsterdam: Benjamins.

———. 1988. Burden of proof. *Argumentation* 2:233–54.

———. 1989a. *Informal logic.* Cambridge: Cambridge University.

———. 1989b. *Question-reply argumentation.* New York: Greenwood.

———. 1990a. Ignoring qualifications (*secundum quid*) as a subfallacy of hasty generalization. *Logique et Analyse* 129–30:113–54.

———. 1990b. *Practical reasoning: goal-driven, knowledge-based, action-guiding argumentation.* Savage, Md.: Rowman and Littlefield.

———. 1991a. *Begging the question: circular reasoning as a tactic of argumentation.* New York: Greenwood.

———. 1991b. Bias, critical doubt, and fallacies. *Argumentation and Advocacy* 28:1–22.

———. 1992a. Nonfallacious arguments from ignorance. *American Philosophical Quarterly* 29:381–87.

———. 1992b. *The place of emotion in argument.* University Park: The Pennsylvania State University Press.

———. 1992c. *Plausible argument in everyday conversation.* Albany: State University of New York Press.

———. 1992d. Rules for plausible reasoning. *Informal Logic* 14:33–51.

———. 1992e. *Slippery slope arguments.* Oxford; Oxford University Press.

———. 1993. The speech act of presumption. *Pragmatics & Cognition* 1:125–48.

———. 1995. *A pragmatic theory of fallacy.* Tuscaloosa: University of Alabama Press.

Walton, Douglas N., and Erik C. W. Krabbe. 1995. *Commitment in dialogue.* Albany: State University of New York Press.

Walton, R. E., and R. B. McKersie. 1965. *A behavioral theory of labor negotiations.* New York: McGraw-Hill.

Weddle, Perry. 1978. *Argument: A guide to critical thinking.* New York: McGraw-Hill.

Werkmeister, W. H. 1948. *An introduction to critical thinking.* Lincoln, Neb.: Johnson Publishing.

West, Nigel. 1987. *Molehunt.* New York: William Morrow.

Whately, Richard. 1846. *Elements of rhetoric.* London: John W. Parker. Reprint (of the 7th British edition), ed. Douglas Ehninger. Carbondale: Southern Illinois University Press, 1963.

———. 1859. *Elements of logic.* New York: Sheldon and Co.

Wheelwright, Philip. 1962. *Valid thinking*. New York: Odyssey.

Witte, Charles L., Ann Kerwin, and Marlys H. Witte. 1991. On the importance of ignorance in medical practice and education. *Interdisciplinary Science Reviews* 16:295–98.

Witte, Marlys H., Ann Kerwin, and Charles L. Witte. 1988. Seminars, clinics, and laboratories on medical ignorance. *Journal of Medical Education* 63:793–95.

Witte, Marlys H., Ann Kerwin, Charles L. Witte, and A. Scadron, 1989. A curriculum on medical ignorance. *Medical Education* 23:24–29.

Woods, John, and Douglas N. Walton. 1978a. Arresting circles in formal dialogues. *Journal of Philosophical Logic* 7:73–90.

———. 1978b. The fallacy of ad ignorantiam. *Dialectica* 32:87–99.

Wreen, Michael. 1989. Light from darkness, from ignorance knowledge. *Dialectica* 43:299–314.

Wright, Richard A., and Ken Tohinaka. 1984. *Logical thinking*. Englewood Cliffs, N.J.: Prentice-Hall.

Yanal, Robert J. 1988. *Basic logic*. St. Paul, Minn.: West Publishing.

Zeligs, Meyer A. 1967. *Friendship and fratricide: An analysis of Whittaker Chambers and Alger Hiss*. New York: Viking.

Zweig, Richard M., Anu Singh, Joseph E. Cardillo, and J. William Langston. 1992. The familial occurrence of Parkinson's disease: Lack of evidence for maternal inheritance. *Archives of Neurology* 49:1205–7.

Index